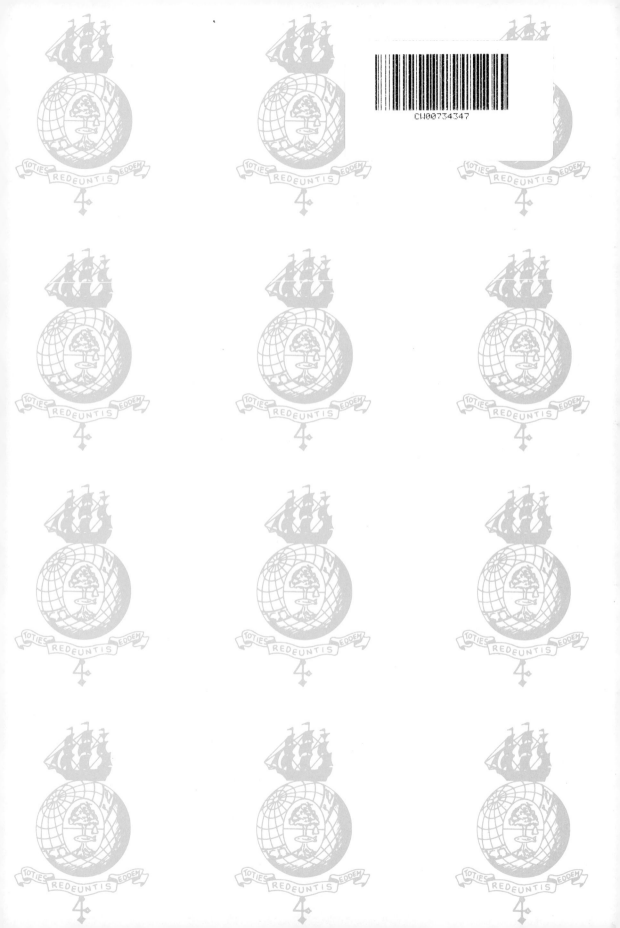

THE MERCHANTS HOUSE
OF GLASGOW,
1605–2005

THE MERCHANTS HOUSE OF GLASGOW, 1605–2005

SUSAN MILLIGAN

based on J. M. REID,

A History of the Merchants House of Glasgow (1967)

First published in 2004 by The Merchants House of Glasgow, 7 West George Street, Glasgow, G2 1BA

Designed and typeset by Digital Imaging

Printed in Great Britain by Scotprint

ISBN 0-9503602-1-X

A catalogue record for this book is available from the British Library.

CONTENTS

Illustrations

Acknowledgements

In 1967 the Merchants House published *A History of the Merchants House of Glasgow* by J. M. Reid. The present volume is a revised and augmented edition of J. M. Reid's compact text. James Macarthur Reid was the editor of *The Bulletin* from 1943 till 1955 and assistant editor of the *Glasgow Herald* before that, and the author of several thoughtful books, on Scottish historical subjects in particular. Such was his concise mastery of his Merchants House subject that I feel no apology is needed – though much grateful acknowledgement – for following in his footsteps.

It is my pleasant duty to thank those who have assisted in a number of ways in the creation of this book. It could not have been written without the support and encouragement of several individuals in the Merchants House, notably Lord Dean Andrew Primrose and Collector David Ballantine, ex-Lord Deans Geoffrey Duncan, James Laird and Alastair Denholm, and the ever-helpful staff in the Merchants House office. I would like to thank all the ex-Lord Deans, as well as others connected with the House, for their willing contributions in the form of interviews and information.

I am grateful to Dr Irene O'Brien of Glasgow City Archives and all her staff for making available the archive sources and for much advice. The staff of the Mitchell Library's Glasgow Room have been most helpful and I would particularly like to thank Mrs Enda Ryan for her assistance in selecting and making available illustrations from the Mitchell's collection. I would also like to thank Helen Avenell of Glasgow Museums.

Mr Andrew Jackson has been outstandingly generous with his expert advice on all matters to do with the Glasgow Guildry and in reading and interpreting early documents. I am also very grateful to him and to Professor Michael Moss for reading my typescript and for their invaluable comments.

All of us involved in the production of the book owe a great debt of gratitude to Mr Rob Cunningham for the immense pains he has taken in photographing many of the paintings and objects in the Merchants House, assisted by Mr James Hardie.

I have benefited from Mr Ronnie Scott's expertise on Glasgow Necropolis, and from Mr Nigel Willis's research on James Ewing. Mr George Fairfull-Smith provided valuable information on the attributions of artwork in the Merchants House's collection. I am grateful to Dr Robert Prescott for information about the Merchants House model ship.

Finally, all at the Merchants House gladly acknowledge the generous contribution from the Joan Weston Trust.

Foreword

Often during the past year, I have been asked at civic receptions in the City Chambers, 'What is the Merchants House?' I have been very proud to take visitors to the window and point out to them the sailing ship atop the globe on the Merchants House building across George Square.

'That's our building', I've said, 'but the Merchants House is much more than that. The House has been totally intertwined in the history and development of Glasgow for at least 400 years. The merchants pioneered Glasgow's overseas trade and industry and controlled its government. With typical Glaswegian resilience, as these avenues narrowed, they have concentrated on using their resources to support their fellow citizens in times of need. They have emerged as a major charitable institution, which has helped Glasgow's regeneration in the last twenty years.'

As we celebrate the quatercentenary of the signing in 1605 of the Letter of Guildry, which settled the organisation and privileges of the guildry of merchants and tradesmen in the city and created the office of Dean of Guild, his Council and Court, we want to tell the story of an historic organisation which deserves to be better known in its native city and beyond.

We invited Dr Susan Milligan to bring our history up to date and our choice was inspired. She takes the reader through the old city from the Cathedral to the Briggait and then up to Glasgow Cross; then west into the Merchant City and Hutcheson Street. She paints in the real characters who lived, traded, prospered, fell on hard times and died there. The merchants established the Necropolis, continued to influence the development of the city and moved on into George Square. Though no longer playing the leading role in the city's government or enjoying exclusive trading privileges, they still worked with determination and pride for Glasgow and its people. Echoing the famous advertisement for Johnnie Walker whisky, the Merchants House is 'still going strong'.

The History will give every reader a lively insight into Glasgow's history and character. It will be an inspiration to the members of the Merchants House who can go forward for the next four hundred years, supported by the achievements and wise investments of their predecessors. The Merchants House will continue to be 'a meeting place and centre of assistance' for the people of Glasgow.

Producing your own history is a challenging and exciting project. Susan Milligan has worked tirelessly at her sources and has produced a most readable and attractive book. Her quiet enthusiasm has encouraged help from all sides for which the Merchants House is most grateful. We hope that you will enjoy reading our History as much as we have enjoyed creating it.

Andrew H. Primrose
Lord Dean of Guild

1
BEGINNINGS

There have been merchants in Glasgow ever since it became a burgh. This is surely the meaning of the Charter granted by King William the Lion in or soon after the year 1175, which declares that its burgesses 'shall have my firm peace throughout all my land in going and returning' – evidently in the course of trade. The town itself was to enjoy 'all the liberties and customary rights that any of my burghs possess'.

These were very important privileges. Glasgow was, of course, a very old place even eight hundred years ago, but it was a very small one, known only for its church, which had become the seat of a bishopric stretching from Loch Lomond to the Border. For Scotland in those days organised towns were something new. They were recognised by the king, as a place where markets and fairs could be held, sometimes under the protection of castles. There merchants and craftsmen could gather safely. They could deal with their own problems and settle their disputes in courts held under the guidance of the king's representatives, called bailies, aldermen or provosts.

This was a kind of life not known till then. Everywhere outside the little burghs, affairs were managed by feudal lords or chiefs, or by the king's sheriffs, most of whom were lords themselves. The new burghs were the germs of self-governing communities. They were given the right to be the only centres of trade in wide districts. Custom duties were paid on the goods sold in their marketplaces, and this revenue went to the Crown.

Most of the new burghs were built on land which belonged to the king. Their people were the king's tenants, just as the feudal lords were, though the patches of ground on which they built their houses – and raised most of their own food – were tiny. But in this Glasgow was unusual. Its land belonged to the bishop. The castle which protected it was the bishop's. Its burgesses were the bishop's men. Not trade but the affairs of the Church – including the bishop's important law courts – gave it its chief business. Yet its merchants were granted the same rights as those of the royal burghs. When Rutherglen, Renfrew and Dumbarton, all of them royal burghs, tried to interfere with Glasgow's trading or to raise tolls on the goods brought to its market, they were forbidden to do this, though quarrels with them over Glasgow's trading rights persisted for centuries.

All the same, King James VI was not so very far wrong when he declared that Glasgow was 'at the beginning one very mean and simple town without ather trafficke or nowmer of inhabitants'. When the burgh was new it had perhaps 1,300 people. Up to the Reformation, though it had become a university city and the ecclesiastical capital of the West, under an archbishop after 1491, it does not seem to have had a population much greater than 4,500. Its relatively slow growth was partly due to its western location: Scotland's trading partners were in Europe, and more accesible to east coast towns. Until the mid-sixteenth century, the Cathedral was more important than the city, and Glasgow's institutions were slower to develop than those of some other Scottish burghs.

The early guilds

Even in the thirteenth century merchant guilds seem to have existed in some Scottish towns. This was natural, since guilds – associations of burgesses whose members paid something to belong to them – were common in England and other parts of Europe. 'Guild' is related to the word 'gold'; in the Glasgow Merchants House the record of membership was to be called the Gold Book.

The guilds served many different purposes. They organised special religious services for themselves, often in honour of their patron saints. They were friendly associations which helped members and their families when they fell into difficulties, as the Merchants House does still. It was their function to protect the business interests of merchants or particular groups of craftsmen, but a 'gildrie' could also become the body responsible for effective local government in a town, electing councillors, and perhaps provosts and bailies, when these became officials of the burgh and not of the king or ecclesiastical lord. Many medieval cities were, in fact, ruled by their guilds; in others the guildry seems to have been little more than another name for the whole effective body of burgesses, the 'community'. In Scottish towns the Dean of Guild, normally the head of the Merchants, was sometimes elected by the town council; there might indeed be a dean without any guild.

Glasgow's records are missing before January 1574; if they had survived we might have a clearer idea of the merchant guild's first beginnings in the town. In the bigger Scottish burghs control of town affairs tended to fall into the hands of the merchants during the later Middle Ages, when Head Courts that could be attended by all the burgesses became less important and new councillors and bailies came to be chosen by the existing ones and not by the citizen body. Some merchants were only shopkeepers, but others were the richest burgesses, those most important to royal governments which looked for taxes from the towns.

Partly in reaction against this state of affairs, craftsmen began to organise themselves into separate guilds for each occupation, whose heads, called 'deacons', claimed the right to act with the town councillors. These were the Incorporated Trades. In Glasgow it was not until 1516 that the first of them, the Skinners, was granted a charter or 'seal of cause' by the town council. As new guilds were organised no artisan was allowed to practise his craft unless he belonged to the appropriate body.

Though Glasgow's foreign commerce was growing – particularly in salmon and herring from the Clyde – there was still no official merchant guild; however, the merchants were drawing together, and by 1569 they had a voluntary association with a president and funds of its own. For taxation purposes they had already been recognised as a group distinct from the craftsmen. In 1582 their president, George Elphinstone, asked for an official writ of incorporation. It was not granted, but this shows that at this date Glasgow's merchant guild was ready to be born. It was his son, Sir George Elphinstone, provost and leader of the Merchants in 1605, who was principally responsible for the Letter of Guildry.

Sir George Elphinstone

Sir George Elphinstone, knighted in 1594, was the son of the richest merchant in Glasgow, owner of the lands of Blythswood, Woodside and Gorbals, one of the great Glasgow estates. He was remembered by later generations, however, for the startling contrast between his attainment of high position (a Lord of Session, Gentleman of the Bedchamber to James VI, Lord Justice Clerk under Charles I) and his final financial ruin.

Nominated provost in 1600 by the burgh's superior, the Duke of Lennox, and apparently also each successive year until 1605, Sir George was at the height of his power and influence in the year of the Letter of Guildry, which was the outcome of his successful management of the crisis between Merchants and Craftsmen. But a position of power in municipal government at that date could be a precarious one. In 1605 he was delegated to ride to London to secure from the king permission for the council of Glasgow to select its own provost, without consulting the superior; the king assented, but the Lennox supporters took exception to this and a fight in the streets ensued, as a result of which the leaders of both factions were thrown into prison.

Sir George and his brothers secured their exoneration and release, but in the following year were embroiled in another dispute, this time over the milling of grain. The council decreed that all grain was to be milled in one of the mills from which it received revenue. Sir George and his tenants refused and continued to use the family mill, whereupon they were fined and imprisoned. After years of argument before the Privy Council, the council's monopoly was eventually ratified. Perhaps it was disillusionment at this turn of events that made Sir George retire from public life. His own affairs took a downward turn and shortly before his death in 1634 he lost his home and all his lands to Viscount Belhaven.

Sir George Elphinstone certainly fell from a great height, but complete financial ruin was not very unusual among merchants of his day. A Hospital for 'poor and decayed merchants' would have no lack of occupants.

The origin of the Merchants House

The Reformation might have killed the little city of the archbishops, which had depended so much on the power and wealth of the Church. In fact Glasgow soon began to grow fast, and the population had probably reached around 7,000 by the end of the sixteenth century. Bishop Leslie in 1578 described it as having 'a verie fair situatioune and plesand, abundant in gairdine herbis, aple tries, and orchardis. Farther it hes a verie commodious seyporte, quhairin litle schips ten myles frome the scy restis besyde the brig . . .'. The same account tells us that from its market fat cattle, herring and salmon, oxhides, wool and skins, butter ('nane bettir') and cheese went to the East Country, and corn to the Western Lowlands, while to Argyll and the Isles and Ireland went liquid cargoes: French wine, ale, a kind of mead called brogat, and 'aqua vitae' which 'heir in place of wine thay commonlie use'.[1]

Fig. 1.1   Detail from Blaeu's map of 1654
The Clyde had many obstacles to river traffic in the sixteenth and seventeenth centuries.

As Bishop Leslie suggested, Glasgow at this time was a market town trading in country produce and basic locally manufactured goods, along with a few luxuries imported from Europe. It had not yet taken its place alongside the east coast towns of Edinburgh, Dundee and Aberdeen as one of the 'four great towns of Scotland'; it was only halfway through the seventeenth century that the city overtook Perth in the national taxation figures. Glasgow's modest importance is explained by the fact that international trade was almost entirely with European markets, and east coast ports had the advantage.[2] But the merchants of Glasgow were at the threshold of their era of dominance and prosperity, and had begun to send out ships from the Potterig, a roadstead on the Clyde above the future Port Glasgow, to Argyll, the inner Hebrides, Ireland, and occasionally to England, France and Holland.

This was the setting for the origin of the Merchants House, which was brought into being not so much by the pressure of the Glasgow merchants themselves as by a general view of the proper shape of town government. Leading Glasgow merchants already controlled the burgh and were in no hurry to concede power to their rivals, the craftsmen. In many Scottish burghs, rivalry between craftsmen and merchants had led to long disputes, and even riots. There was almost certainly tension between the two groups in Glasgow: it came to a head in an incident in 1583 when a craftsman tried to insist on ranking himself with the merchants at a wapinschaw, the parade of burgesses equipped with arms to keep order in the city or defend it, and the dispute ended in a riot. The following year in Edinburgh the young King James VI had to head a court of arbitration between craftsmen and merchants to work out a new constitution for his capital city. An Act of the Scottish Parliament in 1593 laid down that in all burghs a Dean of Guild and his Council should be established on the Edinburgh pattern 'to Juge and decerne in all actionis concerning merchandis . . . according to the Lovable forme of Jugement usit in all the guid townis of france and flanderis', especially Paris, Rouen, Bordeaux and La Rochelle.[3] Two years later the Convention of Royal Burghs followed this up with a letter to the provost, bailies and council of Glasgow declaring that its members were 'nocht a litill offendit that thai [the Glasgow magistrates and councillors] conforme nocht themsellfis to the comlie ordour of uther fre burrowis in haifing ane deyne of gild and electing of gild brether'.[4] The Convention was a powerful body, a sort of supplementary parliament for the Third Estate of the national Parliament in which all royal burghs had a right to be represented. Glasgow was not yet a royal burgh, but because of its importance it already sent commissioners to both Parliament and the Convention. A merchant and a craft deacon were specially delegated to discuss the Convention's message at its next meeting.

A proposal of this sort, said the Glasgow men, was a novelty for their town. It might cause disputes. They hoped the Convention would not press it. The Convention sent them home with a copy of the Edinburgh form of guildry, which their town council, merchants and craftsmen were asked to consider. Glasgow still refused to be hustled, even though the proposed change was backed by the Convention, Parliament and the king himself. The Convention raised the matter more than once again, but dropped it after 1598, defeated by the quiet intransigence of the Glasgow men. The seeds of change had been sown, however, and on 8 November 1604 'the whole body of the Merchant Rank' present in the city and the Deacons of the Crafts met, separately, to appoint commissioners to discuss the ending of controversies between Merchants and Craftsmen and the election of a Dean of Guild and his Council. Two days later the commissioners actually came together – eleven from the Merchants (including two bailies) and thirteen from the Crafts (with one bailie). They, in turn, appointed oversmen or arbiters to draw up a final agreement. It is interesting to note that only eight of those present, seven of them Merchants, were able to sign their own names.

Fig. 1.2   Detail of stained glass window in the Merchants House representing the meeting on
6 February 1605 at which the Letter of Guildry was produced (W. and J. J. Keir of Glasgow)

At last, on 6 February 1605, the oversmen – Sir George Elphinstone, Provost of Glasgow, and the three bailies, David Weemis, John Bell and Robert Scott – with the agreement of the commissioners, produced the Letter of Guildry which still forms the basic constitution of the Glasgow Merchants House and Trades House and in fact fixed the form of local government in the city for more than two hundred years. In our day, when every important change in town affairs has to be made under parliamentary authority and with the guidance of government departments, it is worth remembering that, in spite of the pressure of the Convention of Royal Burghs, this long-lasting reform was finally worked out and enforced solely by Glasgow people themselves. As soon as it had been approved by the town council it came into force. Certainly it was confirmed by an Act of the Scots Parliament in 1672, but by that time it had been working for more than half a century, bringing (says the Act) 'great peace, unitie and concord amongst themselves' to the inhabitants of Glasgow. With the Letter of Guildry the history of the Merchants House had fully begun.

Notes

1. P. Hume Brown, *Scotland before 1700 from Contemporary Documents* (Edinburgh, 1893), pp. 120–1.
2. T. M. Devine and Gordon Jackson (eds), *Glasgow*, vol. 1 (Manchester, 1995), pp. 3–4.
3. *Act. Parl.* iv. 30.
4. *Records of the Convention of Royal Burghs of Scotland 1295–1597*, vol. 1 (Edinburgh, 1866), 1 July 1595, 41.

THE LETTER OF GUILDRY

The original Letter of Guildry no longer exists, but there is an official extract in the records of the Trades House, as well as various copies, the earliest dating from 1611. It is a fairly lengthy document, in its printed form running to some twenty-five to thirty pages. It sets out the background and reasons for the new arrangements and names the commissioners of the Merchants and the Craftsmen; the regulations concerning the Dean of Guild and his Council, their powers and responsibilities; regulations for burgesses becoming guild brethren, and for the sons, daughters, wives and apprentices of guild brethren; regulations and restrictions on burgesses who are not guild brethren; fines to be levied by the Dean of Guild and his Council, and regulations concerning trade to be enforced by them; regulations governing the office of Deacon Convener, and his powers and responsibilities; regulations governing the sale and quality of malt and meal, and of other produce offered in the market; regulations and restrictions on the making of malt; a request for ratification by the provost, bailies and council, followed by the signatures of the Merchant and Craft commissioners.[1]

Glasgow in 1605

The Letter of Guildry tells us a good deal about the life and business of Glasgow in 1605, as well as about its institutions. For instance, substantial citizens (or their wives and servants) brewed their own beer and baked their own bread – probably in the form of oat or barley bannocks. They would salt beef, herring and salmon for their own use, and even make their own candles. Of course they could buy all these things in shops or the town's market if they chose. Butter, eggs, fresh herring, pears, apples, onions, kail and milk were so common that to sell them was 'not agreeable to the honour of the calling of a guild brother' – that is, of the superior class of citizen, either merchant or craftsman, who might hope to have something to do with the management of the town's affairs.

Home-grown foods and things made in Scotland were not all that a Glasgow man might enjoy four centuries ago. He could buy wine, spices, sugars, 'confections, wet or dry', drugs, silks, lawn, taffetas or hats from France, Flanders, England, or other foreign parts. Only guild brothers, however, were to be allowed to sell these things or deal in the products which were the Glasgow merchants' chief exports: plaiding, superior woollen or linen cloth (and the dyes and yarns that went to the making of cloth); salt fish and meat wholesale; sheepskins, hides, and the skins of wild animals (particularly foxes and otters); and tallow wholesale.

Commodities reserved for trade by guild brothers

From the Letter of Guildry:

'It shall not be leasome to a single burgess who enters hereafter to be burgess, and becomes not a gild brother, to tapp [retail] any silk or silk work, spices or sugars, druggs or confections, wet or dry, or launs or camricks, nor stuffs above twenty shilling per ell [yard], no foreign hats, nor hats with velvet or taffety that comes out of France, Flanders, England, or other foreign parts, nor to tapp hemp, lint, or iron, brass, copper, or ache [ash wood]; neither to tapp wine in pint or quart, great salt, wax, waid [woad], grain, indigo, nor any other kind of litt [dye]; neither to buy nor sell in great within the liberties of this burgh salt beef, salmond nor herring, nor yet to salt any of them to sell over again, but for their own use allenarly [only]; neither to buy plaiding or cloth in great to sell again within this liberty; nor to buy tallow above two stones together, except only candlemakers to serve the town, or any honest man for his own use, nor to buy any sheepskins to dry and sell over again, or hides to salt and sell again, nor any wild skins, within this liberty, as tods' [foxes'] skins above five together, otters' not above three together, and other like skins. And sicklike not to sell any kind of woolen cloth above thirty-three shilling and four pennies per ell, except such cloth as is made in their house, which they shall have liberty to sell as they can best; neither buy wool to sell over again within this liberty, nor to buy any linen yarn to sell over again, or to transport out of the town either in great or small parcels, excepting the weavers of the Burgh, who buy yarn to make cloth, and sell the same at pleasure.'

Craftsmen sold their own work, usually made to the customer's order, but it does not appear that, cloth and cured skins apart, much of their produce found its way into trade outside Glasgow and the neighbourhood. The little city had its merchants, but manufacturers were only beginning to have a place in its trade.

Though the Letter of Guildry laid the legal foundation of both the Merchants House and the Trades House, it mentions neither of them by name. It refers repeatedly to the Merchant rank and the Craftsman rank as things already recognised and existing, and also to 'both the estates of the said Merchants and Craftsmen' – within the burgh these were evidently 'estates' in the same sense as the Three Estates of peers, barons and burgesses which made up the Parliament of Scotland. However, the framers of the document set out to establish something different, something new for Glasgow. This was the Guildry, from which the Letter took its name.

In 1605 Glasgow was trying to organise itself according to the best municipal models at home and abroad. For men of the time this meant finding a place for each of the inhabitants and putting and keeping him firmly in that place. We might perhaps compare it to the emergence in the twentieth century of a trade union for every wage-earner, an official society or college or council for each grade of every profession, and trade associations for all employers and businessmen. In modern industrial society there were employers' associations and trade unions long before everyone concerned was expected to belong to one of them, or at least to be guided by the rules and agreements that they made. Similarly craft guilds and a merchants' association had been growing for a long time in Glasgow before they were brought formally into the fabric of the town's life.

From Glasgow's beginnings as a burgh there had been two main classes among the inhabitants, as there were in other towns: burgesses and unfreemen. To begin with, the burgesses were men who held 'tofts' of burgh land and paid dues for this to the bishop – as in a royal burgh they would have paid them to the king. They shared the burden of 'watch and ward', which meant that they policed the town and defended it, and met in the Head Courts (originally assemblies of all the burgesses) to nominate officials, make regulations and see justice done. They alone shared the privileges of regular trade and craftsmanship. The unfreemen were their servants or casual workers, or incomers who had not established themselves properly in the town.

Men qualified themselves for burgess rank by buying the freedom of the burgh; and, though they still bore the burdens of taxation and watch and ward, the burgesses no longer gathered to decide on the town's affairs in the Head Court – perhaps because there were too many of them. A council ruled the city, choosing candidates from among whom the archbishop or his representative named the provost (usually a prominent local landowner) and the bailies. The council's members were chosen by the bailies, ex-bailies, councillors and ex-councillors in a complicated way. Of the three bailies two, as we have seen, were Merchants and one a Craftsman. The provost was always a Merchant, and the whole council consisted of Merchant or Craft burgesses.

But in 1605 it seemed necessary to tighten up this system still further. Apparently there were too many burgesses. Some did not live in Glasgow. The burgh was losing revenue 'by strangers and unfreemen using and usurping the privileges and ancient liberties of this burgh as freely as the freemen and burgesses indwellers' (something that twenty-first-century Glaswegians might view as a fiscal problem not yet resolved). Others were not 'bearing burden' in the old way. There were among them 'infamous and debauched men of evil life and conversation' – perhaps included in this category were those who did not obey the town's regulations for trade and craft work and possibly hankered after rather more freedom than the authorities were prepared to allow them.

The Guildry

Such citizens were now to be excluded from most of the privileges of burgess-ship by the creation of the Guildry. Its head was to be a new official, the Dean of Guild,

Fig. 2.1 Carved relief in the Merchants House

This relief on a freestone slab came from the Merchants' Hospital of 1659 in the Bridgegate. It was positioned on the façade in the space between the upper pillars, above the main entrance (see Fig. 3.5). It depicts three merchants, two of them wrapped in voluminous cloaks and wearing high hats and with long staffs in their hands. A third, clerk-like, figure with a skull cap stands in the background. It has been suggested that they may represent the first Dean of Guild, Matthew Trumble (Trimble or Turnbull in today's spelling), Archibald Faulis, or Faulds, the first Collector, who succeeded him as Dean of Guild, and Archibald Heigait, Town Clerk of Glasgow, who was the first Clerk of the Dean of Guild's Council. Another possibility is that they represent pensioners of the Hospital. The stone is now mounted above the doorway of the entrance vestibule to the Hall, on the first floor of the present Merchants House building.

who would have a Council of his own consisting of four Merchants and four Craftsmen. Every Dean was to be a Merchant, a merchant sailor and merchant venturer (that is to say, an overseas trader). He would be a town councillor *ex officio*. A Dean would be elected every year (though it was evidently assumed that he would normally hold office for two years running) by the provost, bailies and town council, reinforced by the deacons of the Craft Guilds and a sufficient number of Merchants to make the two ranks equal at the election; the choice would be made from a list of three names proposed by the retiring Dean with the advice of twenty-four Merchants. Thus he would, in effect, be the leader of the Merchants in particular. He could call all the Merchants together for the ordering of their hospital and other necessary affairs.

It is in these provisions of the Letter of Guildry that the Merchants House begins to take shape. The hospital in the Bridgegate, built in 1601 as both a meeting place and the centre of assistance for merchants and their women and children who were threatened with destitution, was the material 'house', and the Dean's twenty-four advisers were the predecessors of the Merchants House Directors of later times.

Matthew Trumble

The first Dean of Guild was Matthew Trumble (or Turnbull). He was admitted as a burgess in 1584 on the death of his father, and served on the town council several times from 1594. He inherited some land from his father in the Gallowgate, and later built a large tenement there. He traded to France and Holland, and also to Ireland and the Western Isles, and was accused in 1602 of supplying arms and other goods to Irish rebels. He served as Dean of Guild again in 1623, 1624 and 1626 and died in 1628.[2]

The Craftsmen were also to have a new head, again a town councillor *ex officio* – the Deacon Convener of the Trades. They were to have their own council of deacons and 'assisters' and their hospital, the future Trades House.

It is significant that, unlike the Deacon Convener, the Dean of Guild was, in effect, a magistrate of the town. Next in rank to the provost, he was later to be known as the Lord Dean. His Council of eight lyners, half of them Merchants, half Craftsmen, was evidently intended to be the executive of the new Guildry (Fig. 2.2). It could make regulations – 'laws and statutes, heads and articles to be observed for the weel of the town' – though these must be approved by the town council.

The Dean and his Council were evidently to control entry to the Guildry. It was provided that every existing burgess actually living in the town and not 'infamous and debauched', could become a guild brother on paying the nominal fees of one merk (13s. 4d. Scots)[3] to the Dean and 40 pennies to 'the hospital of his calling' – this condition meant that he must choose to be ranked as either a Merchant or a Craftsman. Even the 'infamous and debauched' were to be allowed to continue their work in the town under supervision, and their sons, if they were found worthy and able, were to have the same rights to follow their fathers' trade and become guild brethren as those of other burgesses.

Future candidates for the Guildry were to be more severely tested, however. A guild brother's lawful son could be admitted if he paid 20 shillings to the Dean of Guild and 5 shillings to the Merchants or Trades Hospital, but he must also have property of 500 merks if a Merchant or 250 merks if a Craftsman. A guild brother's daughter who married a burgess could have him admitted to the Guildry at the same rate. This, the Letter of Guildry points out, was an inducement to apprentices who had served their time and become burgesses to marry their masters' daughters; otherwise they would have to wait longer for membership of the Guildry and to pay 33s. 4d. A merchant or craftsman who came from outside the town had to pay £30 Scots to join the Guildry and 13s. 4d. to his hospital, but 20 shillings and 40 shillings respectively if he married the daughter of a guild brother.

Fig. 2.2 Stained glass window in the Merchants House, representing the first Court held by the Dean of Guild (W. and J. J. Keir of Glasgow)

The Dean of Guild's Council

The Dean of Guild and his Council were also to have power to tax guild brethren not more than £100 Scots in all at one time 'for the wellfare and maintenance of their estate and help of their decayed gild brethren, their wives, children, and servants'. It is doubtful whether this tax was ever actually levied, as there is no trace of its collection in the books. However that may be, the new hierarchy was essentially based on wealth: the financial requirements for entry alone were beyond the means of all but the more prosperous merchants and craftsmen.

The Council could fix fines and penalties, for it was also a law court. It could punish unfreemen 'using the liberty of a freeman within the burgh' by trading as merchants or practising crafts. It could judge 'in all actions betwixt Merchant and Merchant, and Merchant and Mariner, and other Gild brothers, in all matters of merchandize and other such like causes'. It was to oversee weights and measures. With an existing town official, the Master of Work, it was to decide 'on all questions of neighbourhood and lyning' – that is of building and encroaching on neighbours' property and rights. This function was retained by the Dean of Guild and his lyners for over three and a half centuries. The Council of 1605 later became the Dean of Guild Court. One rule laid down by the Letter of Guildry – that lawyers should never practise in this court – was soon abandoned, but the principle had been established that the court should be essentially pragmatic rather than bound up with legalistic minutiae and precedent.

The entry money of guild brothers and part of the fines imposed by the Dean of Guild's Council was to be divided between the Merchants' Hospital and the Trades House for the use of decayed merchants or craftsmen or for 'any . . . good and pious use which may tend to the advancing of the commonwell of this town'. The Merchants' share was to be distributed by the Dean of Guild with the advice of the Merchant Council – presumably the four Merchant lyners – 'and such other of the Merchant Rank as he shall chuse for that effect'.

The first lyners

The first four merchant lyners were named in the act book of the Dean of Guild Court a few days after the ratification of the Letter of Guildry: they were William Stirling, Archibald Faulds, George Muir and James Bell. William Stirling was a tacksman (tenant) of the king's customs on the Clyde and factor to Sir George Elphinstone – as provost at the time and one of the leaders behind the Letter of Guildry, he was probably responsible for Stirling's election. Archibald Faulds, elected Dean of Guild in October 1605, was an overseas trader especially to Flanders. George Muir was Dean of Guild in 1609 and then a bailie. James Bell made a large fortune trading to Flanders and Denmark, was Dean of Guild for four years between 1609 and 1614 and a bailie. Of his four sons, two became Deans of Guild and then provost, and a grandson, John Bell, who fought at Bothwell Bridge against the Covenanters and received a knighthood, was Dean of Guild for three years in the 1650s and provost ten times.[4]

Glasgow after 1605

The picture of municipal Glasgow that the Letter of Guildry gives us is a curiously complex one. There were still unfreemen who had no rights as citizens, and simple freemen burgesses who could trade in a small way or work as journeymen in the crafts but whose privileges as citizens were very limited. They could trade in everyday foodstuffs and ordinary household wares, such as butter, herrings and eggs, and tar and oil; it is perhaps just possible that the more ambitious and energetic among them might have bought up linen cloth and taken it to England, or taken butter, oats and hides in little open boats to Ireland, and by means of such enterprise, they might have accumulated enough money to apply for the full commercial privileges of guild membership.[5] But the majority of these small traders would have remained in their lowly rank. Above them stood the brethren of the Guildry, divided between Merchants and members of the Craft guilds – the Incorporated Trades. Only they could be wholesale traders or act independently as artisans and makers of goods for sale. For the Merchants was reserved the right to sell silks, spices, sugars, drugs, confections, fine textiles and hats, hemp, lint, brass, copper, potash, wine, salt, wax, woad and other dyestuffs – in effect to act as oveseas traders, as all these goods came from France, the Low Countries and the Baltic. They had the power to regulate their own work, and, through the Dean of Guild's Council, to judge disputes among themselves and prosecute outsiders who tried to share their privileges. They did not actually choose the town council, but it was, in fact, made up of guild brethren – an equal number of Merchants and Craftsmen according to a ruling of King James VI in 1606 – and the Burgh Treasurer could not spend more than £10 without the consent of the Dean of Guild and Deacon Convener. They provided a sort of social security for themselves and their families which other citizens did not share, but they were also expected to spend part of their joint funds for the good of the town in general.

Under Glasgow's constitution of 1605, the town's government, Guildry, the general community of burgesses, and the two ranks of Merchants and Craftsmen were sometimes mixed up together in what seems a confusing way. Even the Dean of Guild, though at once head of the Guildry in general and chief of the Merchants in particular, was actually named by the town council, specially reinforced for the purpose. But, in fact, under the Letter of Guildry every mature Glaswegian was duly ranked and knew precisely where he stood in the town's society. It was still possible, as the burgess roll of the century beginning with the Letter of Guildry shows, for the son of a craftsman burgess to become a merchant burgess by paying the specified rate, and several men made the even greater climb to become merchant burgesses by taking the intermediate step of marrying the daughter of a craftsman burgess. This degree of social mobility gave the opportunity by means of business sense and, perhaps, a canny marriage, to rise to considerable heights of success within the Merchant rank. In a city already beginning to boil with commercial enterprise, which was to grow stronger with each generation through the following centuries, the framework of the Letter of Guildry provided a pattern for town life which was felt to be necessary almost everywhere in Europe at that time, but one sufficiently flexible to admit able and ambitious men to the ranks of wealth and influence. By the standards of Scottish cities of the time, the government of Glasgow was fairly broad-based, a fact which may have contributed to the remarkable period of expansion that was about to dawn.[6]

The four corporations of Glasgow in 1605

The government of the city: the town council, bailies and Lord Provost

The Guildry: the Merchants and Craftsmen, who each elect four lyners or members of the Dean of Guild Court, chaired by the Dean of Guild

The Merchant rank or Merchants House, headed by the Dean of Guild

The Craft rank or Trades House, headed by the Deacon Convener, presiding over fourteen Incorporated Trades

---

The Merchants House, though not yet named, had come properly into being. It had its head, the Dean of Guild. It was soon to borrow its chief permanent official, the Collector, from the Dean's Council; the first Collectors were members chosen to gather fines and the entry money of Merchants. It was already beginning to receive bequests for the good of its members and their families in distress. The work of safeguarding the interests and relieving the distresses of businessmen and their families, which has usually been its first concern through the centuries, had made a proper beginning.

Notes

1. H. Lumsden, *Records of the Trades House of Glasgow 1605–1678* (Glasgow, 1910), pp. 529–52; W. H. Hill, *View of the Merchants House of Glasgow* (Glasgow, 1866), pp. 55–81.
2. Andrew M. Jackson, *Glasgow Dean of Guild Court: A History* (Glasgow, 1983), p. 19.
3. One shilling Scots was the equivalent of a penny sterling.
4. Jackson, *Dean of Guild Court*, p. 20.
5. T. C. Smout, 'The Glasgow merchant community in the seventeenth century', *Scottish Historical Review* 47 (1968), pp. 53–71.
6. Ibid., pp. 68–9.

THE FIRST HUNDRED YEARS

Glasgow under Guildry control

The Letter of Guildry had granted the city's craftsmen a similar status to the leading merchants, thereby putting an end to the damaging disputes about representation in the city's affairs. It had also enabled the Merchants to restrict the entry to their rank to men of substance and reputation. In the first list of Merchants and their assisters there are 214 names. A similar list for the Craftsmen has 363. Although outnumbered by the Craftsmen, the Merchants had the upper hand in the city's government. According to King James VI's ruling of 1606, there were to be as many Craftsmen as Merchants among the town councillors. But the provost was always a Merchant, so that their rank had an assured majority – thirteen to twelve. Moreover, the Deacon Convener, the Dean of Guild, the Treasurer and the Master of Work were additional town councillors *ex officio*, and the last three of these were also always Merchants, as were two out of the three bailies. Essentially, though, both ranks of the Guildry were privileged people, the organised middle class of the city, and the most wealthy and politically skilled among them became the leaders of the town. The Merchants and the Crafts, in place of the Church, had become the new ruling elite.

It was a contributory factor in this that the Guildry had been founded at a time when the Protestant archbishop of Glasgow had very little power. Although he had the right to appoint the town's provost and nominate the bailies from a leet submitted to him, a power which the archbishop retained until 1690, over the election of Deans of Guild and Deacon Conveners he never had any such control.

To begin with the Dean of Guild and his Council had to assert themselves firmly. They were a novelty in the town and, as always, there were citizens suspicious of innovation. At their first meeting the Dean and lyners found reason to declare 'that sundrie malicious and deboschit personnis of this toune' slandered and blasphemed 'the guid establischit ordour of the Letter of gildrie', particularly at their dinner tables 'to the greit disgrace of the deine of gild and his counsall, in presence of strangeris'.[1]

It was decided that if any were found guilty of slandering the Dean and Council in future they must be punished and fined. The next day a Merchant, Robert Broune, agreed that if he should slander or blaspheme the new order of things he might be banished from Glasgow, losing his freedom as a burgess of the city 'and he nevir to injoy na benefite within the samin'.[2] This would have been a harsh penalty. There is no indication that any erring guild brother was actually expelled from the city for criticising the Dean or the Letter of Guildry.

Increasingly, Glasgow society became divided between the wealthy and the not-so-wealthy, rather than between burgess and unfreeman. All the burgesses were free to make money, but some made much more than others, and these became the leading men of the Merchants and Crafts and the leaders of the council. Meanwhile the overseas merchants in particular became a very prosperous class.

Fig. 3.1   Relief of ship in the Merchants House
The second of the two reliefs from the Merchants' Hospital of 1659 shows a ship, three-masted and high-pooped – a symbol of the future of Glasgow and a reminder that all the early Deans were overseas traders. The carving was, like Fig. 2.1, originally on the façade of the Merchants' Hospital in the Bridgegate, and is now on display in the Merchants House building.

The merchant community

The size of the class of overseas traders in the seventeenth century has been calculated at between one and two hundred men, out of a total of perhaps between four or five hundred merchant burgesses. The most numerous group of the merchant community was made up of small traders who sold goods within Glasgow, or at least within Scotland; another, smaller, group sold linen cloth in England. Some of these 'English merchants', according to John McUre, Glasgow's first historian, 'became sea adventurers afterward'. An example of such a man, mentioned by McUre, is Matthew Cumming, who regularly travelled to London with a pack of linen cloth on his pony's back, and used credit built up by sales of his cloth to import dyestuffs from Holland to Bo'ness. Perhaps it was with profits from this that he purchased a share in a boat that brought sugar from Barbados and tobacco from Virginia to Glasgow, and on one occasion arranged for sending the cargo onward to Holland because of a glut in the Scottish market.

Among the sea adventurers, or foreign merchants, there was an elite of thirty or so individuals from around twenty families who in any given decade controlled a large proportion of the city's wealth and power. There was much intermarriage between these families, and also with the families of landowners: from the point of view of wealth and social class there was nothing to choose between seventeenth-century Glasgow lairds and rich merchants, and a laird's son might be apprenticed to a merchant, while a merchant's son might marry into a laird's family.[3]

The Merchants House

The Merchants had their hospital in the Bridgegate, the short street leading from the Saltmarket to the old Glasgow Bridge at the foot of Stockwell. It was founded in 1601, the date given in an inscription on a stone from the later Merchants' Hospital on the same site (see below). A hospital in that age was not primarily a place for the sick, but an almshouse for pensioners. From the first, no doubt, the Merchants' Hospital provided such shelter, but most of the assistance was by way of pensions or precepts (occasional grants) paid to 'decayed' Merchants or widows and daughters in distress who were living elsewhere in the town. Many of the petitions from these individuals from the second half of the seventeenth century onwards survive.

Petitions from 'a borne doune woman'

'To the most worthy Lord Dean of Guild of the Merchants of Glasgow and to all the brethren in his Council
Supplicates I Margrat Speir widow & spouse to umquhile [deceased] Alexander Coningham merchant burgess of Glagsow I am ane distressed woman and come to many yeares which is more than fourscore I desyre that your godly wisdomes would consider my low estate and grant me pairt of your christian charity wich you doe bestow towards the releife of the poore and I shall ever continue to pray
Margrat Speir widow

6th Nov 1685: Ordaines the supplicant forty shillings – Robert Robertson'

* * *

'To the worthy Dean of Guild and to his brethren of the Merchants of Glasgow these be presented
Supplicates I Margrat Speir widow and relict of umquhile [deceased] Alexander Coningham merchant a borne doune woman and come to a great aige and is lyable to several diseases as goutt and gravell and at a point of stariving for fault of maintenance the Lord knowes my neidful condition I desyre that your godly wisdomes would consider my necessity and grant me pairt of your christian charity which you bestow on the poore and I shall ever continue to pray

April 24th 1688: Ordains forty shillings Scots to the petitioner – Robert Robertson clerk'

* * *

A resident pensioner

'Unto your Lordship Dean of gild and remanent bretherin of the Merchand Ranke
The humble supplicatione of John Wallace Merchand burgess of Glasgow
Sheweth
That quhair it hath pleased God to take from me my means and estait by Robberie in Ingland and badd debtors both here and there Whereby I ame altogether unable either to provyde for my selfe or familly And it pleased your Lordship's predecessors in office to bestow upon me some Litle thing quarterly which naewayes is able to maintaine me nor my familly which I hop is notour [known] to your Lordship and severall of your bretherin and except that your Lordships thinke upon some other way for my supply I know not how to Leive or my familly.

'May it therefore please your Lordship and remanent bretherin to take my poor caise and condition to your consideration and out of the bowells of your charitie and compassion to Install me as ane of the pensioners of your house and the benefit thereof as others and before your supplicant shall ever pray.

October 29 1674
Admits the supplicant to the house he residing there and no otherwise – J. Graham'

The first recorded endowment for the hospital was a ground annual (an annual payment forming a burden on land) of 40 shillings Scots given in 1602 by John Mure, Skipper, for 'the poore merchants that feirs God within the said citie to be stallit in the almous hous biggit in the Briggait', that is, for resident pensioners. It is interesting that this first bequest to the Merchants was made by a man who two years later was one of the Commissioners for the Crafts. In 1605 he was one of the Craft lyners. Most 'skippers' owned a share in the vessels they sailed, and Mure part-owned a ship, *Gift of God*, which traded to the Hebrides.[4] Other ground annuals, feu duties and sums of money were given or bequeathed from year to year.

The Letter of Guildry provided a regular source of income in the form of entry money of Merchant Guild brethren and in Dean of Guild Court fines. There were also fees for the use of the Merchants' mortcloths, velvet palls for covering coffins on their way to the grave. In seventeenth- and eighteenth-century Scotland there had to be a pall of this sort at every well-conducted funeral, and many kirk sessions relied on the hire of mortcloths to provide money for poor relief. The Merchants had their communal palls, elaborate affairs, if we can judge by a receipt issued by the Collector, James Bogle, in January 1687, for £183. 19s. Scots to William Napier, merchant (Dean of Guild in 1689 and 1690), for velvet, silks, dimity and serge for the mortcloths. They seem to have employed a boy to take the mortcloths to and from the funerals – they received a petition on his behalf for winter clothes in 1687 or 1688.

The mortcloth boy's petition

'Unto the right hounourable the deane of guild and rest of the reverend Bretherene Humblie Sheweth

That whereas I your poor supplicant Jean Gilchrist* relict of umqhuile [deceased] David Sinklar merchand burgess of Glasgow am ane verie poor widow womane oppressed with severall deseases and not able to worke alsoe have the charge of two fatherless childrine wherin ther is one of them that is your poor servent and has nothing upon him and now winter is come one [on], exspects your Lorship will ordaine him to be clothed for putting him by the cold saesoune of the year in regaird he is your servent in bearing the mortclothes home and afield and little thing he gets from them for the doing of the samine, Therefore expects your Lordship's favourable answer according as our poor caise and conditione requires.

Beseeks

24 April 1688: Ordaines a full duket to the petitioner – Robert Robertson clerk'

*Her name is given as Jean Gilchrisoune in an earlier petition, see below.

* * *

A petition from the mortcloth boy's mother

'Unto the right honourable the Dean of Guild and rest of the Bretherine of Court Humblie sheweth

That where I Jean Gilchrisoune relict of umquhile David Sinchler merchant burgess of Glasgow am ane verie poor woman & has nothing to live upon & also has the charge of two poor fatherless boys & nothing to give them, neither have I whereupon to educat them at school which is ane great pitie soe that I am necessitat to make my moan unto your lordships.

'May it therefore please your lordship and bretherin of Court to take this my poor caise to your serious consideration & grant me some of your charitie as my poor caise & my two fatherless boyes require & in soe doing I shall ever pray

Beseeks

Jean Gilchrisoune

December 24th 1686: Ordains the petitioner a rex dollar.'

(A rex dollar or rix dollar was a silver coin current in various European countries at this time.)

They also drew 'bucket money', 8s. 4d. paid by each new burgess, which was shared between the Merchants and the Craftsmen. This provided a primitive form of fire service. When at least the upper storeys of most houses were built of wood, fires were frequent and dangerous. The Merchant and Craft ranks had the duty of providing leather buckets, which every householder could use in case of fire. From time to time the town council had to urge them to repair their old buckets and supply new ones, but the bucket money was usually treated as ordinary revenue, until the Merchants House gave up its share in 1807, when the first effective public fire service was set up.

To a gradual surplus of these sources of income were added over the years legacies and 'mortifications' – bequests or gifts of money or other property for charitable purposes. This formed the capital, or stock, of the House, which yielded revenue by means of investment in lands, houses, loans, and so on. The capital was classified into free stock, owned outright by the House, and mortifications, the rents or incomes from which were administered by the House as trustees, and were usually directed at specific classes of beneficiary. The oldest surviving account book of the House is for 1624. It shows an income of £3,174. 10s. 2d. Scots and expenditure of £2,957. 9s. 4d. Part of the money was spent in quarterly pensions, though the oldest roll of pensioners, twenty-four years later, shows sums ranging only from 10 shillings to £5 Scots quarterly, amounting in all to £66. 16s. 8d. – presumably £267. 6s. 8d. per annum.

The House was, in fact, able to invest money in its first half-century in spite of the long wars of the Covenant, first against Charles I and finally against Cromwell, in which Glasgow lost both men and wealth.

Cromwell's legacy: a petition of 1675

'Unto your Lordship deane of Gild and remanent brethren of the merchand ranke, the supplicatione of John Nisbite merchand burgess of Glasgow

Humblie sheweth

That Whaire without being burdensome to any incorporation within this burghe I have these many years bypast lived by my onwe industrie and Labour, And as it is weel knowne to your Lordships I might, and willinglie would have so continued, had not the great and many losses I have susteaned by having my cropt of vittaill [crop of oats] eaten up and destroyed the tyme of the English usurpation and the death of many of my wark horse which I purchased sensyne [since], Crossed and made oppositione to my inclinatione [sic], by which means I am not onlie reducted to extreme poverty, but all means are taken away from me to provyde for ane lyvliehood to my selfe and familie in tyme coming.

'May it therfor pleas your Lorships to take my caise to your consideratione, which In regaird of old age now come upon me being now 64 years, makes my incapacitie of provyding for my selfe as said is the more appeare, And being considered that ye wold allow me ane speedie supplie as your Lordships shall think fitt and convenient for relieving and supplying my urgent necessities and the supplicant shall ever pray etc.

19 October 1675

Ordaines the supplicant four dollars – J. Grahame'

By far the largest legacy received by the Merchants at this time came from the formidable minister of the Barony parish, Zachary Boyd, who denounced Cromwell to his face in a sermon when the English conqueror visited Glasgow in 1650 (Fig. 3.2). All the other ministers of the town had fled. By his mortification of 1635 he gave the Merchants House £1,000 Scots on condition that it would pay him the interest during his life. Thereafter the House was to apply the income from this sum to the education of a student of theology of their choice, 'the most godly and fitting', either living in the college or at home with his parents. The choice was to rest, if possible, on a burgess of Glasgow, of the Merchant rank, preference to be given to qualified persons of the name of Boyd. This gift gave the House its first direct link with education in Glasgow (Fig. 3.3).

With this and other sums land was bought in and around Glasgow. By far the most important of these possessions were the lands of Easter and Wester Craigs, acquired in 1650 from Sir Ludovick Stewart of Minto, the impoverished head of a family which gave six provosts to Glasgow (and to the coinage the lady who was the first model for Britannia). The Craigs, bought for 23,250 merks Scots (£1,291. 13s. 4d. sterling), stretched from the glen of the Molendinar Burn at the Cathedral into what is now Dennistoun. The House soon sold Easter Craigs, but part of the western lands – the rocky ridge opposite the Cathedral – remained its property for over 300 years. This land was to be developed first as a public park and then as the Glasgow Necropolis,

Fig. 3.2   Zachary Boyd (after painting by George Jameson)

Zachary Boyd was born around 1585 into a wealthy family in Carrick, Ayrshire. He was educated at school in Kilmarnock, at the university in Glasgow and at Saumur in France, where he was later made regent of the college. He spent some years in France as the minister of a Protestant church, but in the face of religious persecution returned to Scotland. In 1623 he was made minister of the Barony parish of Glasgow, where he remained until his death in 1653. At that time the cathedral crypt served as the place of worship for the Barony Kirk, which was where Boyd delivered the famous sermon to Cromwell and his men in 1650. A contemporary account from one of Cromwell's company describes the incident: 'There was one Scotch minister who stayd and preacht on the Lord's-day, and we gave him the hearing Morning and Afternoon with all his poore Stuffe, and Railings of course. I doe believe the Man's Ambition was to have been a Sufferer by us, but we would not honour him so farre.'[5]

Boyd suffered frequent bouts of ill-health. He was forced to face his own mortality when, soon after his appointment to the Barony, around the age of forty, he suffered from a near-fatal illness, and recovered to find a winding sheet prepared for him among his books. This inspired his great prose work, *The Last Battell of the Soule in Death*. He lived for another twenty-six years after this illness, and produced verse translations of the Psalms and some other parts of the Bible, as well as other poems of a spiritual nature (much parodied by later generations), and several volumes of sermons and devotional writings. He held various university positions, including the rectorship in 1634–5 and 1645. He was married twice; his second wife (in her teens to his fifty-plus years) survived him, but neither marriage produced any children. He was a very wealthy man at his death, and left over £20,000 Scots to the university, along with his library and all his writings, on condition that it arranged publication of all his works, with the remainder of the legacy being used for building the new college. The executors never got around to publishing Boyd's writings, and devoted the money to completing a phase of the new college building.

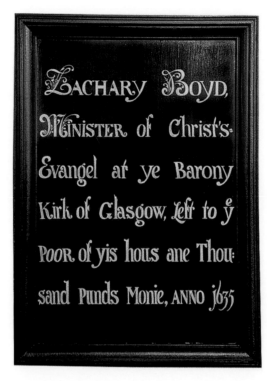

Fig. 3.3   Mortification board of Zachary Boyd

but in the seventeenth century the House had farming tenants in Wester Craigs, which brings into the records a whiff of Covenanting history.

In January 1681 'my Lord Dean of Guild and brethren of the Merchant Ranke' received a petition from David Monteith and John Cuming, tenants of the Craigs Park, asking for a remission of rent. The previous summer they had had crops lying in their barn and barnyard enough to pay what was due, but then came the battle at Drumclog and rising of the Western Covenanters against Charles II. Armed men descended on Glasgow, first rebels and then the King's forces,

> who, without any order or Licence, came at thir pleasure, quartered in the park, did draw the stables, trampled, spoiled, and brocked the corne, took of quhat was readie thrashine to thir horse in great quantaties, and sent thir horse upon the growing grass and corne, and trampled and abused the same without controlment, most shamfullie, ther being seven score of the rebells horse on the grass and corne, four nights, besyd the King's troupe and uther troupes and Companies of dragounes, and by the proveist [Provost's] order ther was at one tyme nyne boolls corn given and a command to lett none of the King's troupe want corne, for quhilk we never got any satisfactione.[6]

It was duly agreed that a year's rent need not be paid.

A new Hospital for the Merchants

The years of Cromwell's rule had scarcely been a prosperous time for Scotland, but in Glasgow they had been, remarkably, a great age of building (Fig. 3.4). It was then that the fine baroque home of the University took shape in the High Street, and perhaps this stimulated the Merchants' ambitions. Their hospital in the Bridgegate was in 'a decaying condition'. At a meeting in January 1659 the Merchants unanimously agreed that they would all contribute to the cost of rebuilding it. A delegation was appointed 'to go to every Merchand, to the end, he may, under his hand, if he can write, or if he cannot, ane notar for him, on this book subscribe what he will contribute to the re-edifying of the said fore-wark and buying the said tenement, whose names are to remain in recorde herein to future ages'.[7]

The Merchant City in the seventeenth century

A traveller to Glasgow around 1660 described it as 'the second city in Scotland, fair, large, and well-built, cross-wise, somewhat like unto Oxford, the streets very broad and pleasant'. He referred to 'several fair hospitals, and well endowed, one of the Merchants, now in building'.[8] The new Merchants' Hospital was notably similar in design to Hutchesons' Hospital, which had been built in 1641 fronting on to Trongate, the town's widest and busiest street, more of a market than a thoroughfare (this Hutchesons' Hospital was demolished in 1803). The Tolbooth had received a new five-storey addition to the west side of the tower in 1626. A House of Correction was built in 1635 in the Drygate, and soon afterwards Rottenrow was graced with a new Grammar School. The Faculty of Physicians and Surgeons built their new home in Trongate in 1697. The crowning glory was the College, completed in 1656.

Many of the town's wooden buildings were destroyed by the fires of 1652 and 1677. After the 1677 fire the council ordered the rebuilding of the High Street to be in stone, and by the end of the century a regular pattern was emerging out of the medieval jumble. A visitor in 1689 noted that 'the two main streets are made cross-wise, well paved and bounded with stately buildings, especially about the centre, where they are mostly new, with piazzas under 'em.' (Piazzas were arcades, housing shops.) He too mentioned 'several hospitals, or houses of charity, and many spires more for ornament than use'.[9]

The book in which the list of subscriptions was made was the House's first Gold Book (or Guild Book), which later became the recognised record of membership. Over 270 members subscribed amounts ranging from £1. 4s. to £66. 13s. 4d. Scots, in total £4,393. 12s. 4d. Scots. The town council was asked to contribute too, given that the new hospital was to have 'ane steiple . . . heigher at least then that of Hutchseounes Hospitall' with a clock and a bell in it, which would be 'not only . . . ane great decorment and ornament to the streit quhair it standis but also verie commodious to all the inhabitants theraboutis'.[10] The town contributed £100 sterling.

Fig. 3.4   Glasgow from the south-east, c.1695 (John Slezer)
The steeple of the Merchants' Hospital takes centre stage.

But by the end of the following year, the Merchants found that the building work had proved unexpectedly costly, that much of their capital had been exhausted and that the contributions had 'not ansuered according to the expectatioune thereof'. The Dean of Guild again had to turn to the town council for help. He argued that 'now the steiple of the said hospitall is to be raised, quhilk will prove far moir profitable to the toune than to the hospitall' it would be 'a shame and disgrace' if it could not be completed.[11] The town, too, had little money to spare but it gave what it could, on condition that the Craftsmen should have similar help if they came to rebuild. The steeple must have been completed by 1665, for in December of that year the town council record that the town had been 'slightit' by one John Brodbreidge, who had not performed the work he had contracted to do in completing the clock, and ordered that 'he be seased upon by the magistratis and compellit to performe' the work.[12] This he must have done, for the town's accounts record payment to him in 1668 'in compleat payment of his making the knock [clock] in Briggait' (Fig. 3.5).[13]

The architect of the new hospital was later said to have been Sir William Bruce of Kinross, who, as architect to Charles II ('Surveyor-general and overseer of the King's Buildings in Scotland'), was to lay the foundation of the great age of Scottish classical building. Merchants House records shed no light on the identity of the architect: the minute books of the Merchants House are not extant before 1676, and although the account books for the building of the hospital still exist, they do not record payment to the architect, though they do tell us that the main contractor was William Boyd. Bruce is unlikely to have been the architect: his authenticated buildings are all dated later than 1659. If the architect was the same man who designed Hutchesons'

Fig. 3.5 The Merchants' Hospital and steeple in the Bridgegate
On the ground floor were apartments for the pensioners of the Hospital. In the late eighteenth century these were converted into four shops and houses to be let out for rent. The hall with its sash windows was on the first floor.

Hospital of 1641, to which the Merchants' Hospital bore a close resemblance, it cannot have been Bruce (who was a child at the time).[14]

More than seventy years after it was built, John McUre gave an admiring description of the hospital:

It was rebuilt in a most stately manner in the year of 1659, Sir John Bell late provost being then dean of gild.[15] It is of length from east to west seventy-two foot, the steeple thereof is of height one hundred and sixty-four foot, the foundation is twenty foot square, it hath three battlements of curious architecture above one another, and a curious clock of molten brass, the spire whereof is mounted with a ship of copper finely gilded in place of weather-cock. . . . The gild-hall, which comprehends the breadth and length of the house, is beautified with the gilded broads [boards], names, designations, and sums mortified for the use of the poor old members of the merchant rank, . . . likewise a large written broad with scripture directions how to buy and sell with a safe conscience . . . The hall is illuminated with fourteen chess [sash] windows

*together with the apartment for the dwellings of four poor old men. The steeple hath
a stately bell, being ten foot in circumference, which rings for the behoove of the
churches, [and] meeting of the merchants house; and hath a large flower garden
fenc'd about on the east, south and west, with a strong stone-wall of nine foot high . . .*[16]

Though the new hospital resembled the old Hutchesons' Hospital in Trongate,
the tower, as the Dean of Guild pointed out to the town council, was grander and
higher. The main façade was also similar to the house built in the Bridgegate by
James Campbell of Blythswood, Dean of Guild in 1659.

The spire is now almost all that remains of what must certainly have been an
exceptionally attractive building. Of the other remains, three are in the present
Merchants House building: the oak door is displayed in the Committee Room, and
the two stone reliefs of the three merchants and the ship are above the entrance
vestibule of the Hall.

Another stone is now in the care of Glasgow Museums. It stood above the entrance
to the hospital, and has an inscription – gilt in its day, though the gilding is now gone
– in Latin, garnished with a little Greek, stating that the hospital was founded 'by the
pious liberality and contributions of the merchants of the city of Glasgow of the
common era 1601. It was newly rebuilt, enlarged and adorned by the generosity and
returns of the same rank in 1659. Whoever gives bountifully to the poor lends to
Jehovah and he will return his gift to him.'[17] This inscription stone had been found
among 'a quantity of old stones' in the Cathedral around 1836 by one Thomas
McGuffie, who recognised it for what it was and, for safe keeping, built it into the
wall of a house he was building in Parliamentary Road. Ten years later he sold this
property and offered to extract the stone and give it to the Merchants House.
The House evidently did not take him up on his offer, for the stone was rediscovered
only in 1945 when the house was demolished. At that point it was acquired by
Glasgow Museums and it was at one time on display in the People's Palace.

The Scripture Rules

For the guidance of the Merchants in their dealings, the House set out 'Scripture
Rules to Be Observed in Buying and Selling', displayed on a 'broad' in their new
hall. Cleland, in his *Annals* of 1816, attributes it to the year 1695, when John Aird
was elected Dean of Guild. Certainly the painter of the Scripture Rules, William
Waddell, was given many assignments by the Merchants House around that time to
paint mortification boards and a board with the names of all the Deans of Guild.

'First take heed', the inscription runs, 'that you do not discommend those
Commodities that are very good, which you are about to buy, so that you may bring
down the price of the commoditie and get it for less than it is worth . . . Prov. 20. 14.
It is naught, it is naught, saith the buyer: but when he is gone his way, then he
boasteth. . . . So should not the seller over praise & commend a Commodity when
it is naught.'

Buyers are not to protest that they will not go beyond a certain sum when, in
fact, they are prepared to pay more. They are not to give counterfeit money 'though

you yourself took it for Commodities', or to use false weights in selling. They should pay promptly. 'It is the badge of a wicked man in Scripture, not to pay his debts, in Psal. 37. 21. The wicked borroweth and payeth not again.'

The merchants must not monopolise any kind of goods 'that by that means you may sell the commoditie at your own price: this is a meer oppression, destruction to a Common wealth, and to all trading'. He must not take advantage of the other man's mistakes; 'as suppos you should come to a shop and buy so many yards of cloth, or the like, and he should give thee more than is thy due, or take less money of thee than is his due, you should take no advantage of him . . . , but restore it again'. There must be no buying or selling on the Lord's Day. It is wrong to take advantage of a poor man's need by giving a low price for what he has to sell. 'Be not among the first that shall raise the price of a Commoditie. . . . When you are found to be deceitful in your dealing do not justifie your deceit.'

Finally, the merchant must not buy or sell 'those things which are not fit to be bought and sold'. He must not buy or sell stolen goods, or 'monuments of Idolatry . . . as Crosses, Beads, and Images, and Crucifixes', or trade in men for slaves. He must not sell spiritual things. He must not sell himself 'as Ahab did, to work wickednesse'. 'You must not sell those things that are for no other use, but to commit sin in the using of them; as for to sell stuffe to paint harlots faces is a sin, because it is for no other use but to commit sin in the using of it.'

A hundred years after it was set up, the board no longer hung in the Hall. Exactly when and why it was removed and when it was restored is not known. A Glasgow historian of the end of the eighteenth century says that it had been removed and implies that its advice was out of fashion: 'the present race of merchants, it is presumed, direct themselves by a more lasting monitor'.[18] It now hangs in the vestibule outside the Hall in the Merchants House building.

Income and investments in hard times

The building was a fine achievement, especially in such uncertain times. King Charles II had just returned from exile to London, and though his Restoration had been welcomed with joy in Scotland, since it brought about the withdrawal of Cromwell's English garrisons, the new government quickly proved to be expensive. The financial difficulties of the Merchants House may also have been partly due to the nature of its investments. In those days, when there were no banks and actual coined money was scarce, even the landed gentry were eager to borrow from all who had capital. The House had made loans on bond to an impressive series of landowners, beginning with the Countess of Glencairn, whose husband had led a rising in favour of Charles II. As too often happened, the lairds were not always able – or willing – to pay their interest. The town council itself owed the House £2,000 Scots. By 1676 the revenue of the House had actually shrunk. Two years later, before the Covenanting troubles cut off the rent from Wester Craigs, pensions had to be reduced by one third 'till it pleas God to incress the house stocke' – £500 more was being paid out than was received in income.

This was the one period of Glasgow's known history before the planned overspill of the 1960s when the population of the city actually fell. The fire of 1677 had destroyed many buildings, and in the years that followed, the town council did what it could to encourage rebuilding. In the case of some ruined buildings, it was impossible to trace all the original owners, or the parts owned by the various individuals had become virtually worthless and none had an interest in rebuilding. It was on such a derelict site, at the corner of Trongate and Saltmarket, that the council persuaded the Merchants House to build 'a large stane lodging, for the use of the poor' in 1682.[19] It acknowledged that the Merchants could not afford to build without help, and so the council undertook to pay the whole cost of the stonework for the building. The Merchants set about raising subscriptions for the rest of the cost and the building was erected in 1683. The various apartments in it, including, by the end of the century, a coffee house, were rented out to produce income for the House (see Chapter 4 and Fig. 4.6). (This was the sense in which it was 'for the use of the poor', in the Merchants House's use of income from investments to relieve hardship.)

A legacy from a German immigrant

In the account book for the building of this 'new house at the Corse [Cross]', the list of sums credited is headed by £2,277. 9s. Scots (around £190 sterling) bequeathed by one Zacharias Zebbes. This mortification, much the largest received at that date, dates from 1679. Zacharias Sibecen or Zebbes was born in Rostock in Germany around 1643, and had been working as a master-boiler in an Amsterdam sugar house, when in 1675 he received an invitation from Andrew Russell, a Scottish factor at Rotterdam, on behalf of John Cross (or Corse) of Glasgow's Easter Sugar House (Dean of Guild in 1694 and 1695), to come to Glasgow and take charge of the sugar boiling operation there, there being at that time no native Scotsman with the necessary knowledge and skills. The terms were a year's trial in the first instance, and 800 guilders a year with free board, lodging and laundry, and travel expenses. The Easter Sugar House had been having difficulty finding a satisfactory sugar boiler, but the arrival of Zebbes – 'the best we ever had' – was the turning point in the business's fortunes. He trained a Scottish apprentice, who was able to succeed him after his untimely death in 1679.[20]

The Merchants House had to defend its right to this legacy in a lengthy legal battle which reached the Court of Session in Edinburgh early in 1695. Zacharias's testament was contested by his family in Germany: his brother, Dominus Joannes Sibecen, minister at Rostock, and his sister Margaret, who was married to the town's chamberlain. The testament nominated Robert Cross, his employer at the sugar house (Dean of Guild in 1685), as his executor, and left several legacies including one to Robert Cross himself: 'the soume of ane thousand and fiftie Guilders Hollands money with his Trunk he had in the suggar house watches and goods therein with his sword pistolls and foulling peice', on the understanding that he would have him 'honestly buried'. The whole remainder of his estate he left to the Merchants House, referred to in the Court of Session decree as 'the hospitall of Glasgow'. The family alleged that Robert Cross and Robert Campbell, another merchant (Dean of Guild in 1679–81, and again in 1688 and 1689) had extracted a deathbed agreement to the will from the young foreigner, who was 'taken with a most virulent and hot fever' and 'distempered and distracted in his mind'. According to the family, Cross had had the will drawn up without consulting Zacharias and then 'prompted [him] to say Yea Yea to everie question'; he then brought a notary to the bedside and got him to ask questions about the will's provisions to which the sick man answered Yea Yea. They asserted that Zacharias would never have neglected to mention any of his family in his will if he had been of sound mind. Robert Cross, they said, had only included the Merchants' Hospital in the will 'the better to collour his own unjustice'. They claimed to have evidence that Zacharias had cried out on his deathbed that there were devils behind the bed coming to take him away, and that a few hours after he had agreed to the will, others had come into the room and tested his mental capability by asking if he would leave legacies to his horse, dog and cat and that he had answered Yea Yea to this too. Cross countered this with testimony of lucid conversations he had had with Zacharias on his sickbed about the will.[21]

Did Robert Cross and his friends take advantage of the incapacity of a foreign employee in the throes of a fatal infection? Or did Zacharias truly intend to leave his money to the Merchants' Hospital? At any rate, the Court of Session in 1695 sustained the testament (which was just as well, as the money had already been spent on the new building). Zacharias Zebbes was added to the list of benefactors of the House and a 'broad' was set up recording it (Fig. 3.6).

Fig. 3.6 Mortification board of Zacharias Zebbes (here spelled Gebbes)

Turbulent times and new opportunities

Helping to erect this 'great Lodging' at the Cross was one of the stated purposes of an unusual mortification of 1682: Provost Sir John Bell and Bailie Robert Cross (or Corse) assigned to the Dean of Guild and his Merchant Councillors all the fines which should come to them for 'Disorderlie baptismes, marriadges, keeping of hous or field conventicles, withdrawing from the public ordinances [worship]' – in fact from the persecution of the Covenanting Presbyterians in Glasgow.[22] Perhaps the provost and bailie were doing something to salve their consciences, though it does not appear that the House actually received any money as a result of the gesture. The next year it was laid down that the Dean of Guild, his Council and electors must take the anti-covenanting Test.

In 1686 King James VII and II, who was interfering in the election of magistrates and officials throughout Scotland, nominated the Dean for the next year – the only case of such government interference in the House's history. The king's intervention was why George Johnston served only one year as Dean; his brother John Johnston was stripped of his position as provost the same year. Both men had acted while in office to combat what they saw as abuses of public authority and funds: the Dean of Guild had had a dispute with the maltmen over excise payments, which he lost before the Privy Council – he spent a short time in the Edinburgh Tolbooth; Provost John Johnston had acted to recover money embezzled by the previous town administration and was imprisoned and ousted from office for defamation of Archbishop Ross, formerly of Glasgow, one of the beneficiaries of the corrupt administration's largesse. In October 1686 the king nominated not only the Dean for the following year, but the provost, bailies, town council, Deacon Convener, and deacons and visitors of each of the trades.

The hard times did not end with King James's fall in 1688. Six years later the House was supervising the raising of a tax of 13 dollars per head on all 'fenceable men' – those of an age to fight – to meet the cost of forty-four recruits raised by Glasgow for King William's wars. Two years later it was decided to invest £1,000 sterling – a very large percentage of the House's capital – in the new Company Trading to Africa and the Indies on which Scotland built hopes of colonisation and commerce, which were disastrously disappointed at Darien. At the same meeting of the Merchants, it was resolved to advise the town council to invest £3,000 sterling 'at least' of the town's money. The century ended with terrible years of famine when the crops failed throughout Scotland and other parts of northern Europe. At the height of this crisis, on 9 May 1699, it was unanimously resolved by the House 'that the haill poor belonging to the Toun be maintained'. Five Merchants were chosen to act with a committee of five members each from the town council, the Trades House and the kirk session 'to cast on a subsidie for the maintenance of the poor'. Perhaps this climate of depression and hardship was behind a decision in 1703 that the families of lawyers should no longer draw help from the House 'in regaird the wryters in Glasgow [the Faculty of Procurators] keep a box for ther own poor, and give the Merchants poor no pairt thereof'.[23]

The Darien Scheme

In 1698 Scotland attempted, and failed, to set up a colony for trading purposes in Darien, on the Isthmus of Panama. It was called the Scots Company Trading to Africa and the Indies, and £400,000 was pledged in subscriptions, estimated to be half the capital available in Scotland at the time. Merchants, mainly in Edinburgh and Glasgow, contributed over a quarter of the capital. The town of Glasgow subscribed £3,000, the Merchants House put forward £1,000, and Glasgow merchants individually signed for another £23,275. Glasgow hoped to be the trading headquarters and main beneficiary of the scheme, but the whole of Scotland pinned its hopes on the venture, ignoring the few voices warning that the Spanish would defend the territory. English merchants saw the venture as a threat, and King William ordered the English colonies in the area not to assist the Scottish settlers. Many died on the voyages, and the exhausted few who arrived failed to establish more than a toe-hold on the inhospitable and unhealthy territory. Of the 2,500 who sailed, 2,000 never returned.

The subscription lists for the Darien scheme are a useful indication of who was wealthy in Scotland at the end of the seventeenth century. Glasgow merchants contributed 8.6 per cent, compared with their Edinburgh counterparts' subscriptions of 13.7 per cent. The landed classes signed for 48.6 per cent.[24]

The hungry nineties

'Unto the Dean of Guild and his brethren merchants
The humble supplication of Mairie Weir spouse to Robert Johnstoune merchant burgess and guild brother of the burghe that where thrie years and ane half since my said husband went abroad to Ingland and from thence to others parts taken prisoner with the Frenchies and all the meanes & stock he had, he did take it with him only left some plenishing in the house and so having ane chyld named Mairie of the age of eight years old is destitute of learning & I not able to maintain myself & her I humbly request your lordships serious consideration of our sober and mean condition and grant us of your charitie quarterlie as your lordships think fit and to enroll us with the rest of your poor
Besikes etc

January 2nd 1691: The petitioner is allowed four pund for present necessity – John Graham clerk'

* * *

'My lord dean of gild And worthie members of the merchand rank
The supplicatione of Robert Craig Sone laufull to umquhile [deceased] John Craig merchand
Humbly Sheweth
That quhair By the providence of God I have atained to some litle learning And my genious leiding me to persew the Chapman calling I being now about 13 years

But having noe litle stock to Begin And hithertofor never having trubled your lordships nor expects god willing shall ever in tyme Coming

Wold Humbly Beg your lordships wold look upon me as on[e] of your members sones And bestow alse much upon me as will Be ane litle stock to begin the Chapman trade quhairby I may be keeped from vaging and being trublesome to uthers

Beseeks

28 April 1691: Appoints the petitioner Four punds scots – James Peadie'

* * *

The following petition was addressed to the town council but referred by them to the Dean of Guild and Merchants House:

'My Lord provost Baillies & Counsell

The humble supplication of Robert and Sarah Pirries bairns Lawfully procreat Betwixt umquill John Pirrie & Bessie Glen spousses

Sheweth

That quhare your petitioners are poor Orphans and in ane verie destitute and poor condition not able to doe for themselves as is known to some of your number, And the said Robert being about 10 or 11 yeares of age hes these two yeares bygoin gone throw the Countrie with a Litle pack, but Latlie the time of his mothers sicknes his mother made use of all that the said Robert had being but Litle about the value of tuentie shillings, So that the said Robertt hes nothing to begin the pack and the said Sarah is but ane sickly tender lass of the age of 8 or 9 yeares And hes nothing quharewith to supplie her present necessitie.

May it therfore pleise your Lordships & Counsell To Take the premisses to Consideration and allow the said Robert what ye think fitt to putt him again to the pack which will keep the petitioner from being any more troublesome to the place As also to Allow the said Sara what ye judge fitt for helping her present straitt & condition which is very bad And your favorable etc.

The petitioners are allowed seven punds ten shillings wherof six ll' to the Lad and half a Croune to the Lass – John Grahame'

A port for Glasgow

Thomas Tucker, in his *Report on the Excise and Customs* in 1655 noted of Glasgow:

The scituation of this towne in a plentifull land, and the mercantile genius of the people, are strong signes of her increase and groweth, were she not checqued and kept under by the shallownesse of her river, every day more and more increasing and filling up, soe that noe vessells of any burden can come neerer up then within fourteene miles, where they must unlade, and send up theyr timber, and Norway trade in rafts on floates, and all other comodotyes, by three or foure tonnes of goods at a time, in small cobbles or boates of three, foure, five, and none of above six tonnes, a boate.[25]

The expanding volume and diversity of overseas trade was undoubtedly the most important area of growth in the seventeenth century, but in order to take advantage of this, Glasgow had to overcome the drawback of the lack of port facilities. In 1668 the town council began to invest in the construction of a large deep-water harbour with custom-house, warehouses and in fact an entire town at Newark, ten miles downstream. It was, according to a Minute of the Merchants House some years later,

> *a most safe and convenient harbor, with Lodgings, Sellars, and all other buildings necessar and convenient for loading, livering, preserving, and stouring all maner of goods, . . . with fitt and convenient habitations for seamen, carpenters, and others, for building, dressing, and repairing of vessells . . .*[26]

The new town and harbour, named Newport Glasgow, was the best port in Scotland – surpassing those of Leith, Aberdeen and Dundee – and the only one ever to be built by a municipality as a planned facility on a virgin site.[27] Gone were the days of being restricted to trade in small boats to the shallow port at Broomielaw, or to unload into lighters in the Firth, or to use the unsatisfactory harbours elsewhere, such as that of rival Dumbarton across the river; Port Glasgow alone was judged 'suitable for ships of the greatest burden'. In 1705 merchants were solemnly warned by the House that they must not lay up or fit out their ships at any other port on the Clyde 'except in case of necessitie'.

Such was the effect of the provision of proper port facilities that another visitor was able to observe, in 1689: '[The] river is a great current, called the Clyde, and conduces much to the riches of the inhabitants, and makes it the most considerable town of that nation.'[28] A second port was provided at Greenock, where a harbour was built between 1707 and 1710 (Fig. 3.7). Glasgow's merchants were required to trade via these ports and nowhere else. Neither town had merchant burgesses of its own, and almost all the business of these ports was based in Glasgow.

Fig. 3.7   A view of Greenock from the Clyde (engraved by Robert Paul, 1768)
Greenock's harbour was built between 1707 and 1710, and by the 1760s trade to the port had increased so much that a new harbour, with east and west quays, was built.

The extraordinary career of Walter Gibson

Walter Gibson is introduced to us by McUre, a younger contemporary, in his History of Glasgow. He was born around 1643, the eldest son of a landowner, who evidently apprenticed him to malt-making: 'His first appearance was in malt-making, and his stock being improven in that way, he left that trade, and betook himself to merchandizing, and began first with the herring-fishing, and in one year he made, packed and cured 300 lasts of herring at six pound sterling per last, containing twelve barrells each last, and having fraughted a Dutch ship, called the St Agat, burdened four hundred and fifty tuns, the ship, with the great cargo, arrived safely at St Martins in France [on the Ile de Ré, off La Rochelle], where he got for each barrell of herring a barrell of brandy and a crown, and the ship at her return was loaded with salt and brandy. And the product [profit] came to a prodigious sum, so that he bought this great ship, and other two large ships, he traded to France, Spain, Norway, Swedland and Virginea. He was the first that brought iron to Glasgow, the shop-keepers before bought the same, with dying stuffs from Stirling and Borrowstounness [Bo'ness].'[29]

Gibson appears as the largest subscriber – for £100 Scots – in the Gold Book of the Merchants House before 1691. According to McUre, he launched himself as a sea-adventurer after 1668: he might have managed part of his transatlantic trade by disguising his vessels as English ships, for it was illegal, under the Navigation Acts, for Scottish ships to trade to American ports. (The only legal way around this was to transport colonists, usually prisoners, on the outward voyage: see below.) His possessions included land in Gourock, where he probably cured his herring, and a magnificent tenement in the Saltmarket 'adorned with several orders of architecture', attributed, like the Merchants House, to Sir William Bruce. He was laird of a huge estate, comprising Meikle Govan and Bellahouston, Balshagrie, Whiteinch-meadow, Balgray, Hyndland, Partick, Partick Bridge-end, and Clayslap or Overton (later the site of Glasgow University). He was provost in 1688–9, but it was only a few years later that the town council was taking legal action to recover substantial debts owed to the town. He was made bankrupt and his estates transferred to trustees. His properties were eventually disposed of, but not before Gibson had found himself imprisoned for debt for a short time in the Tolbooth. He died in 1723.

Later commentators liked to connect his misfortunes with what came to be seen as a shameful episode in his past: in 1684 he had arranged for the transportation to the American plantations of Covenanters captured after Bothwell Bridge; those who survived a particularly brutal voyage, in his brother's ship, were sold as slaves. In the same year he was to be found offering to ship out a different human cargo, of free persons, in a scheme for settling emigrants in the American colonies, at the rate of £5 per adult and 50 shillings per child. The transportation of people – both volunteers and undesirables (felons, beggars and political prisoners) – to the colonies was the one loophole that enabled Scots to trade legitimately across the Atlantic in the face of the Navigation Acts, and the consortium headed by Walter Gibson had a contract with the Government agent for transportation to convey regular consignments of prisoners from the Clyde to Virginia and the Carolinas. Commodities could be carried as well, and a full cargo of tobacco on the return voyage.

Notable and enterprising

The Merchants House had plenty of challenges to contend with in its first hundred years, a century of turbulent history in Scotland, but the century too when Glasgow grew in wealth and population at a greater rate than any other burgh in Scotland. The number of inhabitants increased by something between 50 and 100 per cent, and in wealth Glasgow moved from fifth place among Scottish burghs to second, leaving Aberdeen, Dundee and Perth far behind. The mainspring behind this economic progress was the merchant community, which has been described as 'the source of practically everything that is notable and enterprising in this notable and enterprising town'.[30] With their harbour for ocean-going ships, they had expanded their markets from Ireland and northern Europe to Spain, and even to the New World. The Merchants House had initiated a scheme for giving help to 'poor and decayed seamen', the antecedent of the Clyde Marine Society (see Chapter 4). Glasgow was about to become a maritime city.

The merchants had already begun to plough the profits of their trade into new manufactories for fine cloth, rope, soap, glass, porcelain and paper, as well as a tobacco spinning works and sugar refineries. It is noteworthy that the post-1660 expansion into manufacturing came about not through activity by the craft incorporations but by merchants forming companies to manufacture goods for export. It would be a long time before Glasgow became a great manufacturing city, but the foundations had been laid.

Glasgow merchant enterprise in the late seventeenth century

'In the next place, we are to consider the merchants and traders in this eminent Glasgow, whose store-houses and ware-houses are stuft with merchandize, as their shops swell big with foreign commodities, and returns from France, and other remote parts, where they have agents and factors to correspond, and inrich their maritime ports, whose charter exceeds all the charters in Scotland' (Richard Franck, 1656).[31]

Taking a more measured view, Daniel Defoe wrote in 1706: 'I do not believe there's ten in Scotland who deserve the name of Merchants, that is, Men Universally known in Trade.'[32] Even allowing for exaggeration by Defoe, who had an axe to grind on behalf of the English government, it is a fact that by comparison with their English counterparts, Scottish merchants were poor. Their harbours – shallow, and dry at low tide – would not accommodate the largest ships, until the construction of Port Glasgow.

One of the most frequented destinations for Scottish ships was Norway, and much timber came from there to Glasgow, especially later in the century, along with pitch and tar. Bar-iron came from Sweden, a valuable cargo, in worth a third of all imports arriving at the Clyde. Other high-value cargoes came from France, much of them to the Clyde, including wines and salt (essential for preserving fish). Compared with such journeys, the voyage to Ireland was short and involved much less risk.

Thousands of Scots had emigrated to Ulster, constituting a large consumer market, and this Irish trade enriched Glasgow's merchants throughout the century, providing the profits which were to be invested in riskier, faraway markets, including those on the other side of the Atlantic.

In foreign ports, merchant traders relied on factors, who were familiar with the local language and customs and had detailed knowledge of the market. The factors were themselves merchants, or former merchants, and there were several Scottish factors in the West Indies and North America. They were important to Scottish trade, because the English Navigation Acts of 1660 prohibited Scottish merchants from trading to the West Indies and Virginia, and those carrying on trade in defiance of the Acts could not rely on English factors in these places.

Despite the English attempts to keep Scottish trade out of America and the West Indies, Glasgow men did succeed in breaking into this market, at the risk of being heavily fined if caught. The new harbour at Port Glasgow could accommodate ships large enough to carry a worthwhile cargo and to survive Atlantic storms. It was in 1672 that the first ship belonging to Glasgow, the *Glasgow Merchant*, crossed the Atlantic.

One of the commodities available in this region of the world was sugar, raw or semi-refined. Scotland at this time imported most of her sugar, in the form of loaf sugar and candy, from Holland, where the science of refining was understood. Tobacco may be the most famous transatlantic trade, but it was the sugar trade that blazed the way.

The great prosperity of Glasgow in the eighteenth and nineteenth centuries was not founded on trade alone. It was the partnership between manufacturing and commerce that created the enormous wealth of these centuries, a pairing that began in the 1660s. The partners in the new 'manufactories', making glass, rope, soap and sugar, were merchants, who had the capital to start them off and the means of obtaining raw materials and finding markets for the finished goods.

The first sugar-refining house in Scotland was the Wester Sugar House, founded in Glasgow in 1667 by four merchants. They founded it as a joint-stock company and began in small premises, employing a Dutch master-boiler, the skills needed being unknown in Scotland (just as Zacharias Zebbes was later hired by the Easter Sugar House). Before long it had made so much money that they were able to build a large tenement combining factory and offices, to which was soon afterwards added a distillery for making rum out of the waste molasses.

Special parliamentary privileges such as tax concessions and exemption from customs dues on the exported rum helped the industry in its infancy. Two other sugar houses followed in the next few years, also founded by merchants; in the South Sugar House, the distillery side of the business, producing rum, brandy and other spirits, was at least as important as the sugar refining, 'seeing that no trade can be managed to [the Guinea coast and America] or the East Indies, without great quantities of [these] liquors'.[33] The merchants who founded these sugar houses continued to trade overseas, to Holland, Virginia, Norway and elsewhere. Many of them were Deans of Guild and Collectors of the Merchants House in the last four decades of the century.

The sugar masters in their quest for raw material – crude sugars in the form of large, sticky, indigestible crystals, semi-refined – were sending ships to the Caribbean from the mid-1660s, and thus pioneered the way for the tobacco trade. They made large fortunes for themselves and brought prosperity to Glasgow. They helped the balance of trade by producing for the home market commodities that had previously been imported – a consideration dear to the hearts of the economists of the day. And their factories, along with the new soap-boiling and salt-making concerns, were the predecessors of the important Scottish chemical industry.

Notes

1. Acts of Sederunt of the Dean of Guild Court, 10 Apr. 1605.
2. Ibid., 11 Apr. 1605.
3. T. C. Smout, 'The Glasgow merchant community in the seventeenth century', *Scottish Historical Review* 47 (1968), pp. 53–71.
4. Andrew M. Jackson, *Glasgow Dean of Guild Court: a History* (Glasgow, 1983), p. 21.
5. George Downing's letter, 18 Oct. 1650, quoted in Zachary Grey, *An impartial examination of the fourth volume of Mr. Daniel Neal's History of the Puritans* (London, 1739), app. p. 48.
6. Merchants House Minutes, 16 Jan. 1681.
7. Preamble to the Gold Book of the Merchants House.
8. P. Hume Brown, *Early Travellers in Scotland* (Edinburgh, [1891] 1973), p. 237.
9. Ibid., pp. 288–9.
10. *Extracts from the Records of the Burgh of Glasgow*, vol. 2, 29 Jan. 1659.
11. Ibid., 10 Nov. 1660.
12. Ibid. 9 Dec. 1665.
13. Senex, *Glasgow Past and Present*, 3 vols. (Glasgow, 1884), vol. 1, p. 102.
14. The attribution of the Merchants' Hospital to Bruce, found in James Cleland's *Annals of Glasgow* (Glasgow, 1817), is 'more hopeful than credible', according to Andor Gomme and David Walker, *Architecture of Glasgow* (London, 1968), p.45.
15. John Bell was Dean of Guild from October 1656 till October 1658. He was provost in 1659. James Campbell of Blythswood was Dean in 1659 and 1660.
16. John McUre, *A View of the City of Glasgow* (Glasgow, [1736] 1830), pp. 203–4.
17. 'ΑΠΟΡΕΜΠΟΡΟΔΟΧΕΙΟΝ hoc, civitatis Glasguanae mercatorum, pia liberalitate et impensis fundatum, Aerae vulg. cითიci. Denuo eiusdem ordinis reditibus ac munificentia reaedificatum, auctum, et ornatum est cითიclix.

    Mutuat Jehovae, qui largitur pauperi;

    Et retributionem illius reddet ei.'

    The quotation is from Prov. 19:17.
18. James Denholm, *An Historical Account and Topographical Description of the City of Glasgow and Suburbs* (Glasgow, 1797), pp. 113–14.
19. *Ext. Rec. Glas.*, 30 Sept. 1682.

20. T. C. Smout, 'The early Scottish sugar houses', *Economic History Review* 2nd series, 14 (1962), p. 249.

21. Glasgow City Archives T-MH 45.1.2.

22. Merchants House mortification, 2 Oct. 1682: in W. H. Hill, *View of the Merchants House of Glasgow* (Glasgow, 1866), pp. 593–4.

23. MH Minutes, 8 Jan. 1703.

24. T. C. Smout, *Scottish Trade on the Eve of Union 1660–1707* (Edinburgh, 1963), p. 150.

25. Hume Brown, *Early Travellers*, p. 177. See also Fig. 1.1.

26. MH Minutes, 4 Oct. 1705.

27. T. C. Smout, 'The development and enterprise of Glasgow 1556–1707', *Scottish Journal of Political Economy* 7 (1964), p. 205.

28. Hume Brown, *Early Travellers*, p. 289.

29. McUre, *Glasgow*, p. 169.

30. Smout, 'The Glasgow merchant community in the seventeenth century', p. 57.

31. Hume Brown, *Early Travellers*, p. 192.

32. Daniel Defoe, *The Advantages of Scotland by an Incorporate Union with England . . .* (1706), p. 11.

33. Quoted in George Eyre-Todd, *History of Glasgow*, vol. 2 (Glasgow, 1931), p. 40.

THE HOUSE IN THE MERCHANT CITY

The eighteenth century is a particularly important age in Glasgow's history. It was then that, for the first time, it became a great place of business. In the late 1720s it was called by an admiring visitor 'the beautifullest little city I have seen in Britain; it stands deliciously on the Banks of the River Clyde'[1] – but it was, indeed, a little city with not much more than 12,000 people (Fig. 4.1). By the end of the 1780s the

Fig. 4.1   Glasgow from the south-west, 1760 (engraved in the Foulis Academy)
Looking across the river from the old windmill, the cone-shaped glassworks, the Merchants' steeple and the old Glasgow Bridge can be seen.

population was nearer 70,000, which made it not only the second city of Scotland but a great town by the European standards of the time. And Glasgow's wealth came in the main from trade, not from manufacture as it was to do later. Its leading citizens were merchants: the so-called Tobacco Lords, who made it, for a while, the chief centre of the trade in Europe, and the merchants of West Indian sugar.

The tobacco trade

The tobacco trade grew unevenly after the Union of 1707, but after 1740 it increased exponentially. In 1741, 8 million pounds of tobacco were imported by Glasgow merchants, and by 1752 this had increased to 21 million. Soon Scottish tobacco imports had overtaken those of London and all the English ports combined. In 1771, Glasgow merchants brought 47 million pounds of tobacco across the Atlantic, and exported it to twenty-one European ports, from the Baltic to the Mediterranean, returning with cargoes ranging from iron and timber to lemons and olive oil.

It was the strength of a close-knit merchant community and an already-established industrial background that made possible this legendary 'Golden Age of Tobacco', as it has been called. The tobacco merchants themselves were only ever a small minority – around 10 per cent – of the Glasgow merchants, and within that group an even smaller number controlled the bulk of the trade. In a peak period before 1775, more than half of the Clyde tobacco trade was in the hands of syndicates headed by three men: William Cunninghame, Alexander Speirs and John Glassford. A few other networks of merchant dynasties dominated the rest of Glasgow's Atlantic trade.

Involvement in the tobacco trade (and the West Indian trade too) implies an involvement in slavery. There were very few direct slaving voyages from Glasgow, but some Glasgow merchants trafficked slaves through Liverpool and other English ports. In one way or another, the entire transatlantic trade depended on and profited by slavery. Glasgow merchants provided capital, in the form of credit, to the Virginia planters to buy the slaves they needed to run their estates. In other indirect ways too, Glasgow's economic growth was linked to the slave system: for example, colonial markets, where tens of thousands of slaves required to be clothed, were crucial to the linen industry.

Most tobacco merchants continued to trade in other goods, often carrying a freight of supplies for their chains of Virginia and Maryland stores on the outward voyage, and some of the tobacco was exchanged for goods rather than cash or credit. The typical tobacco merchant had interests in other forms of commerce and investment, both foreign and domestic, from Caribbean sugar to European wine and salt, from banking and marine insurance to the acquisition and commercial exploitation of land. Partnership was the key to this expansion and diversification – as it was for the tobacco syndicates themselves. The Glasgow merchant community was sufficiently wide, access to it and movement within it were sufficiently fluid, and there was sufficient wealth and credit within it, to provide openings to many an ambitious man. Industrial partnerships involving tobacco merchants dominated certain industries, such as tanning and glass manufacture. Newer industries, such as textiles and iron-working, soon to become of paramount importance in the West of Scotland, were funded in part by tobacco money.

The tobacco merchants exercised civic power more in proportion to their wealth than their numbers. Between 1740 and the late 1790s, tobacco merchants accounted for all but five Deans of Guild, and all but one provost.

An independent and influential House

It was natural that in a merchant city the Merchants House should be especially important. It was significant for Glasgow that the official organisation of its merchants had kept an independent life of its own much more successfully than the older merchant guilds of other Scottish towns. Nearly all important burghs were managed largely by men of the Merchant rank, who provided the provosts (except where these were local lords or lairds) and at least half the town councillors. But in many of them – Aberdeen, Dundee and Edinburgh for instance – the councils had practically swallowed the old guildries. They appointed the Deans of Guild, not, as in Glasgow, from a leet named by the Merchants, but by their own choice, and they had even absorbed most of the property belonging to the guildries. In Edinburgh an entirely new Merchant Company was founded in 1681, to begin with as a drapers' guild, but it had very little part in the management of the city.

In Glasgow, however, the two bodies that made up the Guildry, the Merchants and the federated Crafts, were just rising to the height of their influence after a century of official life. Their position in the town's affairs was emphasised by the Scottish Parliament in 1705. The city was seriously in debt, and to keep it afloat it was granted a new source of revenue, twopence Scots (a sixth of a penny sterling) on each pint of ale sold. For the town council this was a great boon and privilege, but it was laid down in the Act that the Merchants and Trades should join with parliamentary commissioners in verifying the debts to be paid with the money (Fig. 4.2). Time and again when the town council was in difficulties – over the need to raise money for fortifications during the Jacobite rising of 1715, over the building of a new quay at the Broomielaw, over the cost of Prince Charlie's requisition in the Forty-Five – the Merchants House was asked for its approval of what was being done.

The House now held it to be its duty to state its views on all important public questions affecting the city. In 1768 it could claim that 'it is the right and priviledge of this House, to be informed of every Bill, proposed to be brought into Parliament by the Magistrats and Council, by which the rights and interests of the Inhabitants of this City may be affected, before application is made to Parliament.'[2] The occasion of this pronouncement was a Bill that the town council had brought before Parliament for building a new bridge and an exchange, among various other projects. The House resolved that the Bill should be delayed until they had had time to examine all its implications. The council responded with surprise at the 'unexpected [and] unconstitutional attack' on its rights. The Merchants House rebutted the allegation of unconstitutional behaviour – the clerk had mistakenly missed out the

Fig. 4.2   Thomas Peter (artist: George Scougall)
Thomas Peter (1641–1721) was one of the members of the Merchants House chosen in 1705 to
inspect the list of the town's debts that were to be paid off by the tax of twopence per pint of beer.
A former town treasurer, and a bailie in 1701 and 1712, he was often entrusted with matters of town
finance. He was nominated by the Merchants House to serve as a manager of the building of the new
Blackfriars Kirk in 1701 (for which he had loaned the town council 2,000 merks) and when the kirk
was built he was appointed collector of the seat prices. As an importer of claret, among other things,
he supplied the town with a large consignment of communion wine in 1707. Successful in business,
he was able to purchase the estate of Crossbasket in East Kilbride. He was Dean of Guild in 1708
and 1709, and for many years had been active in the affairs of the House, serving on numerous
committees. He was the first collector of the fund for seamen, set up by the House, which later became
the Marine Society (see below). On his death Thomas Peter left 3,000 merks to the Merchants House
'for ane old, decayed, poor, honest, burges, gild brother and inhabitant of . . . Glasgow, of the
Merchant rank'. His great-grandson, Robert Peter, was the first mayor of Georgetown, Washington DC
(founded 1751), and Robert's son Thomas married a step-granddaughter of George Washington.

words 'it is the opinion of', as the councillors very well knew – and expressed its
displeasure at the fact that the application to Parliament had been made without its
knowledge. The Merchants objected to the plans for an exchange having been made
without consulting them, and without a proper plan or estimate, which might lead
to 'boundless expense'. And they deplored as 'very unbecoming' the implied threat
in the council's response regarding their powers. The following week the Dean of
Guild was able to inform his members that the council had agreed that the Bill would
not be pressed forward, and the House returned the magistrates and council its

gracious thanks. The Merchants House, throughout the century, had a say in most important city matters with its own voice, and not merely through the Dean of Guild and other magistrates and councillors who were Merchants, and it was most unusual for this to be challenged.

The anti-Union riots

In the early part of the century it also had its own share in the crises of the time. There were the anti-Union riots of November and December 1706, when, for weeks on end, Glasgow was more or less in the hands of mobs protesting against the passing of the Act which was to merge the Parliament and Kingdom of Scotland with those of England. It might be thought that the Union would have been approved in Glasgow, which was to benefit by free trade with England and the American colonies; but in fact the change was violently unpopular, though the attitude of the city's Establishment was rather uncertain. When the first article (or clause) of the Act was passed by the Scottish Parliament in Edinburgh on 4 November, Glasgow's representative, Hugh Montgomerie of Busby – of course a Merchant – opposed it. Three days later Montgomerie's brother-in-law, the minister of the Tron Kirk, preached a famous anti-Union sermon ending with the words: 'Up and be valiant for the city of your God!' The streets filled with protesting crowds. The deacons of the Trades met the provost, John Aird, and demanded that the town should petition Parliament to abandon the Union project.

Provost Aird was a notable and influential figure in the Merchants House and the city. He had been three times Dean of Guild and is said to have been responsible for the House's Scripture Rules for buying and selling. His portrait, still prominently displayed in the Merchants' Hall, commemorates the legacy he left to the House (Fig. 4.3). In 1706 he was probably one of the few convinced supporters of the plan for the Union, but he evidently did not find it safe to say so publicly in this crisis. Instead he explained that it would be unwise to 'address' the Parliament lest the famous grant of twopence on the pint to pay the city's debts should be withdrawn. A few days later, when the anti-Unionists had armed themselves, smashed the Tolbooth windows and came looking for him again, he ran into a neighbour's house and hid in a bed which folded up against the wall.

'But the . . . Hand that smote the men of Sodom with Blindness, when they would have Rabbled the Angels, protected him from this many Headed Monster, and so Blinded them, that they could not find him', wrote Daniel Defoe (whose interest in Scotland was that of an agent of the English government).[3] Aird escaped and took refuge in Edinburgh, where there were troops to protect the Unionist authorities. It was John Bowman, Dean of Guild, and himself a future provost, who took the lead in the hard task of trying to restore order. The burgesses, Merchants and Craftsmen were, in effect, the only police force of the town. The Dean and Deacon Convener summoned them to mount a continuous guard. Every householder was to appear for this duty or send a substitute, and even Merchants and Craftsmen not actually on duty were to join in quelling disturbances, though there was little enthusiasm for the work.

Fig. 4.3 John Aird (artist: John Williamson)

John Aird (c. 1654–1730) was one of Glasgow's most powerful provosts, holding office ten times between 1705 and 1723. He was a friend of Daniel Campbell of Shawfield, the city's MP and one of its richest merchants, and he was provost at the time that Campbell succeeded in getting an Act passed in Parliament renewing the town's grant of twopence on each pint of ale; the magistrates rewarded Campbell for his efforts by giving him the surprisingly large sum of £348 sterling, nearly half of the amount restored to the city, while Aird himself and the Town Clerk received £111. 16s. for their 'expenses in London'. When various other fees and expenses had been paid, there can have been very little left for the common good fund.[4]

Well-disposed towards Union and the English government, he was described by Daniel Defoe as 'an honest, sober, discreet gentleman, one that had always been exceedingly beloved, even by the common people, particularly for his care of, and charity to the poor of the town'.[5] It was through the Merchants House that he conveyed much of his charity: having no surviving children, he mortified to the Merchants House in 1723 his house and ground at the corner of Bridgegate and the Old Wynd, along with other property in the Bridgegate; the rents were to be used for the support of poor elderly merchants and widows after the death of his (third) wife, who remarried and became Lady Craigends. The properties were sold for £480 in 1753, and Lady Craigends continued to receive her annuity until her death in 1757. It can only have been then that the poor began to benefit from Aird's mortification.

Aird was Dean of Guild in 1696 and 1697, 1700 and 1701, and 1704 and 1705. In his handling of the anti-Union riots of 1706 his attempts to placate the mob by certain concessions seem only to have had the effect of making them bolder, but there is no doubt that he was in a dangerous position. He was assaulted by the mob, and had dirt and stones thrown at him, his house was ransacked and a number of muskets and some other property seized, and on at least one occasion he was in fear for his life. For much of the last two months of 1706 the city was under mob rule, but perhaps the provost might have been able to console himself with the reflection that there was no loss of life.

John Bowman and the Deacon Convener then set off for Edinburgh with an anti-Union address, which was duly presented to the Parliament. This was not enough to satisfy the protesters, however, and an armed party from Glasgow set off for Hamilton, in the mistaken belief that an anti-Union army was gathering there. The riots subsided when troops, under the Duke of Argyll's brother, rode into Glasgow, but they revived again when the soldiers left and only ended when the Act of Union was passed.

The Malt Tax riot

In 1725 another Dean of Guild, John Stark, was arrested with the Lord Provost, bailies and Deacon Convener, on a charge of having encouraged the mob that had sacked the house of the city's MP, Daniel Campbell of Shawfield, in protest against the new Malt Tax, which Campbell had supported in Parliament. As the provost and Dean had confronted the mob and attempted to persuade them to withdraw, before being attacked themselves and having to flee for their lives, the arrest may seem surprising. A loyal band of forty to fifty fellow merchants accompanied them to Edinburgh where they were held in the Tolbooth, and on their release they were met on their way into Glasgow by a large crowd of triumphant townspeople. There is some suggestion that the provost and bailies were victims of local rivalries, having recently displaced 'Aird's party', known to be friends of Campbell. Campbell did not come too badly out of the fracas: the city had to pay him punitive damages for the destruction of his house, with which he was able to buy the island of Islay from a fellow clansman.

Glasgow in the Forty-Five

Danger came to Glasgow again with the Forty-Five rising, when the Merchants House was convened to consider a petition from 'the principal inhabitants' to the magistrates and town council 'setting forth that the City is threatened to be attacked by a [Jacobite] force which they are in no condition able to resist, and that the inhabitants, and their trades, and dwellings are in Imminent danger of being exposed to irreparable losses and inconveniences'. The magistrates and council were asked to approve the choice of a committee, including eight eminent Merchants 'upon the approach of any such force, To meet with their Leaders and make the best terms possibly they can, for saving the city and its trade and inhabitants from these dismal consequences'.[6]

The delegation had to meet with Prince Charles's agent, John Hay of Restalrig, bearing a letter from the Prince coolly demanding 'a sum of money . . . not exceeding fifteen thousand pounds sterling' and all the city's arms. The entire annual revenue of the city at this time was about £3,000. They bargained fairly effectively with Mr Hay, persuading him to take only £5,500, and the House, under Dean of Guild George Bogle, agreed that, 'as necessity has no law', those burgesses who had money should make contributions on the understanding that it would be repaid by the people of Glasgow 'according to their respective abilities'.[7] Provost Andrew

Cochrane wrote on the occasion that 'partly by advances from the inhabitants, partly by borrowing money, the sum has been made up, and, with the goods, delivered Mr. Hay. I wish even this may procure us safety from plunder and rapine.'[8]

The Bogles of Glasgow and the Merchants House

The man who was Dean of Guild at the time of the Forty-Five, George Bogle, came from an important and numerous Glasgow family, many of whom were merchants. John Bogle and Marcus Bogle were at the first meeting of the Merchants House in 1605. Early in the seventeenth century, two important branches of the family were founded by the brothers George and Robert Bogle, which became known as the Bogles of Daldowie and Shettleston respectively. George Bogle (1693–1753), Dean of Guild in 1741 and 1742, 1745 and 1746, and 1749 and 1750, was from the Shettleston side. He was elected a bailie in 1732 and again in 1739. He was married three times, and acquired part of the lands of Easter Craigs by his third marriage. At his death he left £100 Scots to the Merchants House. A later Dean of Guild, James Bogle (Dean in 1847 and 1848), was his great-great-nephew. It was James Bogle's brother Archibald who sold the lands of Gilmorehill which were soon afterwards acquired by the University for its new campus (see Chapter 9).

Another George Bogle was the younger contemporary of Dean of Guild George Bogle. He was known as George Bogle of Daldowie, and was town treasurer in 1729, and Rector of the University several times in the 1730s and 1740s. He was on the Dean of Guild's Council of twenty-four (that is, a Director of the Merchants House) for many years. He had been sent to the Continent to broaden his education in the 1720s, and travelled around representing his family's business interests in various countries, from time to time enrolling in a course at a college in subjects that interested him. He became a prominent merchant on his return and was involved in the tobacco trade, and several other concerns including the Easter Sugar House, George Macintosh's cudbear works (Chapter 5), a tannery and an iron works. He built a large house at Daldowie, in what is now the Mount Vernon area, and at the time of the Forty-Five received a demand there from the Jacobite Pretender for large quantities of provisions. His estate was then looted of further stock, and on complaining to the Prince he received a letter of royal protection. His younger brother Matthew was Dean of Guild in 1743 and 1744, and was one of the delegation appointed to meet and negotiate with the Prince's representatives in September 1745.

In November, Provost Cochrane summarised the 'unhappy situation' of the country, and of his own city in particular:

> *For eight weeks there has been no business; our custom-house is shut up, though we*
> *have 4000 hds. tobacco lying in the river undischarged; our manufactures at a stand*
> *for want of sales and money; no payments of any kind; no execution; our country*
> *robbed, plundered, and harassed by partys.*

He adds: 'I have had great care and fatigue, and would not go through such another scene for a great deal of money: God grant it were well over.'[9]

It was, of course, far from over. Repeated requests for assistance and instructions from the king's representatives in Edinburgh met with prevarication, delays and many changes of plan. (Arms were eventually obtained from the government, and a battalion of 600 Glasgow men was raised, and sent to Stirling to help guard the pass under the Earl of Home; this force was later sent to Edinburgh to assist in defending the capital.) At Christmas, the remains of the Prince's army arrived in Glasgow, and demanded an enormous levy of clothing and shoes. The inhabitants 'for fear of being plundered' were again obliged to comply, but the Jacobite army was received with no enthusiasm. They hinted that some mitigation of the levy might be obtained if the magistrates and principal burgesses would pay their respects to the Prince, but they declined. Provost Cochrane estimated the total amount taken from the city to be about £10,000, much of it in goods:

> It is impossible to describe the distress we are in; the lower and even midling inhabitants ruined by want of business, and entertaining from ten to twenty of these guests at free quarters, so many days; the more substantial burgesses in a very desponding state, brought under a heavy debt at a time when no business is stirring, and the publick stock quite exhausted and ruined.[10]

The Prince, having lodged for a week at the house of John Glassford, one of the big tobacco merchants, marched out to win his last victory at Falkirk.

The next year, after the defeat at Culloden, the House was asked to lend its weight to the town's application to the government for some 'relief and reimbursement' of the debts and expenses incurred. This it readily did, but it took Andrew Cochrane and his brother-in-law, Bailie George Murdoch (Dean of Guild in 1751 and 1752), a full six months of argument before ministers and Parliament in London. Eventually the government paid £10,000 in recompense for the Jacobite requisitions; Andrew Cochrane, on being offered a sum by the city in recognition of his serivces, declined to accept anything for himself.

Changes in constitution and membership

The depredations of the Jacobite army evidently had a serious effect on the Merchants House's resources. A committee appointed in March 1746 reported 'that the provisions [sic] for the maintenance of the poor of the merchant rank is extremely scanty and small, and that there is no Fund for supporting and defending the just right and privileges of the fair traders', that is, of the merchant burgesses themselves. Resources for these purposes might be considerably increased, the committee thought, if 'all traders in the place who are willing to contribute', were admitted to membership of the House.[11] It would seem that, in spite of the terms of the Letter of Guildry, which evidently intended that all respectable merchant burgesses should be members – indeed that they must be members as a condition of their right to trade freely – the Dean of Guild had acquired the right of nominating those to be admitted. The reigning Lord Dean, John Brown, offered to abandon this power, provided that the House ruled that his successors must do the same.

In these circumstances some changes in the House's constitution became possible. It was decided that all traders 'of a fair character' who were willing to pay five shillings sterling immediately and four shillings yearly should be admitted 'as the only members of the Merchants House'. In time of distress, such members and their indigent widows and children were to have the first claim on the House's charity.

The Letter of Guildry had, in effect, given the Dean of Guild two councils. The first was the Council of four Merchants and four Craftsmen, who with the Dean formed what, until its abolition in 1975, was called the Dean of Guild Court. This had the power to enforce certain regulations for the public good, mainly concerning building and lining (encroachment on a neighbour's boundaries and other disputes between neighbours relating to property), weights and measures, and burgess privileges; it was also a normal civil law court for actions of debt between merchants or merchants and craftsmen. The second was the body of twenty-four Merchants chosen by the Dean himself, who were to join in nominating candidates for the Deanship and to be his advisers in the affairs of the Merchant rank.

In future, it was now decided, all members of the House should have a share in choosing this second council, which was to be expanded to thirty-six. On the second Wednesday after the election of the city magistrates in October, the House was to meet. The Dean himself would then choose twelve councillors. The next stage of the election may sound strange today, but was characteristic of old Scots ideas about the election of committees. The Dean was to arrange the names of all the remaining members in twenty-four leets, twelve consisting of overseas traders and twelve of home traders. The members of the House would then vote to choose one man from each leet. These twenty-four, with the Dean's own twelve, would form the Council of the House. And the Council, with the Dean, the Lord Provost and Merchant bailies, would choose (again through leets) the names of three candidates for the deanship to be submitted to the town council for their final election. These changes in the rules of the House, with some minor ones, had to be submitted to the town council for its approval. This was given on condition that all the House's members must be burgesses and guild brethren before matriculating in the new form.

Eight years later, in 1754, the House appointed the first of a long series of important standing committees. This Committee on the Books and Affairs was to meet four times yearly and to consist of the Dean, the provost and three other members. It was, in fact, a form of executive. It had to scrutinise the financial affairs of the House, and to examine the applications for pensions and grants, and decide who was to benefit from them.

A page from the Minute Book of the Committee on the Books and Affairs, March 1755

'Glasgow the fourth day being the first Tuesday of March one thousand seven hundred and fifty five years

Present

The Dean of Guild & other members of the annual Committee

1st: That care be taken that the merchants' house be not abridged of any of their just privileges, as it is at present attempted to be done by taking away from their Clerk the benefit of writing the indentures of the apprentices on Auldhouse's mortification contrary to an Express award of the Magistrats and Town Council on the 5th June 1745 which expressly declared the payment of the apprentices' fees and making out their Indentures to belong the merchants house.

2nd: That as the whole of the mortifications and pensions on the house are restricted to certain sums excepting only the Dean of Guild's precepts which for many years backwards are from fourty shillings to five pounds sterling yearly. To prevent this privilege being indefinitely extended and to avoid a multitude of applications which the funds of the house cannot supply, It is desired by the present Dean of Guild and is now Entered by the House that these precepts in all time coming be only allowed and issued to the extent of [blank space] yearly which the Collector is ordered to pay accordingly.

3rd: That George Buchanan's bond of Cautionry be turned into a principal bond as the Cautioners otherwise will soon be free.

4: That £10. 2. 8 sterl. Interest due on Bandalloch's bond be recovered by dilligence.

5: That the House will further Inforce the payment of matriculate money of former years as well as the last which is refused by some, and if not speedily Levied will have a very ill Effect on the whole subscription.

6: That they will likewise give directions what's to be done with a debt of about thirteen pounds sterl. due to the poor of the hospital by Doctor Woodrow, and that they would give publick notice that the prosecutions carried on against any person for debts due to the House are by their Express order to free the Dean of Guild and Collector from the reflections of unreasonable people.

7: There are some persons now in the town's hospital who were formerly and still continue pensioners on the Merchants' house, such as Jean Atchison and Widow Lyle, the first of which is very unruly. This seems to be contrary both to the rules of the Merchants house and Town's hospital.

8th: That some method be fallen upon to Represent to the Lady Craigends the Great Loss the poor of the Merchants' house have suffered by the payment of her annuity which has quite exhausted the fund intended by the late Provost Aird for the relief of the poor of that hospital.

9: That the act of the house of the first of January 1714 anent writing the indentures of apprentices and Booking apprentices in three months and paying the Dues be again Inforced and put in Execution.

10: That a Committee be appointed to sollicite Gold book subscriptions as was formerly ordered on the 18th April 1712, and that they likewise have recommended to them to get what matriculate subscriptions they can.

[signed] John Bowman'

The Merchants House was strengthened financially and its Members were given a greater chance to take an active part in its management. But its character was slightly changed. It could hardly claim, even formally, to represent all burgesses who were traders. Merchants who were not prepared to pay the special contributions remained outside it, though, in theory at least, the Dean of Guild and his Council could still compel them to come in. In 1771 the payment was consolidated into £4 sterling of entry money, and in 1792 it was raised to 10 guineas. Around this time a list was compiled of traders whose names did not appear on the register of freemen, who were to be 'cited by the Guild Court Either to produce their Burgh [burgess] tickets, to Enter with the Town immediately, or give over Trading'. If neither was complied with, the Court was to fine them 'for Trafficking as Unfreemen'.[12]

Glasgow's commercial aristocracy

Throughout the eighteenth century, as Glasgow grew richer, the foremost men of the town took a leading part in the activities of the House. There was Provost Andrew Cochrane, a tobacco merchant with interests in several manufacturing ventures and a founder of the Glasgow Arms Bank, who had guided the city through the troubles

Fig. 4.4 Mary Buchanan (Mrs Alexander Speirs) (artist: Sir Daniel Macnee, PRSA, after Sir John Watson Gordon, RA, PRSA)

of the Forty-Five. The main beneficiary of his generosity was Hutchesons' Hospital, with which he was closely associated, but he acted for the Merchants House on many occasions, for example in representing the House in its application for a parliamentary Act to erect a lighthouse on Little Cumbrae in the Firth of Clyde. He was the founder of the Political Economy Club, which met to discuss the theory and practice of trade, to which he introduced his friend Adam Smith. Smith developed some of his ideas that later went into *The Wealth of Nations* during his time in Glasgow in the 1750s and 1760s, when he knew many of the leading merchants and observed their methods of trade, the investments they made and the social and economic structure of Glasgow. Adam Smith was made an honorary burgess of Glasgow in 1762, when Cochrane was provost and Archibald Ingram was Dean of Guild, though he does not appear in the Merchants House membership list. Another of the notable members of Cochrane's Club was Alexander Speirs, whose tobacco firm was one of those large enough to be able to take advantage of the rise in prices due to the scarcity of tobacco when the American War broke out in 1775 (Figs. 4.4 and 4.5). Others avoided the worst effects of the collapse of the trade by their successful manufacturing investments, such as Archibald Ingram, one of Glasgow's first industrialists, a pioneer of the business of textile printing which was to be immensely important to the West of Scotland in the age of cotton which followed that of tobacco.

Archibald Ingram

Archibald Ingram (1699–1770) typified many things about Glasgow tobacco merchants. He had shares in two tobacco firms, as well as in an inkle (linen tape) manufactory and the Glasgow Arms Bank, and invested his profits into a new manufacturing venture, starting up Glasgow's first bleachfield and printworks in Pollokshaws in 1742, in partnership with his brother-in-law John Glassford of Dougalston and others. Linen printing had been introduced to Scotland only in 1738, and founding his works took Ingram several years of hard work and much perseverance. In the end the works covered a thirty-acre site and were a thriving business; by the end of the century there were more than thirty printfields in and around Glasgow.

Ingram was a self-made man, from humble beginnings – tradition says that he made his first money selling 'a peck of haws' – and rose to become one of Glasgow's wealthiest citizens. By his first marriage, to Janet Simpson, he was admitted a burgess, and by his second, to Rebecca Glassford, he allied himself to one of the wealthiest and most successful tobacco merchants, John Glassford. By the end of his life he too was a very rich man: as well as his grand town house, he owned an expensive chaise, a gold watch, an extensive library, and his own estate, Cloberhill in East Kilpatrick. He took an interest in the arts, having shares in the Foulis brothers' Academy of art and design. He was provost in 1762–3 and 1763–4 and Dean of Guild twice. Ingram Street, formerly Back Cow Lane, was laid out in 1781.

Fig. 4.5   Alexander Speirs (artist: Sir Daniel Macnee, PRSA, after William Cochran)
Alexander Speirs (1714–83) was one of the top four tobacco merchants of Glasgow (with William
Cunninghame, John Glassford and James Ritchie). He was the son of an Edinburgh merchant and came
to Glasgow attracted by the prospects of the tobacco trade. He very quickly prospered, was one of
the founders of the Glasgow Arms Bank, and at one time was the largest importer of tobacco in
Glasgow, itself the largest tobacco port in Britain. Not all his business went through legal channels:
Speirs was actively engaged in 'reloading' (smuggling) goods from the Isle of Man.[13] He bought the
Virginia Mansion, the most splendid of all the tobacco merchants' houses, from the trustees of George
Buchanan (the younger).

His second wife was Mary Buchanan, the daughter of Archibald Buchanan of Auchentorlie,
one of the four sons of George Buchanan, founder of a great Glasgow dynasty, who included some of
the most prosperous tobacco merchants.

Speirs' success as a businessman funded his transition to the landed gentry. He bought up numerous
properties and added to them the estate of Elderslie in Renfrewshire, had the whole consolidated into
a barony under the name of Elderslie, and in 1777 began to build an impressive mansion. It was
finished in 1782 and Speirs removed his family from the Virginia Mansion, but enjoyed his new
property only a matter of months, dying the following year.

Alexander Speirs was active in the Merchants House in the 1760s and 1770s, serving on various
ad hoc committees, usually alongside other prominent tobacco merchants. On his death he left £20
to the Merchants House, and in 1850 his daughters gave £2,000 to the House in fulfilment of the wish
of their late mother, in remembrance of Alexander Speirs of Elderslie.

The merchants met informally and read the newspapers in the town's coffee houses, one of which, the Old Coffee House, was in a tenement owned by the Merchants House at the corner of the Trongate, on the west side of the Saltmarket, which had been built in 1683 (see Chapter 3) (Fig. 4.6). The town council subsidised the supply of newspapers for the Old Coffee House, but withdrew this in 1738 when a coffee house opened in its new town hall next to the Tolbooth. The Old Coffee House was the venue in December 1745 for the dinner Prince Charles gave for his supporters. It was sold in 1752, described as 'the Merchants Great Tenement at the Cross, viz. the first story thereof, called the old Coffee House, with the Cellars and Office houses belonging thereto',[14] and was later used by the Foulis brothers as an auction house for their book-selling business. From its projecting 'lantern storey' patrons could see who was doing business on the 'plainstanes' in front of the Town Hall, a promenade in front of the piazza (or arcade), fenced off by a row of stone pillars. This pavement was the area used by the merchants as their exchange, the adjacent piazza being used in wet weather, until the Tontine Society bought part of the Town Hall building in 1781 and opened an exchange and news-room in it. Later the corner window was a vantage point from which to observe public executions at the Cross. (Hangings took place here between 1788 and 1813.)

Merchants and Masons

In the Glasgow of the clubs and coffee houses, merchants established a strong connection with freemasonry, when the city's oldest masonic lodge was founded in 1735. The Glasgow Kilwinning Lodge No. 4, somewhat confusingly, never had any official connection with the Mother Kilwinning Lodge. Its number was changed to 4 in 1816 in honour of the merchants' mark based on this numeral. It usually met in the Old Coffee House, in the building owned by the Merchants House. The festivals of St John, the masons' patron, in 1740 and 1741 were held in the great hall of the Merchants' Hospital, the members foregathering at the Old Coffee House and making their way in a torchlight procession to the Bridgegate. Most of these members, in the vigorous first forty years of the Lodge's life, were merchants, including eight Deans of Guild: one of them, George Murdoch, Dean of Guild in 1751 and 1752, provost in 1755–6 and 1767–8, was Master of the Lodge in 1741–2. All the founders of the Glasgow Ship Bank and many of the founders of the Glasgow Arms Bank, both established in 1750, were members. In a membership list of the 1740s and 50s, nearly 70 per cent were merchants. Such was the preponderance of merchant membership that the effect of the American War was to put the Lodge's activities into abeyance for the next thirty years or so after 1775.

Involvement in improvements

The House took an active part in almost all the improvements undertaken by the city in the eighteenth century, especially, but not exclusively, those that affected the practice of trade. In 1755 it promoted a Bill in Parliament for the building of the first Clyde Lighthouse, on the Little Cumbrae, guaranteeing the expenses for obtaining the

Fig. 4.6   A view of the Trongate of Glasgow from the east, 1770 (engraved by Robert Paul and William Buchanan)
The building at the left, with the projecting storey, is the 'new house at the Cross' built by the Merchants House in 1683. Within the arches on the ground floor were, originally, cellars, rented out to merchants for storage of their goods; later they were made into shops, which brought in a higher rent. The Old Coffee House was on the first floor. Opposite is the Tolbooth, which housed the old council chamber, court and prison. Next to it is the new Town Hall, completed in 1740, supported on its piazza of ten arches, each with a carved head on its keystone. The statue of King William on horseback now stands near the Cathedral. On the 'plainstanes' in front of the town hall can be seen several groups of merchants.

1756 Act, thereby originating the Clyde Lighthouse Trust. The House also supported the first Clyde Navigation Act to improve the navigation of the river, at a time when the town's revenue from the harbour was only £147 a year. Two years earlier, in 1757, it had encouraged a member, John McCaull, to push forward a plan drawn up by the engineer John Smeaton for the deepening of the river, undertaking for the members of the House 'to subject their shipping which shall discharge at any of the ports of Glasgow, and all gabarts, boats, or other vessels . . . to such tolls or duties as shall be thought necessary, to Reimburse the City . . . in whatever money shall be expended' on the improvements.[15] After the Act was obtained work was actually started on making locks and weirs, but was abandoned when insurmountable difficulties were encountered. The House supported the plan that was eventually adopted, John Golborne's work to deepen the river up to the Broomielaw, contributing money to reward him for its success in 1775. In 1767 it encouraged a scheme for the Forth and Clyde Canal, which was to give the city an outlet to the North Sea; it appointed a committee to consider the plans for improving the harbour of Port Glasgow (Fig. 4.7); and it supported the bill before the Irish Parliament for a lighthouse in the North Channel on rocks off the coast of County Down.

Fig. 4.7 A view of Port Glasgow from the south-east, 1768 (engraved by Robert Paul)
This view of Port Glasgow shows the town and harbour 100 years after their foundation. The long building in the foreground is the ropework.

It lent its weight to early plans for giving Glasgow a water supply other than the wells the old city had relied on, and for lighting the town. Even before there were steam-driven factories it concerned itself seriously about the cost of coal supplies. It began to press for a regular post to London via Carlisle, a facility achieved only in 1781. Again and again, in years of scarcity, it pressed for free trade in corn, an almost revolutionary idea in that century when grain-growing landowners and farmers were carefully protected, and it took the practical measure of contributing to the cost of ensuring the supply of meal in the market at an affordable price, staving off hunger for the townspeople.

An early Glasgow philanthropist

James Coulter (1740–88) was a merchant whose name was connected with the foundation of several Glasgow institutions for the public benefit. He was a tobacco importer who was also involved as a partner in several other businesses, including the Wester Sugar House, and the stocking manufactory of Archibald Ingram and Co. He was a Merchants House Director in 1783, and in his will left several legacies, including £25 to the House. His most famous benefaction was the £200 he left in the care of the Faculty of Physicians and Surgeons for the rescue and recovery of drowning persons, which became the founding capital of the Glasgow Humane Society a few years later (see Chapter 9). He left £400 to establish a public Bridewell or workhouse, and a mortification of £1,200 for annual pensions to indigent persons, both of these to be administered by the town council. His will also provided £200 as a fund for an annual premium for the benefit of trade or manufactures of Glasgow, to be given as prize money or a medal to the person 'whether mechanic or manufacturer or merchant' who 'shall have invented or improved or confirmed in practice any machine or method of working a valuable manufacture in Glasgow, or within ten miles of it'. The judges were to be the provost, the Dean of Guild, and six assessors, three from the Merchants House and three from the Trades House.

Coulter's Prize for Inventions

From the Minute Book, 12 June 1796:
'The House, upon the Petition of Archibald McVicar, Clockmaker in Glasgow, appointed Messrs. David Dale, William Wardlaw, and George McIntosh, to judge, along with the Provost, Dean of Guild, and three Craftsmen to be named by the Trades House, whether an invention by the said Archibald McVicar of a Machine for working finger flowers and spots, in the loom, be worthy of the annual premium appropriated by the late Mr. James Coulter for the benefit of the Manufactures and Trades of Glasgow.'

The Merchants House and the Clyde Marine Society

What was to become the Glasgow – and later the Clyde – Marine Society had its beginnings in 1687, when the Merchants House received a mortification subscribed by over fifty 'shippers and mariners' of Glasgow – most of them merchants involved in seagoing trade – for the aid of 'poor and decayed merchants and mariners'. They undertook to pay 'thankfully and punctually at the return of each voyage' eight pence for every pound Scots earned, half of which was to be paid to the Collector of the House for the poor of the Merchant rank, and half to a Collector to be appointed for the mariners. There was some difficulty in collecting the money in the first few years (perhaps partly owing to the intervention of the 1688 Revolution), but in 1696 members of the Merchants House who were overseas traders and concerned in shipping re-established the scheme, this time for levying four pence Scots in the pound from the wages of masters and seamen in order to create a fund for the relief of their poor. Their first minute explains that:

> *The stock and rents of the Merchant house of the Burgh of Glasgow has been hitherto under considerable burden in supplieing the necessities of poor decayed seamen and their wives and children And wee being fully convinced that it is Just and reasonable that the said Merchant house should in tyme comeing be eased and releived of the said burden . . . hereby bind and oblidge us . . . To stope and keep in our owne hands off and from each Master and seaman to be employed by us . . . the soume of Four pennies off every pound scotts money.*[16]

A committee of six was set up, with the Dean of Guild at its head, and its own Collector, who was instructed to pursue those who refuse to pay. This body was to have power to use these funds for needy seamen 'not only residing within this burgh but of strangers who may be passing throw this Burgh in distress'. The Dean of Guild at the time was John Aird, and the first Collector chosen was Thomas Peter; William Cross was also on the first committee. The fund was known at this time simply as the Seamen's Box, and soon seamen and their widows were being entered on its roll as quarterly pensioners.

In 1758, under the deanship of Archibald Ingram, the Glasgow Marine Society was formed, incorporating the earlier fund (now known as the Seamen's Club) which had evidently become insufficient for the calls made upon it. The new Society was able to raise more funds and do more for needy seamen than the previous arrangement had done. In 1760, for example, it undertook to augment and administer the sum of money collected for the support of a sailor who had been wounded and was unable to work. In 1762 it incorporated the Greenock Marine Society, and in 1786 it was incorporated by Act of Parliament as the Clyde Marine Society. By 1816 over 800 persons were receiving money from it: about £150 was distributed in Glasgow every year, and much more in Port Glasgow and Greenock. The Glasgow director of the Society was the Dean of Guild *ex officio.*

Aid for a disabled sailor

Minute of the Glasgow Marine Society, 3 January 1760
Colin Dunlop, Dean of Guild, in the chair
'The said day it was Represented to the society in behalf of Andrew Gardner formerly a sailor on board the ship Bolling of Glasgow That in the defence of that ship when Engaged with a French privateer He received a shot in his right Leg which so shattered the bones that he is thereby rendered quite Lame and disabled from Earning his bread and has lost the use of said leg – In consideration of which a subscription was lately opened for him by which the sum of thirty one pounds two shillings & six pence sterling was Collected by Hugh Brown the society's Collector now deceased from which he paid the said Andrew Gardner two pounds sterling so there remained for him in the Collector's hand twenty nine pounds two shillings & six pence sterling and the Dean of Guild has since received of

subscription money for him One pound Eleven shillings sterling making in whole Thirty pounds thirteen shillings and sixpence sterling which sum the said Andrew Gardner proposed to sink forever into this Society provided they in lieu thereof Establish on him a pension of three pounds sterling yearly during his Life on account of the said sunk sum which proposal the Society agree to, and further in consideration of his faithfull Services, they install him as a pensioner or poor Sailor for one pound sterling to be paid yearly to him by the society during his Life, the said two pensions making together four pounds sterling payable half yearly during his life on his receipt & an attestation of his being on Life . . .'

The Dean of Guild and his Council in the eighteenth century

Presiding over the Marine Society was one of the Dean of Guild's duties, the list of which grew considerably during the course of the eighteenth century. He was, of course, the president of meetings of the Merchants House and usually the convener of its committees. He was head of the Dean of Guild Court, and *ex officio* a member of the town council. All these rights were enshrined in the Letter of Guildry. By the end of the century, the Dean had been appointed convener of several important committees by the town council, including the Lighthouse Trust. In this connection he had various duties to do with convening commissioners for erecting and maintaining a lighthouse on Little Cumbrae, and he had similar duties in administering the River Trust. He was a Justice of the Peace for the County of Lanark. He was a director of the Town's Hospital, Hutchesons' Hospital, Wilson's Charity and the Royal Infirmary (see Chapter 5).

The dignity of the office was given visible form in 1766, when the House approved the provision of a new gold chain of office 'to be at all times worn by the . . . Dean of Guild'.

The office of Dean of Guild, along with those of provost and bailie, might involve considerable personal expense, and on several occasions threats of fines and disfranchisement had to be used to compel those who had been elected to serve. In 1788 the magistrates and town council obtained an Act of Council fining Archibald Grahame, who had been elected Dean of Guild and had refused to serve, the sum of £40.

He was

> summoned . . . to have compeared [appeared] before the Magistrates and Council of this Burgh within the Laigh Councill chamber on the date hereof at two of the clock afternoon to have accepted of his office as Dean of Guild of the Burgh for the ensuing year . . . And the said Archibald Grahame being three several times called on at the Councill chamber door by the Councill officer and failing to compear and accept of his office . . . Therefore the Magistrates and Councill do hereby Fine and amerciate the said Archibald Grahame in the sum of Forty pounds sterling money and decern [decree] and ordain him to make payment of the said sum to James Hill Collector of the Merchants House in Glasgow . . . for behoof of the poor of the said Merchants House.

The Dean of Guild's Council of thirty-six, reconstituted in 1747, were the legal representatives of the Merchants House, and had five regular meetings annually, as well as occasional meetings if needed. Among their primary duties were the election of the four Merchant lyners for the Dean of Guild Court and the election of the Committee on the Books and Affairs. They also had to choose the Collector, Clerk and Officer of the House, and to elect one of their number to keep the keys of the boxes and presses which held the books and papers of the House. They had to elect twelve directors for the Town's Hospital, to serve alongside the directors chosen from among various other bodies, and a director for the Royal Infirmary and Stirling's Library. They had the responsibility of administering the Auldhouse Mortification, examining the candidates for apprenticeships and deciding who should be admitted. They had to elect three members to serve on the committee of Coulter's Premium for Inventors (founded in 1788), which made an annual grant of £10 to an inventor or improver of machinery for the benefit of trade.

The Collector

The year 1767 is an important one in the House's internal affairs, for it was then that it chose a Collector who was not an active Merchant to be its chief official, under the Lord Dean. To begin with the Collectors had been members of the Dean of Guild Court. Later they dealt with the House's finances and business, being rewarded by a percentage of the money they drew in. Now no member of the House was prepared to take on this work, no doubt because it was becoming rather more arduous, and James Hill, 'writer in Glasgow', was appointed at a salary of £20 per annum. He was the founder of a respected Glasgow legal firm (which became Hill and Hoggan, and eventually, by amalgamation, Mitchells Roberton) and was the first of a Merchants House dynasty. His son (James), his grandson (Laurence) and a great-grandson (William Henry) were to follow him. His grandson's great-grandson, T. L. Grahame Reid, was Collector and Clerk from 1948 until his death in 1969. For two centuries the collectorship, so influential in the House's development, was dominated by James Hill and his descendants.

The Hill family and the Merchants House

James Hill of Cartside, born in 1731, the first professional Collector of the Merchants House, could trace his family's Glasgow ancestry back over 200 years, to James Hill, parson of Govan parish and the first Protestant minister of Cathcart at the time of the Reformation, who acquired landed estates in Ibrox and Dumbreck through marriage. His son, Ninian, born around 1583, likewise made an advantageous marriage, to Helen Hutcheson, sister of the famous founders of Hutchesons' Hospital and School. Ninian was a merchant, but most of his descendants were ministers and lawyers; James Hill of Cartside was his great-great-grandson.

James Hill graduated from Glasgow University at the age of seventeen and became a lawyer. In the course of his career he became attached in some official capacity to most of the principal institutions of Glasgow: the Merchants House, the University, Hutchesons' Hospital and the Faculty of Physicians and Surgeons. The legal firm he started, now Mitchells Roberton, lost the Hill name only in 1985, and can claim to be among Glasgow's oldest. James Hill had a small, 'beautifully situated' property at Cartside in Cathcart, and his Glasgow home was at the head of Stockwell, and later in Buchanan Street. Of the fifteen children he had with his wife Elizabeth Robertson, his son James, born in 1764, was the one who succeeded him in the family law firm and the various official roles, including the Collectorship of the Merchants House. A nephew of this James was Laurence Hill, LL.D. (born 1791), Collector from 1819 till 1837 (Chapter 5). His son, W. H. Hill, was Collector for forty-six years, until 1912 (see Chapter 7). W. H. Hill's great-nephew, Thomas Laurence Grahame Reid, was Collector from 1948 till 1969 (Chapter 8). In the interval between these two, the collectorship, although not in the Hill family, was in the hands of the firm founded by James Hill (then Hill and Hoggan), as it has been ever since the death of T. L. Grahame Reid.

Gifts and grants

As the city prospered, the House began to receive more substantial legacies and gifts. The first came as early as 1715, from James Govan, £627. 1s. 8d. sterling, which was the Merchants' proportion of 'one thousand ginnies in gold laid by and enclosed in a bag sealed with black wax with the Seal of the Galley'. James Govan stipulated that each of the twelve poor men who were to receive maintenance from the interest of this sum was to be furnished with a purple gown, to be worn to church on Sundays. They were to attend funerals when required, clothed in their purple gowns, walking in procession between the two files of the town's officers, on condition that they received a shilling each from the funeral party. Then there was property in the town left by John Aird which fetched £480 in 1753. A mortification by a prosperous printer, Robert Sanders, or Saunders, of Auldhouse, financed the training of boys for generations to come (Fig. 4.8). He left £611 sterling and his lands of Auldhouse (near Pollokshaws, where his house stood until the late 1960s) to provide for the apprenticing of poor sons of Merchants or Craftsmen burgesses, and to found a divinity bursary at Glasgow University, both apprentices and students to be chosen by the House.

The Auldhouse Mortification

Under the terms of the legacy of 12,000 merks left by Robert Sanders to the Merchants House in 1728, 1,100 merks were to be devoted each year to the apprenticing of eleven boys to trades or callings, and £100 Scots yearly to support a student of divinity. Candidates for the apprenticeships were to be between the ages of eleven and thirteen, and eleven were to be chosen each year, five sons of Merchants and five sons of Craftsmen, with one from each rank in alternate years. The testator's nephew, Robert Colquhoun, had the right to present the candidates, and the town councillors were appointed overseers of the trust. A year and a day after admission, the apprentice and his master were to appear before the Dean of Guild and Collector to give an account of their performance.

In 1743 it was drawn to the attention of the town council that no boys had been apprenticed under the scheme for several years. Most of the 12,000 merks had been lent out and lost, and the interest on the rest had gone to Colquhoun, who also had the rent-free use of the land, as long as he did not present apprentices. The town council acted to put an end to the corrupt practice, ordering that the Trades House was to present five boys as apprentices, but that none from the Merchant rank were to be admitted until the capital of 12,000 merks had been restored. The regulations were tightened up, and two years later the full complement of eleven apprentices was restored and the Merchants House was confirmed in its right to administer the fund (see Minute of Committee on Books and Affairs, March 1755, item 1, above).

In 1855 the town council granted the right to allocate the apprenticeships to boys who did not fulfil the original requirements of the mortification, as there was by then little call for such apprenticeships from the sons of Merchants, but much demand from sons of burgesses in general. In the later nineteenth century, with the advent of universal free education, the intentions of the founder were honoured by the transference of the bequest to scholarships and bursaries for boys at Allan Glen's Institution, and in the 1970s, when the special technical status of this school was lost, the funds were applied to bursaries at Hutchesons' Grammar School.

This marked the beginning of the House's interest in technical education which was to continue for 250 years. There were other substantial gifts for the aid of Merchants and their families in distress. At a time when fortunes could be made and lost within a generation, such a guarantee of protection from destitution must have given many men the courage to invest in the risky business of overseas trade.

In 1754 it was found that the funds had increased sufficiently to allow the grant of pensions of £100 Scots to three men and of £60 Scots to two others. All were to have been 'men of credit' and business in the city, over fifty years of age, who had fallen into poverty. Three widows of Merchants, 'women of good fame, and widows of such merchants as have been men of credit and character', were also to receive £100 Scots each. The records state:

> It is to be hoped that no person concerned in the trade of this place, foreign or inland, will grudge so small a benevolence, as one shilling a quarter for the relief of the poor; as thereby they and theirs only, (preferable to all others) in case of misfortunes, will have the benefit of the stock of this house . . . The book for further subscriptions of such as are willing to promote this good design, lies at the shop of messrs. Black and Clark, under the New Coffee-house.[17]

By 1786 the enrolled pensioners, supported from general funds, were fifteen men and forty women, receiving in all £382. 16s. sterling, besides twenty-three men and women who received pensions from special mortifications and 'precepts' – grants for a particular emergency ordered by the House or by the Dean of Guild personally.

Fig. 4.8   Robert Sanders of Auldhouse (artist: George Scougall)

Robert Sanders inherited his father's printing business around 1696, and also had a bookshop above the Grammar School Wynd and later in the Saltmarket. He described himself as 'one of His Majesty's printers' and was printer to the University. He acquired the estate of Auldhouse in 1710. His mortification to the Merchants House came in several stages: at first he left 1,000 merks for paying for the apprenticeship of a poor boy of the Craft rank; two years later, in 1728, since 'it has pleased God to bless me with a considerable stock of worldly means', he mortified his Auldhouse lands for five apprenticeships, three for Merchants' sons, and two for Tradesmen's, as well as a Divinity bursary; and later the same year, because of 'certain important weighty causes and considerations' he mortified, after certain legacies and expenses, his entire moveable estate, including his books and his printing presses; a few months later he ordained that the capital was to be retained and the income only used, for as many apprentices as the interest from it would afford, divided equally between Merchants' and Tradesmen's sons. It was said that he made the bequests to the Merchants House because 'he was exceedingly disobliged by his relatives, and so put all he had by them'[18] – though he had no children to disinherit. In 1744 the House sold part of the Auldhouse land to the Printfield Company of Pollokshaws, headed by Archibald Ingram.

The end of the tobacco trade

As the century reached its last quarter, Glasgow's first great age of mercantile prosperity was coming to an end. The tobacco trade – imports from the American colonies, exports to the Continent – depended on the Navigation Acts which laid down that colonial goods must be carried only to British ports and in British ships. The war and revolution which converted the colonies into the United States of America put an end to all such restrictions. Henceforth American tobacco could be shipped direct to any part of the world. The position Glasgow merchants had won as its chief importers and re-exporters in Britain quickly lost its meaning.

Fig. 4.9 John Luke of Claythorn (artist: John Williamson)

John Luke of Claythorn (in the Calton district) was born in 1665, the son of a prominent merchant of the same name, who had been Collector of the Merchants House in 1661 and 1662. John Luke the younger was a member of the Council of the Merchants House (that is, what was later termed a Director) for many years, especially during the 1720s. His business interests were many, including the Easter Sugar House and the soapworks in Candleriggs (which had been established by his father and others for whale fishing and soap making, and had five ships and premises in Greenock for boiling blubber and curing fish); he also owned a mill and land at East Thorne. He died in 1731, and six years later his widow, Martha Millar, arranged for the payment of the sum of 4,000 merks, which he had requested on his deathbed be mortified to the Merchants House. His wife had taken a note at the dictation of her husband ('very imperfect Jottings' according to the deed recorded by the House), and in the end all was ordered as he had wished. The House was to pay the interest to 'a poor, decayed, indigent, honest man of the merchant rank', to be named by her and her daughters after her. She named as the first beneficiary a nephew of her husband's, George Luke, who had fallen on hard times, and after his death she ensured, by special petition, that the annuity was continued for the benefit of his children until they were educated and provided for. Martha Millar herself died aged eighty-six in 1762 and left the Merchants House 10 guineas.

Fig. 4.10   Thomas Thompson (artist: George Scougall)

Thomas Thompson was Dean of Guild in 1718 and 1719. He became a burgess and guild brother in 1703 by right of marriage to the daughter of a merchant burgess, by which time he was manager of the Woollen and Stuff Manufactory in Candleriggs owned by John Govan of Hogganfield. Some time later he had made enough money to go into joint ownership, with two other merchants, of several ships, including the brigantine *Hannover*. In 1707 he was the town treasurer. He died in 1720 in his forty-ninth year, leaving to the Merchants House 2,000 merks (£111. 2s. 2d. sterling), the interest to be paid 'on the 8th December, yearly, at two o'clock afternoon, in the Laigh Kirk, to the most indigent and deserving poor, of whatever sex, employment, or age, without distinction, by the Dean of Guild, who is, the day before the distribution, to call one or more of the Ministers of Glasgow, and an Elder . . . of every Parish . . . , with one of Mr Thompson's nearest relations in life, who shall together state what each person is to get, not being above a crown, or below twenty pence, . . . and who shall be present next day at the distribution'.

The House supported recruiting for the American War by agreeing that all men who joined the new Glasgow Regiment, which was being raised in 1778, should be made burgesses and guild brothers without payment when they were discharged, and that the families of any who died on service should have this privilege. But the day of tobacco was over. Soon the House had to consider the feeding of the poor in the distressed city. Glasgow merchants had to look for another staple trade. It was for this purpose that the Chamber of Commerce, which has been a partner of the House in many activities and often (as now) has operated under the same roof, was founded in 1783. One of its founders, and its first secretary, was a prominent Merchant and future Dean of Guild and provost, Gilbert Hamilton (see Chapter 5). The majority of the founding members (130 out of 216) were merchants, and it was significant that its emblem, the flying stork, carried not a tobacco leaf but a sprig of flax. The new basis of the city's business, not only for trade but for manufacture, was to be textiles. Cotton was now to be king.

Notes

1. John Macky, *A Journey Through Scotland* (London, 1729), p. 291.
2. Merchants House Minutes, 28 Jan. 1768.
3. Daniel Defoe, *The History of the Union of Great Britain* (Edinburgh, 1709), p. 64.
4. George Eyre-Todd, *History of Glasgow*, vol. 3 (Glasgow, 1934), pp. 134–5.
5. Defoe, *History of the Union*, p. 61.
6. MH Minutes, 15 Sept. 1745.
7. Ibid., 27 Sept. 1745.
8. *The Cochrane Correspondence regarding the affairs of Glasgow 1745–6* (Glasgow, 1836), p. 22 (28 Sept. 1745).
9. Ibid., p. 31 (Nov. 1745).
10. Ibid., p. 65 (4 Jan. 1746).
11. MH Minutes, 9 Oct. 1746.
12. MH register, 1784, in Glasgow City Archives (T-MH 13).
13. I am indebted to Professor Michael Moss for this information.
14. MH Minutes, 19 Dec. 1752.
15. Ibid. 14 June 1757.
16. Minute book of the Seamen's Box, Dec. 1696 (Glasgow City Archives T-MH 29.1).
17. Printed notice in duplicate minute book of the Committee of the Merchants House (1752–68), Glasgow City Archives T-MH 2.
18. *The Regality Club*, vol. 4 (Glasgow, 1912), p. 85.

THE AGE OF REFORM

A *wind of change*

In spite of the hard times that Glasgow had passed through during the American War and after, there was a certain optimism in the air before the 1780s ended. Business was reviving again. And there was a good deal of sympathy in Glasgow with the political ideas that lay behind the successful American Revolution. A Glasgow professor, John Millar, was the foremost teacher of liberal theories about parliamentary government and constitutional law, on which the Americans had largely based their new republic. And the former Glasgow professor, Adam Smith, had published *The Wealth of Nations*, which was to be a bible of capitalist free enterprise for more than a hundred years. Political reform and economic experiments were in fashion when the centenary of the 'Glorious Revolution', which put reforming Whigs into power, was celebrated in 1788. For half a century a wind of change was to blow through the world.

For a body like the Merchants House in a city like Glasgow this state of things raised special problems. The House had been created largely to preserve the trading privileges of Merchant burgesses, but these were out of tune with the new economic ideas of *laisser-faire*. In some ways its constitution was almost medieval. Yet Glasgow was a centre for new things, for the growing Industrial Revolution and expanding world trade as well as for new ideas. The leaders of the House were immersed in these developments.

The House had to keep one eye on the future and the other on the past, but its forward-looking eye was usually the more active of the two. From time to time it still tried to check trading by 'unfreemen', which was contrary to its original rules and privileges but was constantly growing; yet, in the main, it welcomed change. It could even appear ahead of its time, when, for example, in 1789 it recommended a decimal system of weights and measures. It showed itself willing to adapt to changing circumstances by its response to the question of bucket money, the charge levied on burgesses for the maintenance of fire buckets. As the buckets had become obsolete, the Merchants and Trades Houses continued to collect the money, which was treated as a source of revenue. The town council first pointed out that the money ought to be used for the upkeep of the city's fire engines in 1789, but the matter rested for

Fig. 5.1   Glasgow at Broomielaw from the south, 1784 (engraved by J. Lumsden)
The bridge in the middle is the first Jamaica Bridge, built in 1768–72. Compared with Fig. 4.1, the effect of the deepening of the river can be seen in the size of the boats: those drawing 7 feet of water could now be brought as far as the Broomielaw, though ocean-going ships still had to be unloaded at Port Glasgow or Geenock. To the east of the glassworks, trees have given way to buildings, including St Enoch's Church and the long low ropeworks. Further east, the Town's Hospital stands facing the river just to the left of the opening in the fence (which gave access to the river for watering horses and cattle). In line with the end of the old Glasgow Bridge, the Merchants' steeple (second from right) can be seen.

some years until in 1807 (perhaps belatedly, but several years in advance of the Trades House) the Merchants House agreed to pay its share to the Commissioners of Police, the recent Police Act having given the police the responsibility for fire engines. (The matter of bucket money was not, however, finally resolved until 1884, when the charge was discontinued altogether.)

From the Minute Book

11 September 1787
'The House having taken into their serious consideration the late disturbances in this City, occasioned by the lawless proceedings of certain wicked and disorderly persons, which ended in open sedition, and occasioned the bloodshed which ensued, Resolved unanimously—
    '. . . That this House will give . . . a reward of One Hundred Pounds Sterling, to any person or persons, not being themselves guilty, who shall discover the person or persons who struck the Lord Provost, or any of the other Magistrates, on Monday the Third day of September current . . .'

It was also very much in character for the Merchants House to thank William Pitt in 1788 for standing up for the rights of Parliament by insisting that the Lords and Commons had the power to decide on a regency during George III's illness 'thereby asserting one of the most important rights of the People'. (This was Whig doctrine, but, happily, Pitt had been asserting it against the opposition Whigs at Westminster.)

Parliamentary and political reform were already in the air in the 1780s, and in 1788 the Merchants House discussed proposed reforms to the sett (or constitution) of the self-perpetuating Glasgow town council, approving most of them, but refusing to concede that 'the undoubted rights of [the Merchant] rank should be in any degree impaired, or that the Trades rank should obtain a greater share or influence in [town] government and administration than they have hitherto possessed'. It would be nearly half a century before the Merchants were ready to accept changes which ended their pre-eminent position in civic affairs. In a spirit of progress, however, the House approved the move towards the important municipal reform to create Commissioners of Police elected by householders.

In their own discussions of 1788 the Trades House forecast a diminished role for their traditional rival:

> From the late rapid progress of Trade and Manufactures, and from present appearances, there is good reason to conclude that the Trades rank will, in process of time, become, in most respects, the most important body in the community. The Merchants themselves, by turning their attentions to manufactures, and consequently ranking under the class of Tradesman, will contribute considerably to this end.[1]

In fact this did not happen: although Glasgow did undergo a protean transformation between 1780 and 1830 from a great centre of transatlantic trade to one of the great industrial cities of the North, in the lists of Directors of the Merchants House for these years the names of manufacturers are as prominently represented as those of overseas traders – and several were both. It had been merchants in the earlier part of the eighteenth century who had invested part of their profits in a myriad of small manufactories producing saddles, soap, rope and sugar, to name but a few commodities. The ending of trade restrictions after the American War was a stimulus to industry, which needed raw materials from overseas as much as it needed an international market, and, again, it was merchants who had the incentive as well as the means to channel energy and money into new industrial concerns. And so the Merchants House remained a vibrant force in the emerging industrial city.

The textile and chemical pioneers

In prime place was the textile industry, not only spinning and weaving, but all the finishing processes too, such as bleaching, dyeing and printing. The great names of textile production in Glasgow – David Dale, George Macintosh, Henry Monteith, Charles Tennant, Kirkman Finlay, William Stirling – numbered themselves in the ranks of the Merchants. Robert Dalglish, textile manufacturer and future Lord Dean and Lord Provost, having been admitted a burgess as a weaver, was later readmitted as a Merchant. Glasgow was a hub of experiment and invention in textile

Henry Monteith, 1765–1848

Henry Monteith, Dean of Guild in 1818, was one of Glasgow's greatest cotton manufacturers. His father was an Anderston weaver who, by means of importing fine yarns from the Continent, expanded his workshop of a few looms into a sizeable business manufacturing cambric, and went on to produce the first muslin in Scotland. Henry was apprenticed as a weaver and began his manufacturing career as a muslin producer. His acquisition of David Dale and George Macintosh's Dalmarnock Turkey-red dye-works, renamed Barrowfield, under the name of Henry Monteith, Bogle and Co., led to his position as a leading European manufacturer, specialising in the weaving and dyeing of bandanna handkerchiefs. He perfected a method of dyeing these large spotted handkerchiefs – used throughout Europe as neckerchiefs, as snuff handkerchiefs and for tying up parcels of food – and of mass-producing them at a rate with which no one else could compete, with the result that the articles became known as 'Monteiths' in Europe. In his mills and works in Glasgow and Blantyre he became pre-eminent in bleaching, dyeing, calico printing, cotton weaving and spinning.

Henry Monteith was provost in 1815 and 1816, and again in 1819 and 1820, his first terms coinciding with dire financial crisis and the second with the Radical disturbances. He earned the esteem of many for his handling of both, and was elected MP for the Lanarkshire Burghs in 1821 and again in 1831. His election as provost in 1819 explains why he served only one year as Dean of Guild instead of the usual two. He had first appeared in the list of Merchants House Directors in 1803, and served most years, with interruptions for his terms as Dean and provost, until 1828.

A story is told of his attempted entry as a young man into Glasgow 'society' at a fashionable assembly, where he was not welcomed; the following day, a notice appeared in the Tontine news-room that if he made another such appearance, he would quickly be ejected. This has been taken to illustrate his comparatively humble origins and the snobbery of the self-styled tobacco aristocracy. However that may be, his emergence as a leading figure reflects the transition from overseas trade to textile manufacture as the source of wealth and influence in early nineteenth-century Glasgow.

That Monteith did gain acceptance among the select band of Glasgow's young bloods is shown by his membership of the whist and supper club known as the Board of Green Cloth, in which he was a noted placer of bets on subjects of varying degrees of seriousness. 'Mr. Connell beats [sic] agt. Mr. [Kirkman] Finlay a bottle of Rum that Mr. Jas. Dennistoun will rout as a Cow louder and better than Mr. Henry Monteith' runs one entry in the Minutes. Monteith's social mobility can be traced in the changes in his place of residence, from a flat in a tenement in Bell's Wynd in 1789, via a house in Miller Street, then St Vincent Street, and finally the estate of Carstairs on which he built himself a mansion in 1824, now known as Monteith House.

Robert Dalglish

Robert Dalglish, born in 1770, was one of Glasgow's great citizens of the early nineteenth century, a prominent merchant and Dean of Guild (1825 and 1826). He was a founder of the firm R. Dalglish, Falconer and Co., calico printers, at Lennoxtown in 1803, which, with 1,000 employees, became the largest of its kind in Scotland. He was an ally of Kirkman Finlay in subverting Napoleon's blockade of European ports, boosting British morale as well as trade. He was Lord Provost at the time of the Reform Bill in 1832, a canny and constitutional reformer, who remained in firm control of Glasgow's reform campaign, and celebrated the victory by having his house in St Vincent Place illuminated by 3,000 gas lights.

He was chairman of the River Improvement Trust from 1830 to 1832, a stormy time in the relations between the merchant and shipowner lobby and the councillors who maintained a majority on the Trust: as a council member of the Trust who was also a prominent Merchant, he earned respect for his serious and unbiased work for Clyde improvement. Characterised as 'one of those quiet workers that have helped make Glasgow what it is; a shrewd, cautious, sensible man, looked up to and esteemed by every one', he took a practical approach to charity. 'In a flood which occurred during his provostship, he not only sent relief to the inundated districts, but took it to them with his own hands, sailing about the Briggate in a boat.'[2]

He was well known for being active on the city's relief committees, for the unemployed and in the cholera and typhus crises of the first decades of the century – 'a most useful and philanthropic citizen in his day and generation', according to his obituary.

His son, also Robert, was a Merchants House Director in the 1850s. He had entered the family firm and extended the business. He was elected MP for Glasgow as an independent Radical in 1857, and re-elected subsequently, retiring in 1874.

From the Minute Book

27 February 1801
'Memorial to be presented to the Lords of the Treasury.
'. . . That the Manufacture of Printed Cloth has been carried on in this Country to a considerable extent, and has given bread to a great number of industrious persons of both sexes, many of whom could not easily be employed in the other Manufactures of this Country.

'That your Memorialists observe, by the Votes of the Honourable House of Commons, that it is proposed to lay an additional tax on this Manufacture, of two pence halfpenny per square yard, which, if carried into a Law, is likely to be productive of ruinous consequences to the persons who have embarked large Capitals in this branch of business, as well as to many of the work people employed by them . . .'

manufacture and the related chemical industry. Many of the foremost pioneers in this industrial boom were leaders of the Merchants House.

David Dale matriculated as a member of the Merchants House in 1787 and was elected a Director the following year, serving almost continuously until his death in 1806. He was in business in Glasgow for many years before he opened the New Lanark spinning mills in 1787 for which he is famous. His early business was buying and selling linen yarn, and he progressed to manufacturing inkles (linen tapes), and in another partnership had a factory producing cloth for the printfields. He was the first agent of the Royal Bank in Glasgow, and one of the founders of the Chamber of Commerce. He has perhaps become best known for his innovatory direct and practical care for his workforce. One of those with whom Dale was involved in the 1780s was George Macintosh, born in 1739 (the same year as Dale) in the Highlands, from where he came to Glasgow and established himself as a manufacturer. Macintosh became a Merchants House member and Director the year before Dale and also served until 1806. He built works at Easter Craigs to produce cudbear dye from lichen (staffed by Gaelic-speakers and surrounded by a high wall to prevent industrial espionage), and then in 1785 introduced the Turkey-red dye process to Scotland, establishing in partnership with Dale the first Turkey-red dye-works in Britain, which he sold in 1805 to Henry Monteith. Robert Owen, who is famous, well beyond Glasgow, chiefly for his early work in initiating a trade union movement and for his New Harmony community in the United States, was a Merchants House Director in 1807–8. He married David Dale's daughter, and became manager of the New Lanark spinning mills.

Charles Macintosh, George's son, introduced the manufacture of sugar of lead, and in 1797 had the first Scottish alum works at Hurlet. In 1799 with Charles Tennant he co-founded the St Rollox works for making chloride of lime, an entirely new and very effective bleaching chemical. His important discoveries included a process for converting iron into steel, and a method of waterproofing cloth – whence the mackintosh gets its name. He was a Director of the Merchants House for several years from 1818 onwards.

Corn Laws and Reform societies

Glasgow's prosperity – and the fortunes of many members of the Merchants House – began to depend on the labour of large numbers of industrial workers. When in 1786 the Government's proposed Corn Bill threatened to raise the price of bread in industrial centres such as Glasgow, the House acted to oppose them. It supported the Chamber of Commerce and the town council in their protest, and looked forward to 'that happy period . . . when the landed as well as commercial men of the Kingdom shall see their true interest in permitting *the free importation and exportation of corn, at all times*'.[3] It later demanded that special regulations which had the effect of raising the price of oatmeal in Scotland and especially in Glasgow above the price in England should be abolished – 'any distinction in Laws to the prejudice of Scotland, more especially in such as relate to the Bread of the People, is an intolerable grievance'.[4] The Bill was passed into law, but with many of the alterations recommended by the Merchants House and others, so that Scotland was not unduly disadvantaged. The House continued to campaign against increases in import duty under the Corn Laws for several years.

From the Minute Book

9 March 1819

'That it is the abundance and moderate price of Coal to which the City of Glasgow and surrounding district have been chiefly indebted for the establishment of so many branches of manufacture; and that even a very small tax upon an article of which the consumption is so great, both for the purposes of machinery and among the Labourers employed, would be very sensibly felt at present, and might be gradually rendered more intolerable, were the principle once admitted of taxing so important a necessary of life.

'That to the labouring classes of this Country a tax upon Fuel would be felt quite as severely as one upon Provisions, which every wise Legislator would at once reject as equally oppressive and impolitic.

'That for these reasons this House will adopt every constitutional means of resistance . . .'

It was a time of changing political atmosphere. The French Revolution was welcomed at first because France seemed to many people in Britain to be moving towards a parliamentary government of the British kind. But there was less sympathy when the French deposed their king and defied Europe. What were thought to be French ideas – they were often, in fact, those of an Anglo-American, Tom Paine – began to seem dangerously popular to Pitt's Government. Groups of reformers organised themselves into Societies of Friends of the People which, to the alarm of the Establishment, had working-class members.

In December 1792, the House was disturbed to discover that its clerk, George Crawford, was 'acting as Secretary to one of those Societies which have given occasion to the present alarms with respect to the peace of the Country'. It was decided that 'Mr. Crawford's services shall be dispensed with', though he continued to draw his salary for some months. The House solemnly resolved:

> That we consider it as our duty, and the duty of every loyal Subject and good Citizen, sensible of the blessings we and our Fathers have enjoyed under the present happy Constitution, to declare to the World our firm attachment to that most excellent Constitution, and our determination to maintain and support it, more especially as we are convinced that if any abuses have crept into it, the Constitution contains in itself the means of rectifying them.[5]

The last clause suggests that at a time when Reformers, including a well-remembered Glasgow man, Thomas Muir of Huntershill, were prosecuted for sedition and exiled, some members of the House were still anxious to make it clear that, in their opinion, political change might not be a bad thing. But within two months Britain was at war with revolutionary France; it was a war that was to continue, with one short break, until Napoleon was finally defeated at Waterloo, twenty-two years later.

The effects of the war

With this, ideas of Reform became almost unmentionable for a while. The House gave its support to the Government and the war, though not without some reservations. A motion in favour of peace negotiations was rejected in 1795, but at the same time the House advised the all-powerful Tory 'manager' of Scottish affairs, Henry Dundas, that if the Government wanted more men for the Navy it had better offer them higher pay and a guarantee of discharge 'within some reasonable time, after the expiration of the term of their engagement, or of the next arrival in Britain of the Ship they belong to'.[6] In the same year there was an attempt on the life of George III on his way to open Parliament, and the House sent a petition to the House of Commons in support of bills for protecting the royal person and preventing seditious meetings, with only 'two members dissenting'. In February 1797 the threat of invasion prompted the House to take a leading role in the town's offer to the Government to raise two battalions of 750 men each. In 1798 such was the alarm at the financial crisis caused by the war, that the Merchants House joined with the town council, the Trades House and the Chamber of Commerce in urging that 'a small Tax upon every kind of Property or Stock' – in fact a capital levy – 'would be the best measure that could be resorted to, in order to make the burden fall equally upon all descriptions of People' at a time when 'the very existence of the Country, and of all that is held valuable in Society, depends on the issue of the Contest'.[7]

A letter to the Members of the Merchants House, 27 March 1797

'Sir,

In conformity to the orders of the Council of the Merchants House at last Meeting, we have now to annex you a List of all the Matriculated Members, whether Foreign or Home Traders.

'Should there be any of your respectable acquaintances that are Merchant Burgesses of the City, and who, from forgetfulness or inattention, are not among the number, we request you to mention it to them, and to put down their names at the foot of the List . . . if desirous of becoming members, that the Matriculation and Gold Books may . . . be sent them.

'The entry money for Matriculation is Ten Guineas, a less sum perhaps, in proportion to the present value of Money . . . than it was fifty years ago; and the subscription to the Gold Book is optional.*

'The Revenue of the House is above £900 per Annum; and there are many that now find a comfortable resource from its Charity, who at one period of their lives little expected that either themselves or their children would ever stand in need of such assistance. There are many more, who now unavailingly regret that, by withholding a few guineas in better days, themselves and their Families are for ever cut off from this resource. But independent of all personal considerations for the uncertainty of future events, it may be presumed that it will appear a laudable object of ambition to become Members of so respectable a Society, whose sole aim is to smooth the declining years of those who once walked in the same circle, or to assist their destitute families . . .'

* The Gold Book was a record of subscriptions, at first voluntary and for specific purposes (see Chapter 3). In 1723 it was enacted by the House that subscription to it was a condition of obtaining relief for oneself or one's relatives, but this seems not to have been enforced.

Robert Findlay and Son

The only remaining 'tobacco merchant's house' in Glasgow, at 42 Miller Street, was home to two prominent Glasgow merchants and Deans of Guild, both named Robert Findlay. Robert Findlay Snr, known as Findlay of Easterhill, was a nephew of the tobacco baron William Cunninghame, with whom he was in business in the firm of Cunninghame, Findlay and Co. Robert Findlay was in Virginia when the American war broke out, and could not get back to Glasgow for two or three years. Findlay bought the estate of Easterhill (in what is now the Tollcross area) and in 1780 acquired his city residence at 42 Miller Street, which, as was usual, also housed the firm's counting house. He was a Director of the Merchants House for many years from 1778, Dean of Guild in 1797 and 1798, and then a Director again until 1802. He was also prominent in the Chamber of Commerce, one of its first directors, and chairman three times.

His son Robert was born at Miller Street in 1784. He entered the family firm, which became Findlay, Duff and Co., one of the city's largest mercantile establishments. In 1814 the firm had the Virginia Buildings erected, extending from Virginia Street to Miller Street. Like his father, he was an active member of the Chamber of Commerce, and his contribution to the Merchants House was even more notable: he was very prominent, especially in its public affairs, particularly during the 1820s and 30s, and served as Dean of Guild in 1819 and 1820. Robert Findlay was president of the Chamber of Commerce at the time of Sir Robert Peel's election as Rector of Glasgow University. Peel's supporters in Glasgow invited him to a celebratory banquet in January 1837, in which Robert Findlay was heavily involved. Henry Monteith was in the chair, John Leadbetter was one of the organisers, and the Merchants House was one of the bodies that presented an address to Peel. A pavilion was specially erected in Buchanan Street, on the site of what is now Princes Square, and an amazing 3,435 people sat down to dinner, the largest banquet ever held in Glasgow.

In 1803, when a French invasion seemed possible, £500 was voted towards the cost of raising a volunteer corps in Glasgow – with the caveat 'that nothing but the strong necessity and extreme importance of the measure could induce the House to appropriate any part of their funds to any other purposes than to Charitable uses'.[8] One of the keen volunteers in this effort, a Major in the corps – and Captain in one of the 1797 battalions – was Gilbert Hamilton, a most active Director of the House, who had been Dean of Guild in 1791 and 1792.

Gilbert Hamilton

Gilbert Hamilton (1744–1808) became a member of the Merchants House in 1782 and a Director the same year, serving very actively until his death in 1808, interrupted for only one year apart from his deanship of 1791 and 1792. He was provost for the two years following his deanship. He was a founder of the Chamber of Commerce and its secretary from its inception in 1783 until his death. Preternaturally tall and thin, he was said, when dressed in his provost's black velvet clothes, to look like 'death running off with the mortcloth'.[9] In the difficult years after the end of the American war and at the outset of the war with France, there were many Glasgow bankruptcies, and Gilbert Hamilton acted as trustee on many of these bankrupt estates. The most famous was perhaps that of Andrew Buchanan, the great tobacco merchant bankrupted as a result of the American war, who had intended to open up a street along the length of his garden. After Buchanan died in 1783, Hamilton carried out his intention, selling building lots on both sides of the new thoroughfare, which he named Buchanan Street. He also bought a plot for himself, running back from Buchanan Street and fronting on to Queen Street, almost opposite the future Gordon Street and next to the Cunninghame mansion (later the Royal Exchange and now the Museum of Modern Art). From the counting house at the back of his house, he conducted his business as a partner in the Carron Iron Company and as the first Collector of the Bank of Scotland (before it had a branch in Glasgow). He was also a partner in the Delftfield Pottery and the Westmuir Coal Company.

   He spent much time and energy on schemes to relieve financial distress in the business community, especially in the extremely hard years of his provostship, coinciding with the start of the war. One of his great achievements as provost was to have been a bridge at the foot of Saltmarket, and he laid the foundation stone in June 1794 – but during a flood towards the end of the following year the almost-complete bridge was swept away. He therefore might have had a greater insight than most into the vagaries of the river, when, in 1800, he was a member of a Merchants House committee that recommended the House subscribe to a fund to build flood defences in the vulnerable parts of the town. In 1790 he was one of the founders and the first president of the Humane Society, for rewarding and encouraging the rescue of people from the river (see Chapter 9).

In the disastrous harvest failure of 1799 the House pledged £500 in support of town council plans to procure food for the people of Glasgow, and in 1801 it asked Parliament, not for the last time, that there should be no distilling of grain while supplies were short. The House was 'impressed with a strong conviction of [whisky's] injurious tendency, not only as it respects the Manufactures of the Country and the morals of the people, but also as it will materially abridge the comforts of the lower orders of the Community, whose resignation and fortitude under the heavy pressure of a general scarcity have been eminently exemplary'.[10] The petition was twice renewed in 1810, a year of great scarcity, and a similar address to the Prince Regent in 1811 declared that:

Your Petitioners are filled with fearful apprehensions when they consider how much Grain and Potatoes have been lost and injured by the severity of the weather, . . . and also, when they consider how unable the labouring classes of the Community will be to provide the absolute necessaries of life at advanced rates, while the wages they are receiving are lower than last year's, when Provisions were cheap and in plenty, and when, even at that time, a voluntary Contribution to a considerable extent was found indispensably requisite to supply the wants of these classes, many of whom could not get employment owing to the stagnation of Trade.[11]

A plea on behalf of the engineer of the *Comet*

Merchants House Minute, 4 January 1827
'The House petitioned the House of Commons thus:–
'That your Petitioners, as representing the Commercial Community of the City of Glasgow, feel it their duty to recommend in the strongest manner to the favourable consideration of your Honourable House the Petition of Mr. Henry Bell, of Helensburgh, in the County of Dumbarton, Engineer, who first successfully introduced the practical application of the Steam Engine to the navigation of the River and Firth of Clyde, from whence it has been brought into universal use.

'That Mr. Bell spent many years, and incurred great Expense, in gradually maturing his improvements. He is old, lame, and in narrow circumstances, and appears to your Petitioners to have an unanswerable claim to a liberal remuneration from his Country, for the eminent advantages of his labours to all Classes of the Community.

'And therefore pray this honourable House to take into consideration Mr. Bell's public services, and to allow him such remuneration for his great sacrifices to the general benefit as to your Honourable House shall seem suitable and proper.'

Henry Bell's development of the first commercially successful passenger steamship, the *Comet*, launched on the Clyde in 1812, brought increased prosperity to the river – though not to Bell, who was no businessman. He was living in near-poverty by the 1820s, and friends and supporters began to agitate for a reward, grant or pension, in recognition of his contribution to engineering and the nation's prosperity. The Merchants House letter was part of this campaign, and eventually Bell was given £200 by the Government. The Clyde Navigation Trust, more generously, gave him an income, in the form of an annual grant of £50, later increased to £100, which was continued to his widow after his death.

James Ewing

The long war was drawing to an end, however, and the movement towards reform of many kinds was soon to revive again. One man's influence on the House was particularly important in those years. He was James Ewing, twice Lord Dean of Guild (in 1816 and 1817, and 1831 and 1832), one of the most active and enterprising members in its history and an outstanding benefactor at his death (Fig. 5.2).

Fig. 5.2. James Ewing, MP, LL.D. (artist: John Graham Gilbert)

James Ewing (1775–1853), a Director of the Merchants House from 1814, was the most important influence on the House in the first third of the century, and its most generous benefactor at his death. He effected the sale of the old Merchants' Hall before it became a burden; he added over 360 names to the membership list, reversing the decline in membership; he was the guiding spirit behind the creation of the Necropolis; he set in motion reforms of the House that preserved it some status and usefulness. After his deanship of 1816 and 1817, the House formally thanked him 'for his eminent services' and voted him 'a piece of Plate, value fifty Guineas, as an honorary mark of their approbation and gratitude'.

A reluctant speaker in Parliament ('very seldom intruding on the ear of the House' according to his obituary), but always an effective writer, he published an account of the Merchants House in 1817, and thereafter a stream of papers, pamphlets and reports on a variety of matters of local and national concern.

He married in 1836 at the age of sixty-one, his wife, Jane Crawford, being thirty-eight years his junior. Ewing lived thereafter in virtual retirement from public life, in his house in George Street and his estate at Strathleven, until his death in 1853. They had no children, and Ewing left an estate worth £280,000, of which he bequeathed nearly £70,000 to charities and public causes, including £31,000 to the Merchants House, by far its largest legacy at that date.

James Ewing (called 'of Strathleven' from the estate near Dumbarton to which he finally retired) was an example of what many nineteenth-century Glasgow businessmen most wished to be. The son of a prosperous West India merchant and accountant, he went from the city's Grammar School to Glasgow University at the age of twelve. Trained as an accountant, he was already highly successful when he succeeded to his father's business. He later set up his own business, James Ewing and Co., and his father's firm was eventually merged with this. His enterprise and acumen earned him a considerable fortune, with which he was very generous, giving to many good causes and helping to establish several people in their careers. He was a co-founder of the Glasgow Bank (later the Union Bank), whose notes were at one time 'payable to James Ewing'. In 1815 he helped to establish the first Glasgow Savings Bank, in which people of modest means could make small deposits. Before he became Dean of Guild at forty-one, he was already a town councillor actively interested in education and in the terrible problem of the new industrial poor. This last interest made him a friend and disciple of the minister of the Tron Kirk and leading Evangelical, Dr Thomas Chalmers, who tried to prove practically that urban poverty could be dealt with by the Church. He was president of the Andersonian University, established for working men. In 1819 and 1822 he presented detailed reports on the shockingly overcrowded City Bridewell (the prison in Duke Street) and personally saw that the Bill to establish a new and much improved prison was carried through Parliament.

By the period around the end of his first deanship, therefore, he was establishing himself as one of the city's most dedicated and effective campaigners for social improvements and reforms. He had a success with civic reform at this time too, in persuading Glasgow town council to abandon the burgess oath. This oath, to be sworn by all who 'entered burgess', effectively excluded from public life a sizeable body of townspeople, members of a branch of the Seceders from the Church who argued that the burgess oath, which had been introduced after 1745 as an anti-Catholic measure, implied full recognition of the Established Church. Ewing was asked to inquire into this mare's nest, and his report, concluding that 'the period has surely arrived when we may apply the hand of reform without the reproach of innovation', was hailed as liberal and enlightened, and adopted as policy by the city in 1819.

An experience of quite a different kind in 1820 tested his popularity to the limit. After the pitiful Radical Rising of that year the Government sent commissioners from London to apply the savage law of treason, always so unpopular in Scotland that no Scottish court could be trusted to act on it. James Ewing found himself chancellor (foreman) of the jury at the trial of James Wilson, who had been tricked into carrying a broken sword towards Glasgow (which was said to be in the hands of a force of Reformers) but had turned back after walking eight miles. The jury found him guilty on one count of the charge but recommended him to mercy. The Government, however, wished 'to make an example' and the bewildered man was duly hanged, beheaded and quartered. The city and most of the jurymen were horrified, and there were cries of 'Murder!' at his execution – they had been convinced that Wilson would be reprieved. All concerned in the case became the objects of popular odium, and at the time James Ewing was blamed as being the tool of the Government.

He continued with his public work, however, and regained his standing as a liberal and public-spirited citizen. In 1827 he was the largest single subscriber to the cost of the new Royal Exchange and the chairman of one of the committees for its establishment. He laid the foundation stone of the Exchange building (which was built on the site of the former mansion of William Cunninghame the tobacco lord, and later housed Stirling's Library, eventually becoming the home of Glasgow Museum of Modern Art).

He was elected Lord Provost in 1831, the last of the pre-reform provosts, and standing for election for the first reformed Parliament, he headed the poll in December 1832. But at the election of 1834 he refused to pledge himself to vote against the Duke of Wellington's short-lived Tory Government – on the ground that

Fig. 5.3   James Ewing at his mansion at the top of Queen Street (artist: Augustin Edouart)
Ewing bought the Crawford Mansion in 1815, a substantial property at the head of Queen Street, with a sloping shrubbery and an avenue of trees famous for its colony of rooks. Here he lived for many years, overlooking the site that was to become the eventual home of the Merchants House, before selling his property to the Edinburgh and Glasgow Railway Company, who built Queen Street Station on the ground.

no MP should ever give general pledges. He lost his seat and settled down again as a businessman, a public-spirited citizen and finally a country laird. It was the sort of record that mercantile Glasgow most admired.

Free trade with India

Ewing first appears prominently in Merchants House affairs as the champion of a particular kind of free trade. The East India Company had a monopoly of British commerce beyond the Cape of Good Hope; goods from or for not only India but also Arabia, Persia, China and the Far East generally had to be carried in its ships or by its licence. Kirkman Finlay, the most powerful and enterprising of Glasgow merchants and cotton manufacturers (and a Director of the Merchants House almost continuously for thirty-five years from 1799 onwards), had done more than anyone else to break through Napoleon's ban on British trade with the European continent, by shipping goods through Smyrna (Fig. 5.4). He was ambitious to put an end to the much older British rule that prevented merchants and shipowners from trading freely by the sea routes to Asia. In Glasgow, James Ewing was his chief supporter in this campaign. Together they no doubt inspired a petition by the Merchants House to the House of Commons in March 1812, when the East India Company's charter was about to be renewed, asking 'that no Monopoly be granted of the Commerce and Navigation to the Countries Eastward of the Cape of Good Hope, but that the Trade may be free and open, in the same manner as other branches of Commerce, not only to the Port of London, but to all the other Ports of Great Britain and Ireland'.[12] Merchant supporters of the abolition of the monopoly probably helped to get Kirkman Finlay elected both provost and MP later in 1812, and he was able to press further his parliamentary campaign against the East India Company.

Trade with India was thrown open in 1813, and the first Glasgow ship, owned by Kirkman Finlay and laden with a cargo including three-quarters of a million yards of cotton, reached Bombay in 1816. Fourteen years later, again at the instigation of Finlay, the House petitioned for free access to China, where the East India Company had to give up its monopoly in 1833; in the same year the *Kirkman Finlay* arrived triumphantly in Canton. In 1842 the *Glasgow Herald* counted it among Finlay's achievements that 'we now rarely see the Broomielaw without one or more ships on the berth for Calcutta, Bombay, Madras, Singapore, Manila, and other parts in the East'.[13]

Fig. 5.4. Kirkman Finlay (artist: John Graham Gilbert)

Kirkman Finlay (1773–1842) was one of the greatest Glasgow merchants of all time, with trading connections all over the world, but his significance to Glasgow and the Merchants House lies even more in his political activity, both at civic and national level. His family firm of James Finlay and Co. (still in existence) were important cotton manufacturers, with several mills in Scotland. In 1812, while Lord Provost, he was elected MP for Glasgow, his wildly popular status confirmed by a crowd who hauled him in an open carriage from the Town Hall to his Queen Street house, and silver medals were struck to mark the occasion, bearing the legend 'Faith, Honour, Industry, Independence – Finlay, 1812'. Rejoicing was great in the Merchants House, which formally thanked the bailies and town council for their unanimous support of him. It had been seventy years since they had one of their own number at Westminster. The House kept up its petitions against the East India Company monopoly, Finlay's great cause at the time, and sent him their petition against the Corn Laws to present to Parliament. A few years later, when word came that he had voted (in line with his Tory sympathies) in favour of a Corn Bill, he was not so popular, and the windows of his house were smashed by a mob.

He was provost twice more, and served as Lord Rector of the University and Governor of the Forth and Clyde Navigation Company. A strong opponent of radicalism, he was a close associate of the more moderate James Ewing: while Ewing dominated the Merchants House, Finlay's great sphere of influence was the Chamber of Commerce, of which he was chairman four times. Although Finlay had been the scourge of Radical activity in the years following 1815, when he stood for Parliament in 1830 it was against a Tory traditionalist, James Campbell. With the Merchants House pressing for Reform, Finlay for once had adopted a reforming position himself, motivated by free trade considerations and proclaiming himself the representative of the 'commercial men'. Despite much support for him and for Reform, the highly anomalous voting system ensured his narrow defeat on this occasion.

Finlay acquired an estate on the Cowal peninsula of the Firth of Clyde, where he built Castle Toward and, energetic as ever, had five million trees planted. He was known for his hospitality and the wide range of his interests and conversation. He was best remembered in Glasgow as the man who stood up to the East India Company and opened the East to all comers, and after his death in 1842 the Merchants House placed his statue (dressed, perhaps more appropriately for the statesman than for the merchant, in a toga) in their newly acquired Merchants' Hall. It now stands outside the Chamber of Commerce, in the present Merchants House building.

Saving the pound note

Scotland was outraged in 1826 when the British Government threatened one of her favourite institutions, the £1 note. A financial crisis had emphasised the weakness of the banking system south of the Border, where the Bank of England, with its special privileges, was the only great banking company permitted by law. Other banks worked under severe restrictions and could not have more than six partners, but all could issue as many notes as they liked. In these conditions hard times produced waves of bank failures when the notes of weak firms were suddenly found to be worth nothing. The smallest Bank of England note was for £5. Scotland, on the other hand, had three chartered banks besides a number of other companies with quite considerable resources. Their £1 notes were the usual means of payment in the country and were safeguarded by a clearing house system of note exchange between offices. But in England, local £1 notes had a bad name. It was proposed to abolish them throughout the United Kingdom. There was a national wave of protest, to which Sir Walter Scott contributed his 'Letters of Malachi Malagrowther'. The Merchants House, too, sprang to the Scottish banks' defence.

Kirkman Finlay and James Ewing joined in proposing a series of resolutions. 'The commencement of prosperity in this Country', they argued, 'was nearly coeval with the Incorporation of the Bank of Scotland, in 1695.' They quoted Adam Smith to show the importance of the banks for the development of Glasgow's trade and emphasised the confidence of the people in 'a solid and judicious system of Paper Currency, convertible on demand into Gold':

'[T]he exclusion of Small Notes from the circle, and the obligation on Banks to provide Gold [in place of £1 notes], would materially diminish their ability to accommodate the Public, particularly in times of scarcity and pressure, when their aid is most required. . . . [A]ny attempt to alter the established usages of this Land, to which we have been so long attached, and under which we have so long thriven, is uncalled for by our circumstances, is opposed to our customs, and must be injurious to our interests.'[14]

The Lord Provost, Mungo Nutter Campbell, and Dean of Guild, Robert Dalglish, went to London to assist in presenting the petitions to the Lords and the Commons. The opposition was successful and the Scottish £1 note was saved; nearly eighty years were to pass before the rest of the United Kingdom would have a similar currency. (In the meantime they had to make do with gold coins.) The Merchants House remained suspicious of Government interference with the Scottish banking system and protested against the Act of 1845 which restricted the right of Scottish banks to issue notes without a fixed backing in gold.

The end of the old Merchants' Hall

James Ewing's effect on the Merchants House was that of the proverbial new broom. He was deeply attached to the House as an institution and his first major project as Lord Dean was to write a brief record of its history. His second, in 1817, was to support a proposal that the House's old Hall in the Bridgegate should be sold. A committee was appointed to consider the question of 'improving the Property'.

'That the Merchants' House of such a great Commercial City should have a place of Meeting suited to respectability of this Corporation, there could be but one opinion', it reported:

> *The present Building was renewed in its present form so far back as 1659, which is more than a Century and a half; and when it is considered what was the state of the City at that period – how small was the number of its population, and how restricted the extent of its Trade, compared with the present situation of the Town – it must be admitted that such an Establishment conferred the highest credit on the public spirit of the Merchants of that day . . . A very material change, however, has since taken place. . . . The Bridgegate, which was then the most respectable and fashionable part of the Town, has now become the residence chiefly of the inferior classes, with an awkward access, and a still more objectionable vicinity.*

The sale of the Hall, the committee stated, would be profitable. It would open for new building a useful (if not socially very desirable) strip of land between the Bridgegate and the Clyde; and the expanding city needed all the new housing it could get: 'A site ought to be chosen which would not only be more productive for the rent of the attached Building, but in all respects be preferable for the occupation of so respectable a body. Such a situation, your Committee are satisfied, may easily be procured in a genteel and central part of the Town . . .'.[15]

During the previous seven years the House had actually increased the size of its property in the Bridgegate by acquiring the ground between its garden and Clyde Street, and the property to the west of its boundary wall, perhaps with the intention of rebuilding on the enlarged site. Whatever the original intention, the addition of this ground made the property more saleable, as it was now large enough to accommodate two rows of tenements, whereas previously it had been too broad for one, and too narrow for two.

It was agreed that one part of the old building must be kept in the House's possession – the steeple, which was 'an ornament to the City'. Some thought that it should be stipulated that any plans for new buildings must show off the steeple from its base; 'but as the lower half consists of a naked square Tower, and as the whole elegance is confined to the upper part above the Clock, it was considered a matter of no moment, or rather that it was advisable to conceal the bottom'.[16]

The House accepted all these proposals with an assurance from Ewing that he had personally raised £2,000 by the recruiting of new members, and he was making every effort to raise a further sum by having the Dean of Guild Court compel the entry of new burgesses, as it was no doubt entitled to do under the Letter of Guildry, but had not, in fact, done for a long time past. This, with the price to be got for the old property, would provide funds for the building of a new Hall. The property (excluding the steeple) was sold to a builder for £7,500 in September 1817, with the stipulation that the steeple was to be left intact and the height of the new tenement to be restricted.

The Bridgegate had been a dignified street in the previous two centuries. Several of the rich and powerful had their mansions there. But by 1817 it was degenerating into a filthy slum, as older houses were 'made down' and subdivided. The wealthy families had moved westward to the spacious new streets to the west of George Square. The Merchants' Hall had ceased to be a hospital for pensioners. Probably its garden could no longer bloom among the tenements. With the opening of the Tontine rooms at Glasgow Cross in 1781, patrons of balls, concerts and receptions had a far more elegant venue than the old Merchants' Hall in its now insalubrious surroundings. And the Trades House had moved into their splendid new building in Glassford Street, designed by Robert Adam, in 1794.

Fig. 5.5   The Bridgegate, c.1830
The Merchants' Hospital has now been replaced by a tenement, but the steeple still stands.

More than a quarter of a century was to pass before the Merchants House found its own new home. Meanwhile it held its meetings in the town council's hall next to the Tolbooth. By 1821 the old steeple rose from a block of high housing, Guildry Court (Fig. 5.6). The House proposed to install a new clock and asked the council to take over the ownership of the steeple and maintain it in all time coming. The council after considering the offer rejected it, on the grounds that 'the steeple is now so much surrounded with high buildings that the clock can only be seen to advantage by the tenants in Guildry Court and a very small portion of the inhabitants of the Bridgegate.'[17] Agreement was reached in the end that the Merchants would provide a new clock and keep the steeple in repair 'upon condition of the Magistrates and Council being at the expense of keeping the Clock and ringing the Bell, as in the other steeples of the Town'.[18] At the same time the council decided to let the Merchants House use the Town Hall rent-free. The steeple was later enclosed in the city's fish market.

Fig. 5.6 Guildry Court from the south

The Merchants House clock

From a Report of the Special Committee of the Council on the Public Clocks, c.1835:
'The Bridgegate Clock
'This Clock is in tolerably good repair; and, in moderate weather, ought to keep
pretty good time, but in stormy weather, from its great height and exposed situation,
and particularly from the great length of the pointers, and inefficiency of power in
the movement, it is utterly impossible to calculate upon its keeping correct time.
This Clock requires to be wound up three times every week.'

The Necropolis

After the sale of the hall, the most important piece of property owned by the House
was what remained of its land of Wester Craigs. Soon after the House had acquired
this land, in the mid-seventeenth century, it had divided it up into parks, or fields,
and given them names such as Craigs Park, Goufhill Park and Broom Park, some of
which survive in the street names of Dennistoun. In the mid-eighteenth century the
House had feued out all the usable part of Wester Craigs to various individuals.
The Craigs Park, the rocky hill east of Glasgow Cathedral, including the quarry,
remained in the House's possession, and around 1717 it was walled and planted with
fir trees, and came to be called the Fir Park. In 1804 the park was improved, new
trees were planted and paths laid out, and the name was changed to the Merchants
Park, though 'Fir Park' was the name that stuck. From its heights strollers could look
down on the spreading city. A special committee was in charge of this little pleasure
ground, one of the few places of the kind in early nineteenth-century Glasgow.

In 1824 the Revd Robert Stevenson McGill, Professor of Divinity at the University, had
been allowed to set up there the massive doric pillar carrying a colossal statue of
John Knox, which still stands over the city. James Ewing helped to pay for this
monument. Perhaps it was this that suggested to Ewing and the Collector of the
House, Laurence Hill, a respected lawyer who was active in schemes for the city's
welfare, the possibility of monuments of another kind. Five years later James Ewing
suggested to the committee that the park should be converted into a burial ground.

It was, he thought,

> *admirably adapted for a Père la Chaise, which would harmonize beautifully with the
> adjacent scenery, and constitute a solemn and appropriate appendage to the
> Venerable Structure [i.e. the Cathedral] in its front; and which, while it afforded a
> much-wanted accommodation to the higher Classes, would at the same time convert a
> Property, at present unfrequented and unproductive, into a general resort, and a
> lucrative source of Profit to a Charitable Institution.*[19]

Members of the House, it was stated, made little use of the park. At the same time
the Barony parish 'which now contains so many of the residences of our wealthier
Citizens' had no cemetery of its own except for the crypt of the Cathedral. The rock
was well suited 'for constructing Vaults and Tombs of the securest description',
a serious consideration in the days of body-snatchers.

Fig. 5.7 The façade from the Necropolis Bridge, 1836
The façade, designed by John Bryce, was erected in 1836, serving the practical purpose of a retaining wall after the roadway at that point had been widened to allow carriages to turn, and providing an imposing architectural view as one crosses the bridge. The upper part of the main arch has since been filled in, and the inscription it bears was formerly on the cast-iron gates of this archway (now removed). It begins: 'The adjacent bridge was erected by the Merchants House of Glasgow to afford a proper entrance to their new cemetery combining convenient access to the grounds with suitable decoration to the venerable cathedral and surrounding scenery . . .'. The inscription above the arch reads: 'Erected A.D. MDCCCXXXVI. James Martin, Dean of Guild'. The intended function of the archway was as the entrance to a tunnel which was to have been excavated through the rock linking with the quarry on the other side. This tunnel was to house catacombs, secure burial places for the dead in the days of the 'resurrectionists'. The Anatomy Act of 1832 in fact made this plan unnecessary, and the archway remained a shallow recess, like the four smaller archways, or 'mausoleums', flanking it, all of them purely ornamental.

This was the origin of the Glasgow Necropolis, one of the most extraordinary architectural features of the city, the first thing of its kind in Britain, and for generations an absorbing concern of the Merchants House and its Directors (Fig. 5.7). The plans for the layout of this dramatically situated burying ground were a matter of intense public discussion. The House sponsored a competition, and the resulting designs were modified and completed by two eminent Glasgow architects, David Hamilton and John Baird.

The problem of access from the south-west was solved by the purchase of ground to the west of the burn and south of the Cathedral churchyard and in the Drygate area. This made it possible to join the Fir Park 'with the Cathedral and its Ancient Cemetery, and with the fine large square, displaying in one view the Infirmary, the Cathedral, and our own noble and picturesque wooded Terrace'.[20] The town expressed an interest in purchasing a plot of this ground for burying cholera victims – Glasgow suffered its first cholera epidemic in 1832 – but the committee in charge of the new cemetery refused, 'being satisfied that the respectable Class to whom the House must look for occupying both their newly acquired ground and the Fir Park would consider it an insuperable obstacle that such Cholera patients were admitted . . .'. One of the objects in establishing the cemetery was to provide a more sanitary means of accommodating the dead than in the overcrowded churchyards of the city.

The approach across the valley of the Molendinar, by then a stinking and polluted stream, was resolved by the building of the graceful Bridge of Sighs below the Cathedral (Fig. 5.8). The first burial had already taken place, in September 1832, of a Jew, Joseph Levi (who had in fact died of cholera), the Synagogue having purchased a small area of the park as a burying ground. (The first Jewish member of the House, Salis Schwabe, had enrolled the same year.) This was the first Jewish

Fig. 5.8   The Necropolis, 1866

The ornamental burial ground, though a completely novel idea in Scotland and indeed Britain, was an immediate success, with a forest of obelisks, urns, mausoleums, and temples springing up in the first thirty years. The Bridge of Sighs, designed by James Hamilton, had its foundation stone laid by the Dean of Guild, James Hutcheson, in 1833. It provided a convenient and graceful means of access to the cemetery from the west, and from the Cathedral in particular. The west end of the bridge is bounded by a pair of ornamental cast-iron gates, designed by David Hamilton, bearing the motto of the Merchants House, Toties Redeuntis Eodem, and the name and date of the Dean of Guild, William Brown, 1837–8.

cemetery in Glasgow: the tiny Jewish community had to go to Edinburgh to bury their dead before that date.[21] The Merchants House paid for an ornamental gateway and pillar at the entrance for the Jews' burial ground. The first Christian interment was in 1833.

William Brown

Dean of Guild in 1837 and 1838, William Brown was born in Glasgow's Stockwell, in an upper flat, with views of the braes of Castlemilk in one direction and the Kilpatrick hills in the other. His father James was an oil and colour merchant, and William, upon entering the business, showed a flair for chemistry: he expanded the business and set up his own works, exporting abroad. He was an original partner in the Cunard Company, though investments in other ventures were not so successful.

A keen yachtsman, he built yachts to a new design. He was an Evangelical in religion, and an associate of Glasgow's great Evangelical minister, Thomas Chalmers. He married Jane Wilsone, who had also lived in the Stockwell as a child, and they had two sons, who both died before him. For a while he owned the great country house of Kilmardinny, styling himself William Brown of Kilmardinny, as was the custom in those days.

William Brown was a very active Director of the Merchants House: among other things we find his name associated with Merchants House involvement with legislation on the Poor Rate, reform of municipal corporations and customs reform. He was among those who pressed for Merchants House assistance with improvements to the Cathedral, and his name is to be seen on the gate at the Bridge of Sighs. He was brought back as Dean of Guild in 1856 after the death of William Connal, who himself had replaced the deceased Dean of Guild Robert Baird.

He died in 1884 at the age of ninety-two, seeming to the citizens of the time a solitary figure left over from another era, with his 'punctilious, old-fashioned courtesy', and despite having outlived his children and most of his contemporaries still possessing a bright and cheerful disposition, undimmed faculties and a fondness for reading.

To visit the Necropolis today, even in its weathered and rather time-worn state, is to walk through the pages of Glasgow's Victorian history. On every side are the names of provosts, reformers, poets, professors, industrialists – and, of course, merchants. In the first Necropolis Report the assurance is given that those who purchase a burial lair thereby help 'the poor, . . . the aged, the orphan, and the widow, who are indeed the peculiar owners of this vast city of the dead',[22] and for many years the Merchants House's charitable funds drew a considerable income from this unusual investment.

The establishment of the Necropolis brought the Cathedral into sharper focus for the Merchants. A movement to restore and improve the Cathedral, concentrating in particular on its unusual and asymmetrical western towers, had begun in 1833, initiated by Archibald McLellan, merchant and coachbuilder, the art collector who left his collection and the gallery named after him to the city. By the late 1830s the plans to bring the Cathedral into line with Victorian concepts of good Gothic design had acquired considerable momentum, and money was being raised locally. Archibald McLellan became a Director of the Merchants House in October 1837, serving for three years, and was one of a committee which recommended to the House in 1839 that it subscribe £500 for the 'renovation' of Glasgow Cathedral. The donation was unusual as the object was not directly charitable in nature, and necessitated a full explanation:

> *[T]he character of the City has suffered materially in the eyes of every visitor of intelligence and taste, from the neglected and dilapidated state of the Cathedral, so different from the high state of repair in which the English Cathedrals are maintained, yet to none of which the Cathedral of Glasgow yields in point of Antiquity or in Architectural or Historical interest. . . .*
>
> *The formation of the Necropolis by the Merchants House, and the judicious Regulations under which it has become one of the most interesting Cemeteries in the kingdom, if not in Europe, were based upon its vicinity to our great Civic Monument . . . All improvements, then, upon the property in the neighbourhood, . . . concentrate the attention of the public upon the property of the Merchants House; and no improvement . . . can do this so effectually . . . as the completion of the Cathedral.*[23]

The 'completion' turned out to mean the removal of the two western towers, an 'improvement' which was later regretted by some.[24]

Parliamentary Reform

When the Necropolis was opened in 1833, James Ewing was both Lord Provost of the city, the last under the old order before municipal reform, and one of its MPs, the first to be elected after parliamentary reform. In the Age of Reform, the Merchants House – especially under Ewing's influence – showed itself to be in favour of constitutional change to both city and Parliament. It is true that the House could oppose a Bill for extending Glasgow's boundaries on the ground that the value of its property might suffer (March 1830), but it approved plans for Scottish legal reforms, as it was to do repeatedly in the future – on condition, however, that this would strengthen the work of the courts in Glasgow, rather than in Edinburgh alone (April 1830). But these were preliminaries to the great projects of parliamentary and municipal change which were now exciting the whole of Britain.

On 6 December 1830, a special meeting of the House was held to discuss petitioning Parliament for a reform of the House of Commons which King William IV's new Whig Government was considering. Ten years before, at the time of the Radical Rising in the city, the House had sent an address to King George IV denouncing 'the daily attempts making [sic] by factious and designing men to seduce your Majesty's subjects from their allegiance, and by the degradation and abuse of one of our highest privileges – the liberty of the Press – to instil into their minds principles leading not only to discontent, but even to insubordination and rebellion'.[25]

Now, however, the tone of the House's petition was almost radical:

> *While the Population, Wealth, Enterprise, and Intelligence of the Empire have for ages been steadily advancing, the real state of the Commons House of Parliament, which*

professes to represent, and which ought to represent the People, has been gradually and regularly retrograding from its original purpose, chiefly through the undue influence exercised on the part of the privileged Classes, by which they secure wealth and patronage to themselves and their followers, at the expense and to the great injury of the other and more numerous Classes of Society.

The undue influence thus acquired by the privileged Classes has now become so great as absolutely to threaten the overthrow of the Constitution; for while in many places those who have the ostensible right of voting are the slaves of some aristocratic family, in others their number is so inconsiderable that the Representative is, in fact, the mere nominee of one or two high-born or influential Individuals. . . .

[T]hese abuses . . . are peculiarly and strikingly manifest in the case of Scotland, where the return of Representatives in the different Counties is, with few exceptions, under the absolute control of one or two great families, and the election of Members for Burghs is exclusively confined to Juntos, who, in almost every instance, are self-elected.[26]

When it was published the Reform Bill was welcomed by the Glasgow Merchants. But it was rejected in the House of Lords. The reaction of the majority of the Merchants House was to petition King William to create enough peers to ensure the passing of the bill (18 October 1831), though a minority felt 'that a degraded House of Peers would become much worse than a useless burthen on the Country, and would no longer occupy their place in the Constitution as the protectors of Liberty and Property against democratic fury on the one hand, or against the acts of despotic power upon the other'.[27]

The King evidently agreed with this minority, for the moment, and the Whig Government fell. There was intense excitement throughout the country and in Glasgow great public demonstrations. At the fifth and last of the special meetings of the Merchants House during the crisis (16 May 1832) the House agreed to make two petitions, one to the King asking him to recall his Reforming ministers, and the other to the House of Commons proposing that MPs should 'withhold all Supplies until the Bills pending in Parliament for amending the Representation of the People shall have passed both Houses, unimpaired and unmutilated, and shall have received the Royal Assent'.

Such pronouncements from middle-class bodies had, perhaps, as much influence on the King and the Tory peers as the demands of crowded meetings. Within three weeks the opposition to Reform collapsed. The old system by which, in Scotland, delegates from the self-perpetuating town councils in groups of burghs alone had a share in choosing an MP, while in the counties voting was confined to lairds and their friends, came to an end. Householders where property was valued at £10 were now to be the voters and Glasgow was to have two MPs of its own, instead of sharing one with Renfrew, Rutherglen and Dumbarton. At the first election James Ewing was returned at the head of the poll.

Reforms nearer home

In the years of James Ewing's second deanship the House had been considering two other schemes of reform: that of the town council and of the House itself. It was the

Trades House that had taken the lead in proposing municipal reform some thirteen years earlier, but it was not until parliamentary reform had been achieved that ending the town council's self-election moved to the top of the agenda. This system, along with the leeting method that gave the Dean of Guild so much power in the election of his own Council, had ensured that the circle of men that led the Merchants House was essentially the same circle that controlled the town council for over 200 years, but it was accepted that its day had passed. Both Houses had an interest in civic reform, in that with no existing external control over council borrowing and spending, liability for the debts of a spendthrift council might ultimately lie with them.[28]

So intimately was the Merchants House connected with the town council that any reform of the latter necessitated an overhaul of its own organisation. In September 1831 the House formulated a proposal that in future Deans of Guild should be elected by all members of the House, without any submission of nominations to the town council, and that the system of leets for the choosing of Directors, with the Lord Dean's right to nominate twelve of the thirty-six, should be abolished and that all should be chosen by the members as a body. But under the Letter of Guildry changes of this sort could not be made without the approval of the town council, and the town clerk, James Reddie (who was no reformer) had ruled that Parliament's consent would be needed before such a thing could be done.

A committee drawn from members of the town council, the Merchants House and the Trades House had agreed on a modest scheme of reform for the council itself. It was proposed that the number of councillors should be increased to forty, each to hold office for five years. The Dean of Guild and Deacon Convener were always to be councillors. The Merchants House and Trades House were each to choose one other member each year, and each year the parliamentary voters who were burgesses were to choose four councillors only. The Scottish Burgh Reform Act of 1833 swept aside a good deal of this canny planning; in fact, as it left the Commons, not only would it have ended the representation of both Merchants and Trades Houses on the town council, but it would effectively have given complete control of both bodies over to the council, including control over their property and financial affairs. Both the Merchants and Trades Houses sent urgent proposals to the House of Lords requesting alterations, several of which were adopted, and both bodies were left free of council domination; it is significant that James Ewing was both Lord Provost and MP for Glasgow at this date, and it was largely thanks to his intervention that Glasgow's voice was heard.

Under the new Act as it passed into law, the Dean of Guild and Deacon Convener held their place on the council. The other councillors were to be elected by citizens (not necessarily burgesses) who had a parliamentary vote. Councillors need not belong either to the Merchants House or to the Trades House. The old rule that the Lord Provost and three bailies must be of the Merchant rank disappeared, and consequently 'Merchant Magistrates' could no longer take part ex officio in the direction of the Merchants House as they had done.

The House was given the power to reform itself, and duly did so by instituting 'an annual election of the Dean of Guild and all the Directors by the universal suffrage of every recorded Member . . . , amounting to Twelve Hundred of the most respected Traders in Glasgow'.[29]

The Glasgow Guildry – Merchants House and Trades House – had grown up both as part of the city's governing framework and as a pair of friendly societies who looked after the interests of Merchants and Craftsmen and helped their own members in distress. The Houses had been tied to the town council in two ways: all the councillors were chosen from the two ranks, and the council supervised their constitutions and made the final choice of the Lord Dean and Deacon Convener. Now, for the first time, the three bodies found themselves substantially independent of each other. From the first the Guildry, as a single body uniting both Merchants and Craftsmen, had been rather a theoretical idea than a practical fact. Nothing was heard of it in 1833, or later.

The links between the two Houses and the council were not completely broken. The Dean of Guild Court, containing both Merchant and Trade lyners, continued to do essential work for the city by supervising new building and preventing encroachments on neighbours' properties. This work was especially important at a time when Glasgow was growing very fast; though it should be remembered that much of this development was in suburban districts (some of them independent burghs) over which the Glasgow Dean of Guild Court had no jurisdiction – a state of things which was certainly not for the good of the expanding city.

These reforms were of far-reaching significance for the government of the city, yet there was no wholesale rejection of the old order. Many of the pre-reform councillors were later returned with a popular mandate, among them at least half of the Merchants on the pre-1833 town council. Despite the self-perpetuating system and lack of external accountability, the city had been run fairly efficiently. There had been none of the financial mismanagement that resulted in bankruptcy for Edinburgh and Aberdeen.[30] This relatively creditable record can be partially ascribed to the influence of the Merchants House – politically conservative but not opposed to change that was perceived to be in the city's interests, governed by a wealthy elite but not insensible of the needs of the community, and ever alert to matters of fiscal responsibility.

Changing functions of the Merchants House

All this activity made the early 1830s a particularly busy period for the Merchants House. In 1836 a special committee appointed to look into its management reported that its many and various interests, in particular the recent addition of the Necropolis, added up to a change in the nature of its affairs:

> They are not now confined to a Revenue flowing from a few well-defined and easily-managed sources, and to an Expenditure controlled by restrictions and regulated by long-established rules, but they now embrace an enterprise of great magnitude, requiring for its progressive success much minute attention, and the confidence and good opinion of the public [i.e. the Necropolis].[31]

They recommended that 'although the present Collector has conscientiously and ably discharged his duties', the office of Collector should be made a full-time post and combined with that of superintendent of the cemetery, and they proposed to appoint a new Collector the following month. For the Collector, Laurence Hill, this announcement came as a very unpleasant surprise. He protested that he had discharged his duties faultlessly for seventeen years and pointed out the bitter irony that he had been one of the originators of the Necropolis, the existence of which was now given as a reason for – in effect – his dismissal. He had carried out the Collector's business from the office of his legal partnership, Hill and Davidson, in South Frederick Street, for a modest annual fee.

Despite qualms from some quarters, even on the committee, a majority supported the proposal in a vote of the House. There ensued a vigorous campaign of pamphlets and published letters against the reform, which had been instigated and driven through by John Leadbetter, an active Director and future Lord Dean (see Chapter 6). In the face of the protests, the Directors went ahead and advertised the post – now to be that of Collector and Clerk combined – at an annual salary of £200. Hill presented an interdict against the measure, but judgment was given against him, and in October 1837 Robert Buntine was appointed Collector and Clerk, for one year in the first instance (the idea of combining it with responsibility for the cemetery having been quietly dropped). The unfortunate episode – it is significant that Hill's friend and collaborator in many projects, James Ewing, had retired from active membership – led to the wounded and embittered Hill breaking his ties with the House that three generations of his family had served. Buntine retired in 1850, and was thanked for his faithful services, but, from a Minute of this time, in which it was stated that 'repeated instances [have] lately occurred, where the rights and privileges of the House have been invaded, and its Regulations overlooked',[32] it appears that the detailed knowledge and legal expertise of Hill had been missed. (As a postscript to the affair, it may be noted that the year of Hill's departure, 1837, also saw the birth of his son, William Henry, who resumed the family connection and became one of the House's most influential Collectors.)

The reforms of 1833 had left the House free to manage almost all its own affairs, and with the new challenge of working out its function as a body depending not so much on legal powers as on prestige and on its practical usefulness both to its own members and to the social health of the town. It was represented either by the Lord Dean or by one or more of its Directors on most of the public trusts and governing boards in which Glasgow was interested. As before, it made pronouncements on public questions. It built up its own relief funds for its members, and gradually for a wider public.

Committees of the Merchants House and public bodies with Merchants House representatives in 1835

- Annual Committee on Books, Revenue and Pensions (see Chapter 4)
- Committee on Cemetery and Lands and Quarries
- Committee on New Hall and Post Office Accommodation
- Committee on Auldhouse Mortification, for Apprentice Fees etc. (see Chapter 4)
- Committee for Revising the Lists of Members, and entry of Members

- Directors of the Town's Hospital
- Commissioners for Bridewell
- Manager of Infirmary
- Manager of Lock Hospital
- Managers of Lunatic Asylum
- Manager of Blind Asylum
- Director for the General Lying-in Hospital
- Managers of Stirling's Library
- Committee on Coulter's Mortification for Premiums to Inventors (see Chapter 4)
- Trustees of Statute Labour

The first five of these were, of course, internal committees of the Merchants House. The others were town institutions in the management of which the Merchants House was involved.

The Town's Hospital (always called by that name, rather than by the shameful term 'poorhouse') was built in 1731 on Great Clyde Street. It was founded by the magistrates and town council, the Merchants House, the Trades House and the General Kirk Session 'for employing and entertaining the poor and restraining the scandalous practice of idle begging, and encouraging of virtue and industry', and each of these four bodies provided twelve directors. It was a combination of workhouse, orphanage, asylum and infirmary, and by 1815, with over 500 inmates, was very overcrowded. The Merchants House had contributed £60 a year at the outset, but by 1815 this had been increased to £110, a considerable outlay on top of its commitment to maintain its own poor. In 1843 the Town's Hospital was moved to the premises of the former lunatic asylum in Parliamentary Road.

The first Bridewell, or prison, in Glasgow was opened in 1788 in a former granary, most of its inmates being 'dissolute women' and vagrant boys. The first purpose-built Bridewell was erected around 1798 in Duke Street. This too was very overcrowded by 1814, and new accommodation was built in the Justiciary Court House at the foot of the Saltmarket, facing Glasgow Green. In 1825 a new prison was built, officially the Town and County Bridewell, also known as Duke Street Prison.

The Royal Infirmary was built in 1791 near the Cathedral, and the Merchants House subscribed £400 to the building of it. The Lock Hospital was established in 1805 for 'the care of unfortunate women' (that is, for the treatment of venereal disease) in a house in Rottenrow. In that year the Merchants House subscribed £300 towards the founding of a Lunatic Asylum, for the better housing of the unfortunates who were at that time confined to the lunatic ward in the Town's Hospital. It took several years to raise sufficient funds and build large premises in Parliamentary Road. It was a model asylum of its time, and became the Royal Asylum for Lunatics in 1824, moving to a splendid new home in Gartnavel in 1843. In 1825 the House gave £200 for the new Asylum for the Blind in Castle Street. The Lying-in Hospital, for poor or homeless women, including the unmarried, was established in 1834 in the old Grammar School building, and after many years of struggle against infection and lack of funds, in 1860 acquired more suitable premises in Rottenrow, where a new building, in use until recently, was erected in 1879. This became the Glasgow Royal Maternity Hospital.

Stirling's Library, the first public library in Glasgow, was founded in 1791 by the will of Walter Stirling, merchant, a member of the famous family of textile manufacturers. In 1912 it was transferred to Glasgow Corporation.

Statute labour was originally compulsory work in building and maintaining roads: by a statute of 1719 every householder had to give six days' work each year. This was soon commuted to 3d. per day, or 18d. per householder each year, out of which labourers were paid. This system was ratified by an Act of 1795, and householders paid a local tax towards road building. In Glasgow the Statute Labour Trust was created in 1820, to raise and administer this 'conversion money', used for making and maintaining streets, roads and sewers. Under this system there were fifteen trustees, including the Dean of Guild and four appointees from the Merchants House. By recruiting labour from the ranks of the unemployed, it functioned as a form of poor relief. The powers were transferred to the Police Commissioners in 1837 and a rate was substituted for the conversion money.

On the other hand, one of the most important of its original purposes was gradually dropping out of sight. As Glasgow grew it had become more and more difficult to insist that all important trade must be in the hands of merchant burgesses. There was an attempt to punish all traders who were not freemen in 1755, with only occasional prosecutions thereafter. Later in the eighteenth century (and still more in the nineteenth) the atmosphere of the time grew steadily less sympathetic towards legal restrictions on traders.

The idea of discouraging 'unfreemen' was not altogether forgotten. Under the Letter of Guildry this was the business of the Dean of Guild and his Court. Individual Deans could refrain from pursuing traders who were not burgesses, but an appeal to the Court from Merchants or Craftsmen who felt that they were suffering from what was strictly illegal competition could not be altogether neglected. The House, indeed, went so far as to inform the Commons in 1836 that it neither possessed nor sought 'any monopoly in trade', but this could have been seen merely as a declaration that its members, simply as members, claimed no special privileges – which had been true ever since it had ceased to include all the merchant burgesses of the time.

As early as 1821, however, it had refused to contribute to the expense of a lawsuit which the Dean of Guild of Cupar, in Fife, was pursuing to try to obtain a ruling 'that persons not entered as Brethren of the Merchant Guild have no right to open Shop within Burgh, for the sale of Articles of Foreign Manufacture', and by the 1830s the attempt to insist on the payment of 'fines' by Glasgow merchant burgesses seems to have been abandoned altogether.

A Merchants House disclaimer

'The House derives . . . a very trifling annual sum as the proportion of the fines of entry of Merchant Burgesses; which they have not of late shown any desire to enforce, and which they are perfectly willing to abandon . . .'

From the Report on the Bill for better regulating Municipal Corporations in Scotland by a Committee of the Merchants House of Glasgow, 23 June 1836.

In the years after the Burgh Reform Act of 1833 had confirmed the Lord Dean's place on the town council and the authority of the Dean of Guild Court, the House protested repeatedly (and successfully) against proposals that would have weakened the position of either Dean or Court.

From the Minute Book

10 December 1844
'On the Motion of Mr. Newall, the Meeting resolved that two Ornamental Lamps, with appropriate devices, should be erected at the entrance to the Lord Dean of Guild's Private Residence, as a distinction becoming the official head of the Merchants House, and the Second Magistrate of the City.'

A new home

By the late 1830s it was felt to be necessary for the Merchants House to find a home of its own again. For one reason and another it had not proved to be so easy to build a new hall on a 'genteel and central' site as had been expected when the old Merchants' Hall was sold. The House seems to have met comfortably enough as the guest of the town council, and later in the City Chambers at the foot of the Saltmarket. But Glasgow Corporation (as it now began to call itself) felt the need of larger offices. It was decided to build these and also a new Sheriff Court House for Lanarkshire on a site bounded by Hutcheson Street, Wilson Street, Brunswick Street and Ingram Street, in what is now very much the eastern end of the city centre.

John Leadbetter, energetic Director and future Dean of Guild (see Chapter 6), was chairman of the Court House Commissioners at the time, and also on the Merchants House 'New Hall Committee'. He provided the House with plans and drawings of the proposed new building and persuaded the members to build their new Hall in the courthouse complex. A man of large vision, he championed the most extensive of three possible options for the new premises, and had the satisfaction of seeing his motion carried by a large majority over an amendment to build much more modest accommodation elsewhere. The new Merchants' Hall was to stand between the courthouse and the City Chambers. It was a handsome classical building designed by Glasgow architects William Clark and George Bell, with an imposing hexastyle Corinthian portico facing Hutcheson Street and sculptured reliefs on the frieze (Fig. 5.9).

Fig. 5.9   The Merchants' Hall in Hutcheson Street, home of the Merchants House from 1843 till 1870

The price of the ground allotted to the Merchants House was realised from a debt owed to the House by the corporation. The cost of the building was just under £5,000. It was to bring in an income in rents: the Faculty of Procurators was given approval for renting rooms for their library and meetings, and it was also agreed to lease part of the new building to the National Security Savings Bank; other offices were leased as counting houses to two law firms and a gas company.

Within its new home the House assembled the relics of its past which had been in store for more than a quarter of a century. The boards with the names of benefactors and the 'Scripture Rules for Buying and Selling' were hung in a room which reflected, on a loftier and larger scale, the House's old meeting place in the Bridgegate. The sculptured stones, with the reliefs showing seventeenth-century Merchants and a ship were re-installed. Portraits were displayed (and a few years later also the statue of Kirkman Finlay). In October 1843, the opening of the new Hall was celebrated by a public dinner.

The end of Merchant privileges

When the House entered its new home it was just about to face the last change in its status which the Age of Reform would bring to it. Though the exclusive trading privileges of merchant burgesses had, in fact, been slipping away through several generations they still existed in law. In October 1845, the House was prepared to say

Fig. 5.10   Merchants House membership ticket, 1830

again that traders ought to be merchant burgesses, but by the end of that year Glasgow town council had agreed to a change and the Dean of Guild Court had decided to suspend 'the enforcement of the Laws against persons who have commenced or carried on business in Glasgow from and after the 1st January, 1845',[33] though it still claimed the right to penalise non-burgesses who had been trading before that date, on the ground that it would be unfair to refuse to protect the privilege of those who had previously 'entered Burgesses' in due form.

Already, however, the Whig Government was preparing a Bill for the Abolition of the Exclusive Privilege of Trading in Burghs in Scotland. The House saw this with foreboding. In years to come, it declared, 'a total abolition of the privileges hitherto enjoyed by Corporations', such as the Incorporated Trades and itself, 'must result in the complete extinction of a Civic distinction of ancient standing, intimately interwoven with the Public and Charitable Establishments of this City, and affording a qualification for the reception of Charitable Bequests vested in this House and other Public Bodies'.[34] As an alternative it was suggested that the entry fees paid by burgesses might be cut by half.

In spite of its anguished tone, however, this was rather a formal protest than a convincingly serious one. Its very wording shows that the House recognised that its chief function, though not its only one, was now the building up and administration of funds for the benefit of traders in distress and their dependants. In fact its greatest work in 'the reception of charitable bequests' and their use had yet to begin when the Bill became an Act on 14 May 1846.

What vanished then was the last shadow of the municipal Middle Ages.

Notes

1. Merchants House Minutes, 10 June 1788.
2. [James Maclehose (ed.)] *Memoirs and Portraits of One Hundred Glasgow Men* (Glasgow, 1886), vol. 1, p. 97.
3. MH Minutes, 30 Oct. 1786.
4. Ibid., 28 Jan. 1791.
5. Ibid., 11 Dec. 1792.
6. Ibid., 30 Jan. 1795.
7. Ibid., 17 May 1798.
8. Ibid., 26 Oct. 1803.
9. *The Regality Club* (Glasgow, 1889) vol. 2, p. 76n.
10. MH Minutes, 12 Nov. 1801.
11. Ibid., 29 Oct. 1811.
12. Ibid., 21 Mar. 1812.
13. *Glasgow Herald*, 7 Mar. 1842.
14. MH Minutes, 20 Feb. 1826.
15. Ibid., 22 Aug. 1817.
16. Ibid.
17. *Extracts from the Records of the Burgh of Glasgow*, 24 Aug. 1821.

18. Ibid., 28 Dec. 1821.

19. MH Minutes, 15 Oct. 1829.

20. Ibid., 8 Oct. 1832.

21. Joe Fisher, *The Glasgow Encyclopedia* (Edinburgh, 1994), p. 126; Arnold Levy, *The Origins of Glasgow Jewry*, 1812–1895 (1949?), p. 23.

22. James Martin and Laurence Hill, *The First Annual Report from the Committee on the Necropolis* (Glasgow, 1835), p. 6.

23. MH Minutes, 2 May 1839.

24. James Macaulay, *The Western Towers of Glasgow Cathedral* (Glasgow Cathedral lecture series 6, Glasgow, 1998).

25. MH Minutes, 26 Dec. 1820.

26. Ibid., 6 Dec. 1830.

27. Ibid., 18 Oct. 1831.

28. Irene Maver, 'The guardianship of the community: civic authority prior to 1833', in T. M. Devine and Gordon Jackson (eds), *Glasgow*, vol. 1 (Manchester, 1995), pp. 237–77.

29. MH Minutes, 23 June 1836.

30. Maver, 'Guardianship of the community', pp. 262—70; Maver, 'Glasgow Town Council in the nineteenth century', in T. M. Devine (ed), *Scottish Elites* (Edinburgh, 1994), p. 100.

31. MH Minutes, 20 Sept. 1836.

32. Ibid., 1 Nov. 1850.

33. Ibid., 9 Dec. 1845.

34. Ibid., 25 Feb. 1846.

6

THE MERCHANTS HOUSE
IN THE VICTORIAN CITY

The face of the industrial city

Glasgow in 1846 was one of the most rapidly growing cities in industrial Britain. Its population had much more than tripled since the century began – with its swelling suburbs it was now well over 300,000. To the west of Blythswood, several merchants and future Deans of Guild had built handsome villas in the district that was soon to be further developed with elegant terraces and tenements into the West End. South of the Clyde new streets were breaking through the neat hedgerows of Govan Parish. New church spires were rising round the city, and also great new chimney stacks. The steam engine had drawn cotton factories into the town from the rivers and burnsides where they had first sprung up to use water power. Works to produce such engines were also beginning to appear in the city. On the edge of the southern suburbs a famous iron foundry, Dixon's Blazes, lit the night sky, heralding a new industrial age in which iron was to replace cotton.

With all this came smoke and spreading slums. The business centre of the city had not moved very far to the west when the town council, the Merchants House and the County Court House Commissioners set up their new buildings between Hutcheson Street and Brunswick Street, but around Glasgow Cross and to the east masses of industrial workers were pouring into the older buildings and into new shoddily built 'backlands'. At first this new proletariat had come mainly from the Lowlands, but the dreadful potato famine in Ireland and the Highlands brought scores of thousands of starving refugees in the Hungry Forties to crowd into every possible living space from windowless cellars to garrets. The Merchants House made special grants to provide food for the desperate poor, but in 1848 discontent, unemployment and political Chartism exploded into what looked like a revolutionary outbreak, when mobs raided gunsmiths' shops and the cry *Vive la République* echoed the continental risings of that year. Businessmen, too, suffered 'difficulties and distress', which the House attributed not only to the failure of the potato crop but also to the working of the Bank Acts that had restricted the operations of the Scottish banks.

The battle for the railways

Perhaps the most significant new feature of the second quarter of the nineteenth century was the advent of railways. The most active early supporters of railways were the industrialists, especially in textiles and, increasingly, in iron and coal, whose enterprises depended on transport to bring in raw materials and to send out their manufactured goods and coal. For those with money to invest, railways meant the welcome prospect of financial buoyancy less risky than either banks or seagoing trade. For social campaigners, the building of railway routes right into the city centre and the creation of stations were seen as ideal opportunities to clear the slums. As we would expect, the Merchants House took a close interest in the development of railways, though any attempt to influence their development ran the risk of involvement in the bitter rivalries that grew up between the competing companies and promoters of different lines.[1]

As early as 1808, long before any steam locomotive ran on steel, twenty guineas had been subscribed by the House towards the survey for 'a Rail Road' from the Monkland Canal to Berwick-upon-Tweed, which must have been intended for horse-drawn traffic. The first call for a railway in the later sense came in 1836, when the House resolved to join in a petition for 'the level thorough [sic] line of Railway betwixt Glasgow and Edinburgh',[2] and weighed in against a rival proposal for a shorter line linking North Lanarkshire with the Union Canal which ran from Falkirk to the capital.

One man who became a Director of the House in that year, and Dean of Guild in 1845 and 1846, had a particular interest in the Glasgow–Edinburgh line. John Leadbetter had been brought up in Lanark, the son of a wright, and had come to Glasgow as a young man and taken a job as a clerk in the linen trade. Bent on self-improvement, he attended evening classes to further his education, and meanwhile rose to become a partner in the business that had employed him. On his visits home to Lanark, which he frequently made on foot, he must often have wished for a better mode of transport than the crude carrier's cart that was the only alternative to walking. By 1815 he had his own business buying and selling linen; although cotton had supplanted linen as the most important textile manufactured in and around Glasgow, the city remained a centre of the linen trade, with imports from Germany, Ireland and the East of Scotland passing through Glasgow on their way to America and the West Indies. In those pre-railway days John Leadbetter travelled around Ireland on horseback buying linens to send back to Glasgow; his Scottish linens were produced by weavers in cottages and sent to the city by canal or cart. The advent of power-looms, to be followed by railways and telegraph, changed the textile industry for ever, and Leadbetter was at the forefront of the revolution, establishing power mills in Dundee and Belfast and exporting his products directly from there. In 1832, the year when the Manchester and Liverpool Railway opened, he came back from a visit there determined to bring a railway to Glasgow. He was the first to subscribe for the Edinburgh and Glasgow Railway, and became the chairman of the directors. In the great fight to get the Bill through Parliament, which lasted from 1835 till eventual success in 1838, the Merchants House supported him, sending petitions to Parliament – though refusing to commit any funds of the House to the costs of petitioning.

The Edinburgh and Glasgow Railway opened in 1842, and its success converted a sceptical public into fervid supporters of railway travel. The battle was now on to secure permission for a route from Glasgow to the Border and beyond, fought with relentless ferocity by the competing companies and the speculators who stood to gain or lose large sums of money. When early in 1842 the House met to consider the report of the Government's commissioners into the proposed routes, it gave its support not to the line favoured by the Edinburgh and Glasgow Railway Company, but to a route through Clydesdale and Lockerbie (the future Caledonian line), agreeing with the argument that 'this line is . . . calculated to benefit Glasgow in a peculiar manner' and that it must be vigorously promoted because if not 'the support of Government will . . . be transferred to the line from Newcastle to Edinburgh, by the East Coast of Scotland'.[3] The motion was carried with only one vote against. The dissenter was John Leadbetter, who argued that the most likely eventual outcome, and the best for Glasgow, was that two lines would be built, one by the west coast, the other by the east – linked, of course, by the Edinburgh and Glasgow.

The Caledonian Company came to have a dominating position, which was often countered by the tactical alliance of the two other main rivals, the Glasgow, Paisley, Kilmarnock and Ayr Railway (which became the Glasgow and South Western, with its line through Cumnock and Dumfries) and the Edinburgh and Glasgow. The House again became caught up in the argument in 1845, when a motion expressing 'high satisfaction at the prospect which is now presented of the formation of a direct Railway communication between England and the City of Glasgow, by means of the Caledonian line' (by Lockerbie and Carlisle) triumphed over an amendment, no doubt proposed by the adherents of the anti-Caledonian alliance, 'that the more railways which have their termini at Glasgow, the better for the Community' and that the Board of Trade should 'investigate the different schemes . . . and in the event of one line only being adopted, that it be the Western line by Dumfries and Carlisle'.[4] John Leadbetter was Dean of Guild at this time, but evidently did not succeed in carrying the majority with him on this question. He would perhaps have been heartened by another resolution passed at the same meeting, to petition Parliament in favour of a railway from Perth via Stirling which would link with the Edinburgh and Glasgow Railway.

Railway routes were one battleground, but another no less hotly contested was the sites of city termini. The influence of the Caledonian can again be seen in another Merchants House resolution of 1845, against the West of Scotland Junction Project, sponsored by the Glasgow, Paisley, Kilmarnock and Ayr and the Edinburgh and Glasgow companies, for a high-level steel bridge across the river and a terminus on a site just to the west of what was to become Central Station. The House argued that the project would

> destroy the beauty and amenity of some of the most important streets in the City,
> endanger the lives of the Citizens in its most crowded thoroughfares, particularly on
> the Glasgow Bridge, and by the constant flowing of sparks from the Engines, greatly
> endanger the crowded Shipping in the Harbour, and deteriorate in a material degree
> the Revenues of the Clyde Trust, by interrupting the traffic on the River, carrying to

other and distant Ports goods which would otherwise be shipped or transhipped at the Broomielaw, and deprive the citizens of the ready access to Passenger Steamboats which they at present enjoy.[5]

Fig. 6.1. Crowded shipping in Glasgow harbour, c.1840 (artist: J. D. Nichol)

The alarm at the threat to shipping was real: by the 1840s the Clyde was deep enough at Glasgow for ocean-going ships, half of them employed in the transatlantic trade, chiefly bringing in raw cotton. The scheme was also opposed by the Blythswood Trustees, the Clyde Navigation Trust, the town council and the Tidal Harbours Commission, and was duly defeated. There was to be no rejoicing for the Caledonian, however, as its own scheme, for a similar bridge and a terminus near the later St Enoch Station, was also defeated. The result of all the plotting and counter-plotting was that no company succeeded in getting permission for a railway bridge across the Clyde or a central terminus on the north side of the city for another twenty years.[6]

The Merchants House and the Clyde Navigation Trust

That the Clyde had a harbour at Glasgow deep enough by the 1840s for ocean-going ships was a development in which the House had been closely interested since the 1750s, when it supported the first Clyde Trust Act (see Chapter 4). In 1846 it petitioned Parliament in support of the proposal of the River Improvement Trust, as it was then called, to construct a dock at Stobcross and much-needed lengths of riverbank quay. But in the early years of the century it had come into conflict with the Trust on the matter of its representation – and the representation of shipowners and ratepayers – on this powerful authority. It had campaigned for representation from the Trust's inception in 1809 – unsuccessfully, since membership was confined to magistrates and councillors. A new Act in 1825 had empowered the town council to nominate a further five members for the Trust, thus widening representation, while still leaving the composition of the authority in the control of the council. The next opportunity to protest about this state of affairs had come in 1836, when a new Bill for massive widening and deepening was to be brought before Parliament. There had been concerted opposition from the public bodies representing the shipowners and merchants – led by the Merchants House – demanding a complete shake-up of the composition of the Trust, which they wished to see made up of twenty-five members, twelve elected by the shipowners and by those who paid dues to the Trust, and thirteen nominated by the town council. The House pointed out that since

> the Revenue from the River and Harbour is more than double that of the Corporation from all other sources, it must surely appear very inconsistent that the River Trust should continue to be a mere appendage to the Corporation Trust . . .

and that it was only right that

> those who contribute so largely to the Revenue of the River Trust should have something to say in the representation and management of those large funds, so as to prevent all prodigal expenditure, but at the same time to encourage every rational improvement for the River and Harbour.[7]

The Trustees refused to compromise and the opponents of the Bill took their fight to Parliament, where the arguments raged for almost two sessions, ending in defeat for the Bill and delay for the essential improvements to the river. It was only in 1840 that a compromise was reached, with the Merchants House being given three representatives of its own (four counting the Dean of Guild) on a thirty-three-member River Improvement Trust. The agreement of the Merchants House to accept this limited representation was a major factor in the withdrawal of opposition to the Bill.[8]

The Clyde Navigation Act of 1858 established a new body, the Clyde Navigation Trust, nine of whose members were, for the first time, to be directly elected from shipowners and ratepayers – but, less acceptably to the Merchants House, their own representation was cut to two members. They protested:

> That seeing the Merchants House of this City consists of a Constituency of about 2,000 Members, embracing all classes of Merchants, Manufacturers, Ship Owners, and Traders, and it being acknowledged . . . that the Three Members, with the Dean of Guild, hitherto nominated to the River Trust, have been efficient and desirable Members, this House . . . cannot but consider the present proposal . . . to reduce their number to Two Members, to be founded on imperfect knowledge of the extent of the Constituency and character of the Merchants House, and would venture to express a hope that they . . . may rather extend the number from the Merchants House, as being the best Representative Institution of the Commercial and Trading interests of the City.[9]

Their objections were not sufficient to impede the Bill, which duly passed into law, and the House had to content itself with two representatives on this Trust, whose interests, powers and revenue came to be of enormous importance, not just for Glasgow, but for the whole of the West of Scotland in the second half of the nineteenth century.

The mails and the post office

Postal services were another area in which the House took an interest. It campaigned for better postal services, but not to the extent of a Sunday post: in 1849 it sent a Memorial to the Postmaster General, observing

> *with much regret the contemplated change in the General Post Office, London, in reference to the transmission of Mails on Sunday . . . [I]ts immediate effect must be to increase the amount of Sunday labour in London, as well as in many of the leading Commercial Towns throughout the Country, thus employing many individuals in Secular duties that might be disposed to spend their time in connection with Religious duties on that day.*[10]

Until 1848, when the railway line from Carlisle reached Glasgow, mail and stage coaches had trundled into Trongate every day from first light till midnight. The advent of railways speeded up the delivery service considerably. In 1851 the House petitioned for sending the evening mails from Glasgow and London on a fast train to enable letters to be delivered the following morning. It was concerned too about the Atlantic mail service, and in 1864 asked the Postmaster General that the Mail Packet Station be changed from Southampton to Falmouth, and the mails be sorted on board the steamers before arrival; in 1865 it joined with Liverpool Chamber of Commerce in pressing for the despatching of American mails from London on a Friday instead of Saturday.

The Glasgow post office was another subject that drew forth several petitions from the Merchants House. In 1810 the post office was in Nelson Street (now Albion Street), in premises built by and rented from Dugald Bannatyne, a property developer and for many years secretary to the Chamber of Commerce, who was also the postmaster. (He was a Merchants House Director too, both in the 1790s and again several times from 1810 onwards.) There it remained for the next thirty years, the inadequacy of the premises and the chaos of the arrangements a constant source of grievance to the business community. On a more convivial level, it also served as a club for the merchants and men of business, who met there each evening around eight o'clock. The Laigh Kirk bell (in Trongate) was rung from a quarter to eight till eight o'clock to remind the clerks, porters and messengers from all the offices that the London mail was being made up, and the bag about to be closed and sealed, and as the offices closed the members of the unofficial post office club met to discuss the day's events. During the 1830s a barrage of complaints was directed against the post office by various public bodies. It was only with the retiral of the nearly octogenarian Bannatyne as postmaster in 1838 that an opportunity presented itself to get the post office moved from 'the extremely unsuitable and objectionable locality' into accommodation suited to the greatly increased population and business of the city, and at the same time to appoint a properly qualified person as postmaster, and to end the abuses that had arisen from the fact that the allowance for the office and staff were part of the postmaster's salary. The Merchants House pushed for the new office to be situated in Glassford Street, and there the post office moved in 1840, but even this office could not cope with the volume of business in a satisfactory way. There were only two window clerks to receive mail, who had to keep the office open from 7.30 a.m. till 10.30 p.m., seven days a week – except for the period of divine service on a Sunday. The House and the Chamber both continued to keep up pressure on the post office authorities and Parliament to improve staffing and premises, but this was resisted until 1852, when at last plans were made to build a new office on the south side of George Square.[11]

At the same time as it was campaigning for this new post office to be built, the House had appointed a committee to look out for property to invest in on its own account, and this resulted in the purchase in 1853 of property adjacent to the new post office site, at the corner of George Square and South Frederick Street. The purchase was evidently made with a view to securing a site for future expansion of the – as then unbuilt – new post office. In the meantime the House let the properties. The George Square post office was opened in 1856, occupying about a third of the frontage between South Frederick and South Hanover streets. In 1871 the post office authorities were ready to extend the Glasgow office and the Merchants House sold its George Square and South Frederick Street properties to the Government for £27,000. The House petitioned the Postmaster General about the need for significantly increased staff and services, and for the Glasgow post office to be placed directly under the control of the Postmaster in London, instead of having to direct all business through Edinburgh. The first phase of the post office expansion, on the site of the property sold by the Merchants House, was begun in 1876 and completed in 1879.

Besides these developments in Glasgow's communications, there were many matters of national importance on which the House made its voice heard in those decades. In 1855 it proposed, not for the first time, a decimal coinage: the florin, one-tenth of a pound, already existed, and it suggested the introduction of a silver cent and a copper mil (one-tenth of a cent). The shilling, 'important from its use in quotation of prices and wages', should be kept, along with the sixpence.[12] In 1867, when parliamentary reform was again in the air, the House petitioned (vainly) that Scotland should be given House of Commons seats in proportion to its population. There was a special interest in legal reform. The House repeatedly urged the abolition of arrestment of wages to meet unpaid bills, on the ground that, relying on this expedient, salesmen could tempt wage-earners disastrously into debt. In 1868 it was asking for the removal of the distinction between heritable and moveable property in intestate estates which could put widows and daughters (who at that time did not have property rights) out of their family homes in favour of a dead husband's brother or cousin. It asked for arbitration in mercantile disputes as an alternative to costly litigation. In 1873 it protested vehemently against a proposal to introduce something like the English law of mortmain to Scotland, which would have placed certain restrictions on the conveying of property to charitable institutions; the House pointed out that this would prevent 'bequests of the wisest kind from flowing into the best of Charitable Channels' and that it was far too stringent and quite unnecessary in Scotland.[13] The Bill was eventually withdrawn.

A crisis in the deanship in 1856

In 1856 the Merchants House suffered the loss of two Deans of Guild in one month. William Connal had been a Director of the Merchants House throughout the 1840s and Dean of Guild in 1851 and 1852. By a quirk of fate, he was again Dean at the time of his death. Robert Baird, elected Dean of Guild in October 1855, died suddenly in August 1856, and William Connal was elected Interim Dean on the 22nd of the month. But he died on the 25th while visiting a friend in Forfarshire.

William Connal was born in Stirling in 1790, and came to Glasgow in 1806 to work in the counting house of Findlay, Duff and Co., 'one of the most extensive colonial and general mercantile establishments in the city'. Every Saturday he would finish his week's work at four o'clock and walk back to Stirling to his father's house, arriving at ten o'clock. This suggests an energetic and reliable character, and indeed Connal became a partner in the firm at the age of twenty-two. Not long afterwards he acquired the substantial house in Miller Street where Robert Findlay Jnr had been born (Chapter 5), which is now the only remaining merchant's house in the city. The business went through various metamorphoses and changes of name, and William Connal eventually had his own firm, William Connal and Co., commission merchants and produce brokers. When the China trade was opened up he was the first Glasgow merchant to import directly an entire cargo of tea, and he built a large warehouse in York Street near the harbour for the tea consignments, said to be the finest privately owned tea warehouse in Europe or America. Tea, rather than tobacco or sugar, had become by the 1840s Glasgow's chief import. Perhaps his most far-sighted venture was in supporting Sam Cunard, who had failed to find backers in London for a steam packet company to North America. William Connal became the first chairman of the Cunard Company.

When tributes were paid to Connal soon after his death, the mood in the Merchants House was sombre: they had lost two Deans and a Director, William Morgan, in the space of three weeks.

Victoria and Victorians

In 1849 there was great excitement in Glasgow at the first royal visit since that of James VI in 1617. The House's address to Queen Victoria was presented to her on board the royal yacht which was moored at the landing stage at the foot of West Street:

> *In recognizing in the August person of your Majesty the lineal descendant of illustrious Princes who swayed the Scottish sceptre for a series of ages, we unite with all classes of our fellow-subjects in giving expression to those enthusiastic feelings of patriotism and attachment with which we bid you welcome.*[14]

To celebrate the occasion its pensioners were given a 50 per cent increase in their pensions for the current quarter.

In its exponential expansion, early Victorian Glasgow had to provide itself with the organisations to support a great industrial city. Hospitals and schools were needed for the growing population. It had its ancient university, already anxious to move from the slum-ridden High Street – indeed it claimed to have two, for the germ of what was to become first the Royal Technical College and later the University of Strathclyde called itself the Andersonian University. All these public institutions had to find their own funding. In an age of almost unrestricted free enterprise the state, and even the city corporation, would do little for them. Commercial life was fiercely competitive. Fortunes could be made, sometimes quickly, but they could be lost as easily.

The decayed and the distressed

The Annual Committee of the Merchants House considered twenty-eight applications for aid in September 1850, and made awards, totalling £322. 5s. 6d., to twenty-four of these. A sample, from the Minutes:

5 September 1850

'Misses Ernestine and Charlotte Stewart, daughters of the late Mr Allan Stewart, Merchant in Glasgow, state that in consequence of the death of their Mother who enjoyed a Pension of Twenty-five pounds per annum from the Merchants House, your Memorialists are rendered very dependent, and fondly hope, that seeing their late father was at one time one of the Directors of your Honourable House, and took a lively interest in its prosperity, your Honours would be disposed to continue your Memorialists on the List of Recipients from your excellent charity, for which they will ever feel grateful.

'Respectably recommended.'
A grant of £20 for five years was allowed.

'James McAslan, became a Member of the House in October 1833, That when admitted he was a Merchant trading on his own account. He continued the business untill declining years and a succession of losses compelled him to cease. That he is now reduced to a state of penury and distress, and is now destitute of resources. That Petitioner has maintained a respectable Character, and is not blame-worthy for his misfortunes. That in the month of July last year, Petitioner made application to your Lordship and the Members of the House, and he was humanely allowed the sum of Ten pounds, and a farther sum of Five pounds was granted, with the understanding that the sum of Ten pounds per annum should be ultimately awarded permanently.'
A grant of £11. 2s. 2d. was given from Luke's Mortification.

'Miss Mary Alston, residing in Glasgow, states that she is the daughter of the late Thomas Alston of Cloverbank, who was a Manufacturer in Glasgow, under the Firms of Alston, Jamieson & Company and Thomas Alston & Son.

'That her father died in 1814, leaving her a competency, but that from various causes, particularly rendering pecuniary assistance at various times to her brothers, who have not been successful in business, she has suffered a gradual decay in circumstances which has ended in her means now being exhausted, and the seizure and sale of her furniture for rent. That since this unhappy event the Petitioner's only means of support have been derived from subscriptions raised for her by some friends, and none of these who from their relationship might be liable legally to assist her are in circumstances to do so; that the only income available for her support (her eyesight marring her exertions) arises from Fifteen pounds awarded to her by Hutchesons' Hospital within the last few weeks, and which is evidently inadequate of itself to her suitable maintenance. That the late John Alston of Rosemount a Member of the House was Petitioner's half brother, and she hopes that your Honours will keep his public services in view, and grant such assistance as may be consistent with the Rules of the House.'

No award was given, perhaps because Hutchesons' Hospital had made one.

'Mrs. Susan Scheviz, widow of George Scheviz who states that her late husband was for many years a member of the House, and for some years a Director of it, and a member of the River Trust. In which situations he took great interest and discharged the duties thereof faithfully. He died on the third of March last year, and soon after his Estate was sequestrated.

'Under these circumstances she submits her case to your favourable consideration, in the hope of your granting her, such relief, as you may deem right.

'Petition numerously and respectably signed.'

£25 was granted.

'Miss Helen Douglas states, that her late father Hugh Douglas who lived in Carlton Place, was a member of the House. That he was a West India Merchant, and returned from Demerara with his Property mortgaged. That those in possession of it have hitherto supported the children, but find it impossible to continue to do so any longer. That one of the children is an invalid, and the Petitioner finds it impossible to educate and maintain them on the small allowance she has hitherto received, and

'Prays that your Honourable House will take the Case of the Family into your consideration, and grant them such support as you may deem fit.

'Petition signed by James Ewing, Strathleven, and James Anderson, Lord Provost.'

A grant was given of £20 for four years, from Speirs' Gift, the recently received mortification of the daughters of Alexander Speirs of Elderslie (see Chapter 4).

From the Minute Book

April 26 1865, Meeting of the Directors on Books, Revenues and Pensions

'The Dean stated that he had called this Meeting to consider certain interim applications which had been sent in for the charity of the House, vizt.:

'Mrs. Jane McEwen or Donald, who has frequently been relieved by precepts of

£10 each states that her husband has got a situation in Queensland and that she is anxious for a sum to aid her and her Family to join him there. The Meeting considered that it was not competent to apply the funds of the House to such a purpose.

'Patrick Thomson, Castlemane, Victoria, a Member of the House (No. 1379) applies for aid. This application certified and recommended by the Mayor of Castlemane. The Committee instructed the Clerk to write to the Mayor of Castlemane that as Mr. Thomson has left his wife hitherto a burden upon this House she having received aid from it for some years the House cannot entertain his application.'

For such a society a body like the Merchants House was as important as it had been in the days when it had a more formal part in the direction of the town's affairs. It helped to channel the impulse towards mutual help. This help could come only from private generosity and the active interest of men who had been successful in making money. In the pages of satirical magazines, such as Glasgow's *The Bailie*, founded in the early 1870s, businessmen like William McEwen with a finger in many charitable pies were slyly caricatured. But it was, in fact, such men who made life in the Victorian city more tolerable, who provided it with social organisations, from charitable societies for the unfortunate to colleges and churches. Many of those most active in this kind of work are found among the Deans of Guild and Directors of the Merchants House.

William McEwen, Dean of Guild in 1869 and 1870, and 1884 and 1885, had joined the Merchants House in 1848 and was a Director from 1863 (Fig. 6.2). He was the only man since James Ewing to be re-elected Dean of Guild for a second two-year term, and he served as a Director again after each of his deanships until his death, a thirty-year period of involvement during which he took a particular interest in the House's pensioners. He was also a director of the Savings Bank of Glasgow and served a term as president of the Chamber of Commerce. He had come to Glasgow as a youth and worked in the office of his uncle, John Henderson, before setting up his own drysalting company, R. and J. Henderson. He was the agent for Vivian and Sons, copper smelters, chairman of Young's Paraffin Light and Mineral Oil Company, and a director of the Tharsis Sulphur and Copper Company. His business enterprises were highly successful and he was an extremely wealthy man when in the 1860s he turned his attention increasingly to charitable work. He was chiefly known for his involvement with the Royal Infirmary, serving as manager, and for two decades as chairman of the House Committee, where he was a redoubtable advocate of reforms to nursing practice and a great friend and ally to the nursing side of the hospital, succeeding in establishing a medical school there. Never one to shrink from a battle, he also established, in the face of fierce opposition, the authority of the board of management over the medical staff in matters of management policy. When the City of Glasgow Bank failed in 1878, McEwen was one of the first to help set up a relief fund to assist those who had been most affected. After the disaster of the sinking of the steamer *Daphne* at its launch in 1883, when 146 men lost their lives, again McEwen was at the forefront of the relief efforts that raised over £30,000. He worked tirelessly for the Old Man's Friend Society and started up a similar charity for women, raising money for a new home for the aged and unfortunate (to which the House contributed £100 in 1891). Those who opposed him in any of his many public interests found him a stern and overbearing character, but in contrast the old folk of the Rottenrow home knew him as a friendly visitor willing to while away many an hour by the fireside in chat.

Fig. 6.2 William McEwen (Norman Macbeth, RSA)

The son of an Edinburgh minister, William McEwen (1813–93) came to Glasgow in 1827. He was apprenticed to his uncle, who had a drysalting business in St Vincent Lane, and later set up his own business. His uncle left him a large slice of his fortune as well as the business on his death, and McEwen became a very wealthy man. He became very prominent in city affairs, particularly in his work for the Royal Infirmary, for which he is commemorated by a bust near the hospital's entrance. 'No one would dream of attempting to get up any great public demonstration for charitable, or civic, or commercial purposes without seeking his alliance', in the words of a contemporary sketch-writer.[15]

The portrait was commissioned from Norman Macbeth, RSA, funded by subscription by '150 of the most prominent citizens of Glasgow' and presented to the Merchants House in 1886 'in commemoration of his many public services'.

Sir James Lumsden (1808–79) was another Merchant and Dean who was active in charitable concerns. He was Dean of Guild in 1861 and 1862, and served as a Director and member of many committees for several years. He was educated at the Grammar School (as it still was then) and Glasgow University and then went into his father's counting house in Queen Street, James Lumsden and Son, 'merchant of stationery for home and foreign and colonial use'. His father, also James, was provost in 1844–5, a Director of the Merchants House for many years, and prominent in many benevolent and charitable schemes, in recognition of which his statue was erected in Cathedral Square. After his father's retiral James Lumsden Jnr and his brother became proprietors of the flourishing wholesale business. For many years from 1849 onwards he was a director of the Glasgow and South Western Railway Company, becoming chairman in 1870, and he was also prominent in the Clydesdale Bank. Having first taken his seat in the council as Dean of Guild, he then went on to be a councillor and then provost in 1867–8 – unusually, bypassing the office of bailie. In 1866 Lumsden had been an opponent of the Merchants House's resolution to grant the university £1,000 towards their new building on Gilmorehill, on the grounds that it would be a misuse of funds that were intended for the relief of decayed merchants, their widows and children (he was defeated in the vote); two years later he found himself as provost officiating at the laying of the foundation stone of the new buildings at Gilmorehill by the Princess of Wales. He afterwards entertained the royal party at his house in Bath Street, and received a knighthood in honour of the occasion. He spent his years after 1876 occupied with the railway and the directorship of the Clydesdale Bank; his charitable interests, including the Royal Infirmary and Glasgow Benevolent Society; and his estate at Arden on Loch Lomondside.

Sir James King was Dean of Guild in 1875 and 1876, and again in 1894. Born in 1830, he was educated at the High School and Glasgow University. He became a senior partner in the family business, the Hurlet and Campsie Alum Company, which had taken over the firm of George Macintosh and Company and specialised in the manufacture of cudbear, a red-purple dye, of enormous importance in the dyeing and printing industries before the advent of aniline dyes. He was a member of the Merchants House from 1852 and a Director from 1860. From 1863 till 1892 he was a director of the Chamber of Commerce, serving as president in the late 1870s. He was a director of the Caledonian Railway Company for many years and became deputy chairman. He was director and chairman of the Clydesdale Bank for thirty years. He held several important university offices in the course of his career, and was Dean of Faculty at the time of his death in 1911. He was made Lord Provost in somewhat unusual circumstances: he had not previously been a member of the council, except in his capacity as Dean of Guild, but was 'headhunted' for the job by councillors despairing of finding a suitable and willing candidate within the council. With the Queen's Jubilee and the International Exhibition, not to mention a royal visit, coming up, it was important to secure an outstanding public figure. They assured him that if he stood for election as an interim councillor in the summer of 1886, he would be provost within six months. His provostship proved successful and so did the great events, with a knighthood being conferred at the time of the Jubilee and the Queen performing the ceremony during her visit to the Exhibition in 1888. At his funeral the flags flew at half mast on the Merchants House and all over Glasgow.

Sir James Watson was another of the outstanding Deans of the period. He was provost in 1871–4, knighted at the close of his time of office, and Dean of Guild in 1877 and 1878, these honours crowning a varied and important career. From his early days working for a mercantile firm, he rose to become an accountant in the Thistle Bank, later incorporated with the Union Bank of Scotland, and afterwards worked for a firm of grain merchants, John McCall and Co. When he began, around 1830, to buy and sell shares he became Glasgow's first stockbroker. At a time when there were only a few joint-stock companies in existence and the railway companies were in their infancy, very little of this kind of business had been done before, any such transactions being handled privately. The rapid growth of railway companies provided a popular outlet for spare capital, and at the same time there was a large increase in the number of joint-stock companies. By 1844 Glasgow had several accountants acting as stockbrokers, and a group of them founded the Glasgow Stock Exchange, of which Watson was chairman for its first twenty-one years. One of his commercial interests had been a precursor of rail connections with England, a fleet of steamers that ran between Ardrossan and Fleetwood in Lancashire, part of a system that could get passengers leaving London at 10 a.m. to Glasgow by 12 noon the next day. The rail connection to Carlisle would make this route redundant, and Watson was active in railway enterprise from the beginning, being secretary of the Glasgow and Ayrshire Railway from 1836 till 1839, and then secretary of the Glasgow and Edinburgh Railway. He played an active part in promoting the Bill to get the railway built, and he remained a director for many years. From a young man, Watson had taken an interest in the condition of Glasgow's less fortunate inhabitants. He was one of the founders of the Mechanics' Institute, the first of its kind in the country, and helped to establish two model lodging houses during the 1830s. The model lodging houses could no more than scratch the surface of what had become a festering sore, and Watson along with some like-minded men, notably the social reformer and future provost John Blackie, purchased and cleared away a large block of particularly notorious slum housing, later selling it to the corporation at cost price for redevelopment. Watson was a councillor and a bailie in the 1860s when the City Improvement Trust was formed to put slum clearance on an official footing. This controversial improvement scheme demolished slum housing – much of it giving way to railway development – and later began to build housing for working-class families. Watson was one of its great advocates, turning hostile public opinion in its favour by his skilful championing of the project.

A variety of gifts

The first business of the Merchants House itself was, as Sir James Lumsden had pointed out, to give a sense of security to its own members, but it continued in its steady support of Glasgow's charitable institutions by its influence and its members' work as well as by grants. The great flood of bequests and gifts which has multiplied its funds and expanded its work was only beginning in early Victorian times; but the very existence of the House drew gifts, sometimes of an unusual kind.

There was, for instance, the case of Colin Campbell of Colgrain, who had owned a plantation in British Guiana in the days of negro slavery and had accepted a bill drawn on him there for £400. More than thirty years later, in 1862, he had never been called on to meet this debt and the holder of the bill could not be found. 'Not wishing to retain Money which does not really belong to him', he offered £672, representing the bill with accrued bank interest, to the Merchants House on condition that he should be guaranteed against any further claims.[16] The gift was welcome but the Directors, with proper caution, decided to let the money lie and gather interest until 14 July 1865, after which no demand for payment could legally be made.

The greatest benefactions of that time, however, were those of James Ewing of Strathleven (Chapter 5) and James Buchanan. These were on a scale new to the House and brought new responsibilities for its Directors. James Ewing at his death in 1853 bequeathed £31,000 to the House, £10,000 of which was to provide pensions or allowances for 'decayed Glasgow Merchants', £10,000 for Merchants' widows and daughters in distress, and £10,000 to be spent chiefly 'in educating, training and settling in business the sons of decayed Glasgow Merchants'. The estate was not fully realised until 1906, but payments were made to the House over the years after his death, and the total finally received with accrued interest was £41,721. 19s.

The Directors recorded their sense of obligation in 1854:

> Under any circumstances, liberality so great must have commanded their deepest gratitude; but they feel it to be enhanced by the recollection of the position which Mr. Ewing so long and honourably occupied as a Member of the House; a Merchant of Glasgow from his youth till his death, he never ceased to take the deepest interest in the Institutions of the City, especially in that which the Directors represent, in which he was long an honoured Office-bearer. . . . By means of his liberality the Directors will be enabled to comfort the hearts and cheer the homes of many who, through the vicissitudes incident to Commercial Life, have themselves become the objects of that kindness which they or their friends in times of prosperity have shewn to others, and, at the same time, provide for many the means of education, on which their ultimate success in life so much depends.[17]

Four years later another Glasgow Merchant, James Buchanan, left £10,000 (subject to his widow's life-rent) 'for educational purposes on behalf of the sons of decayed members, . . . and granting bursaries to such of them as give evidence of future eminence' (Fig. 6.3). (Mrs Buchanan died in 1883 and the legacy was paid in the following year.) He also bequeathed a large sum for the founding of a school for destitute boys towards which the House subscribed £500, appointing four of its members as directors of the Buchanan Institution.

The Buchanan Institution

At his death in 1857 James Buchanan left most of his large fortune to Glasgow institutions: £10,000 to the Merchants House, £10,000 to the Trades House, £10,000 to the Royal Infirmary, and £30,000 to the city to found an industrial school for destitute children, on condition that the city would provide and maintain the buildings at public expense. For a trial period of ten years, £3,000 a year was to be spent on the maintenance and instruction of the boys; if the school was successful, the estate was to continue to fund it, with the residue going to the school after Mrs Buchanan's death.

The object of the Buchanan Institution was to maintain, educate and train destitute boys between the ages of six and fourteen, preference being given to those whose fathers were dead or absent. By the express wishes of Buchanan, the boys were to live at home, however overcrowded and unhealthy, and not in the school: the evils of institutional life would be avoided, and the boys were to be given 'no false notions of . . . comforts' but were to be 'brought face to face with the realities of their condition'. The Buchanan's boy in turn was to import into his home habits of cleanliness and other desirable qualities – he would be 'an active social teacher, and to some extent a reformer' in the home, and the foundation would be 'a grand social lever for the improvement of all the families connected with us'.[18] Those who had no home would board with suitable families. This family-centred emphasis was one of the distinguishing features of the Institution.

The children were given three substantial meals a day: porridge morning and evening, and soup or broth, with beef and potatoes or bread for dinner. There was no stinting on quantity. 'No working man's family in Glasgow is better fed' was the Institution's boast – and all on 3d. per pupil per day. It was a matter of pride that the average Buchanan schoolboy was heavier, healthier and stronger than his Glasgow counterpart fed at home. The healthiness of the regime was one of the Institution's claims to advanced principles: junior boys had an hour's free play each day, and games, gymnastics and drill were part of the daily routine. Over the years they acquired a brass band, a garden worked by the boys and a swimming pool.

A large mansion near Glasgow Green was purchased and converted, with funds subscribed by the town council, several public institutions including the Merchants House, and many leading citizens. In its workshops and classrooms, over 300 boys on average each year were instructed in the rudiments of navigation, tailoring, shoemaking and joinery. The Buchanan's boy could make and mend his own clothes, shoes and chairs. The object was not to produce craftsmen in these trades, but to produce 'a class of workmen who can help themselves, in the army, at sea, or in the colonies' – boys, who, like the founder, would seek their fortune abroad. The Merchants House provided four of the board's twelve directors. Several prominent members of the House were very active in the school, notably Sir James Lumsden.

After 1914 the Institution encountered financial difficulties, exacerbated, after 1918, by the rise in teachers' salaries and the withdrawal of government grants to voluntary and endowed schools. In 1922 the building was sold, and the school passed into the hands of the Education Authority. (It later became Greenview School and has recently been redeveloped as flats, still with its distinctive statue of the schoolboy on the façade.) Buchanan's scheme had been successful not for one decade but for six, and seven thousand boys had been educated, fed and sent out into the world.

Fig. 6.3   James Buchanan (sculptor: William Brodie)

James Buchanan (1785–1857), one of the House's greatest benefactors, was the son of a blacksmith and farrier in Stockwell. His mother had died when he was young and he spent most of his free time in his father's workshop, where he came to the attention of two West India merchants who were frequent customers, James Buchanan (no relation) and Moses Stiven, partners in the firm of Dennistoun, Buchanan and Co. They took the lively young lad into their office and, finding that he had an ambition to go to the West Indies, sent him to Grenada in 1800. The letter that introduced him to their manager there was prescient: 'By the *Loiusa*, a young man goes to you, James Buchanan, as an assistant. He has been about the warehouse for some time, and is clever; but it is a doubt whether he is to turn well or ill out. Mr. Stiven is of opinion that this namesake of mine will cut no ordinary figure in the world. He thinks he will either be the cleverest fellow, or the greatest blackguard in the West Indies . . . [W]e think him a wild, spoiled boy, and that he will require to be looked after. I request you do this, for he may do you honour, and he is the son of an honest, worthy man.'[19] When the manager there retired seven years later, James Buchanan was put in charge of the office. He became a managing partner and moved to Kingston, Jamaica and then Rio de Janeiro. He retired in 1816, still a young man but a very wealthy one, and after marrying went to live in Edinburgh for the rest of his life. He was buried in Glasgow, in the Necropolis, where his monument, a circular Greek temple, is among the most graceful.

Up till then the House's chief educational interest had been in administering the Auldhouse Mortification under which it paid apprenticeship fees for the sons of Glasgow burgesses (Chapter 4). There was a standing committee for the purpose of administering the fund. By the 1850s, however, it was finding that some employers of boys were no longer asking for such fees and that parents who applied for them were, by a legal fiction, able to spend the money themselves, perhaps not always for their sons' benefit. Perhaps this was behind the request that the Collector now began to make to employers that they recommend whether the fee should be paid to the boy direct or to his parents. Meanwhile demand for help with apprenticeships from the sons of Merchants had declined by the mid-nineteenth century, and the House obtained the agreement of the town council to waive the restriction to equal numbers of Trades and Merchant applicants.

Auldhouse apprentice correspondence

'Sir,
The Lord Dean of Guild intends paying, in a few days, the Auld-house Apprentice Fee to those Apprentices who were appointed by this House on ＿＿ December 18＿.

'As a step preparatory to this, it is necessary to know whether the Apprentices are diligent in learning their Trades, obedient to their Masters, and in all respects conducting themselves with propriety.

'It will be obliging, if before the 1st January, you will have the goodness to write me with this information as to ＿＿＿＿＿＿ now serving you as an Apprentice; and stating whether you give your sanction to the Fee being paid to him or his parents.

'I am, sir, Yours respectfully,
Wm. H. Hill'

'Glasgow, Dec. 30th. 1876
'From William Munro, Steam-power Letterpress Printer, 81 Virginia Street
To the Lord Dean of Guild of Merchants' House or W. H. Hill Esq.
Auld House Apprentice William Dunn is doing well with me, and I expect him to continue obedient and active. I would suggest that as his parents are dead the fee should be paid over to his sister Janet Dunn, who keeps house for him and his brothers.
Wm. Munro'

'140 Rose Street, Hutchesontown
31st March 1870
Mr Hill.
Sir,
I regret to inform you that I have not been successful in getting James a suitable place for to bind him – Mr. Thomson the Architect to whom he was to be engaged would not give him any wages during the first year and told him that he would require to attend several expensive Classes in the evening, and as I could not do that, he would not suit. He remained in Dr. Black's Consulting Rooms till a Month ago when he went to Mr. Brown Clothier West Nile Street to learn the business of a Cutter – but when only a fortnight there, Mr. Brown failed and his Shop was shut so James was thrown out of employment – I think it best to inform you as it is time that the Schedule was to have been given in.

    Yours Respy. Mrs. Munro
    P.S. I have been very ill since the Middle of Decr. and am still unable to go out.'

'Glasgow 17 Novr. 70
To the Honerable [sic] the Directors of the Merchants House
Gentlemen
Your Honerable Board were pleased to grant to my Son John McBride, the Auld House Apprentice Fee. His Indenture was duly completed and ready for Signature, when his Employer, owing to his having given up the Business, declined to Sign it. He has now got an Engagement for three years, with Thomas Fotheringham 80 Union Street Produce Broker and Commission Merchant. I hope this new arrangement will meet the requirements of your Board and not Prejudice his Claim to the Apprentice Fee, you have so kindly granted him.

    I am Gentlemen your Obedient Servant
    Agnes McBride
    8 Norfolk Court, Laurieston, Glasgow'

Moving House again

The Merchants did not enjoy their second home, in Hutcheson Street, for long. The Merchants' Hall there was evidently valued by others besides the House's members. Early Victorian Glasgow had too few public meeting places, and the handsome hall was a favourite scene for balls and other entertainment as well as for more stolid and serious functions such as company meetings.

The Merchants House in Hutcheson Street

From the Minute book:

15 January 1846

'Meeting of Committee on New Hall

'The Committee having considered an application from the Revd. Mr. Ingram's Congregation for the use of the Hall, to be used on Sabbath days and once a month in the evenings, for which they offer a Rent of £50 per annum, are of the opinion that the offer should be declined, as the Premises and furniture would be liable to be defaced and damaged by crowded evening meetings.'

28 July 1848

'Hall Committee

'The meeting agreed that the Hall should be let to Mr. Anderson, the Wizard of the North, for 2 weeks at £14 per week reserving the use of the Hall for day meetings if it should be required.'

George Simpson Ingram was a Congregational minister, pastor of Albion Street Congregational Church, which moved out of its North Albion Street Chapel around this time, and seems to have been homeless for a while. It was allowed to hold meetings in the Mechanics' Institute in 1847, before setting up in North Hanover Street later that year. Who the Wizard of the North was, history does not record.

Glasgow Herald 29 September 1848

'On Wednesday, M. Chopin, the great French pianist, gave a *matinée musicale* in the Merchants Hall, under the patronage of the most distinguished ladies and gentlemen of the nobility and gentry of the West of Scotland. At half-past two P.M., when the concert was to commence, a large concourse of carriages began to draw up in Hutcheson Street and the streets adjoining. The audience, which was not large, was exceedingly distinguished. Of M. Chopin's performances, and of the style of his compositions, it is not easy to speak so as to be intelligible to unscientific musicians. His style is unique, and his compositions are very frequently unintelligible from the strange and novel harmonies he introduces. . . . M. Chopin is evidently a man of weak constitution, and seems labouring under physical disability and ill health. . . .'
Frédéric Chopin was indeed ill, and died of tuberculosis the following year.

Minute Book

17 February 1863

'The Dean stated that this Meeting had been convened to take into consideration the propriety of illuminating the front of the Merchants House on the 10th proximo, the evening of the day of the Prince of Wales's marriage. This he considered as a proper mark of respect and loyalty on the part of this House, and a similar one, he understood, was contemplated by the Corporation and other Public Bodies in Glasgow. The Meeting unanimously concurred in the views expressed by the Dean; and it was moved, seconded, and unanimously agreed to, that a sum of £25 be placed at the disposal of the Dean for this purpose.'

By 1867 the Court House Commissioners, who were the House's neighbours, were looking for more accommodation. Three years later an arbitrator decided that they should pay £176,673 for the Hall. Meanwhile the Chamber of Commerce, then at 6 Virginia Street, had agreed that the House should use its Hall while the Directors looked for a site for a new one. The House hung its portraits of former Deans and benefactors on the Chamber's walls. Its other objects were packed away.

Fig. 6.4   Bas-relief of Archibald Ingram

Archibald Ingram (see Chapter 4) kneels to receive a civic crown from the Genius of Glasgow; behind him stand Commerce, Architecture and Civic Rule. The marble bas-relief was given to the city in 1809 by Robert Ingram of London, a grandson of Archibald Ingram. It was intended that it should be installed in the Merchants' Hall. For whatever reason, it was not set up at the time, and it was only fifty years later that a mention chanced to be found of it in the old Minutes. A search was organised for it, and it was found, still in its packing case, in a cellar of the new Merchants House, in Hutcheson Street. It was duly installed, only to be put away again in 1870, when the hall was sold. It found its final resting place seven years later, above the fireplace of the Directors' Room, when the present Merchants House was opened.

Thus began a neighbourly association that has lasted from 1870 to the present day when the Chamber is a long-established tenant in the Merchants House buildings. This third Glasgow 'House' has always had close links with the senior body of Merchants. Many prominent Glasgow men have been presidents of the Chamber either before or after their years as Lord Dean – there has been a general understanding that the two offices should not be held at the same time. On public questions affecting the business community House and Chamber often spoke and acted together.

Changes and challenges

By this time the House was involved in a legal dispute which seemed, for a time, to threaten the position of the Lord Dean on the city corporation, as it was now called, and perhaps even its own existence as a historic body. In 1868 revised regulations were adopted which stated plainly that:

> *all persons who have paid Ten Guineas to the funds of the House, and who have subscribed the Matriculation Book, and all persons who in time coming may be considered eligible by the Directors and who shall have paid the entry money of Ten Guineas, or such other sum as may have been fixed by a meeting of the Matriculated Members, and who shall have subscribed the Matriculation Book, shall,* ipso facto, *be deemed to be and become Members of the Merchants House of Glasgow . . .*[20]

This was a formal abandonment of the old rule that the House should consist only of Merchant burgesses of the city. Burgess-ship had, in fact, lost its old meaning since neither voters nor town councillors themselves were required to possess it, and in fact the Merchants House had for many years been admitting members who were not burgesses. The new regulations were duly submitted to the corporation in accordance with the Letter of Guildry, and were approved by it the next year.

Meanwhile the House had been explaining and defending to a Scottish Law Courts Commission the value of the Dean of Guild Court. In the course of their dealings with the subject the Directors had come to the conclusion that the appointment of Clerk and Assessor to the Court needed to be reconsidered. The Clerk and Assessor was the Court's legal adviser. Under the Letter of Guildry 'the Dean of Guild and his Council' were to elect a clerk annually. In fact from the first year of the Court's existence the man chosen had been one of the town clerks of the city council. But there was now only one principal town clerk of Glasgow, and, in a city of more than 450,000 he was an exceedingly busy official. Moreover, Glasgow Corporation owned a great deal of house property and was concerned in schemes of slum clearance and rebuilding which had to be considered by the Dean of Guild Court. It seemed wrong that the Court's chief official should advise it on plans for which his principal employers were largely responsible.

In 1872 the town clerk, Angus Turner, resigned. This seemed a good moment to make a change in the Dean of Guild Court. But here the history of two and a half centuries raised some very natural confusion in the minds of both Merchants House Directors and town councillors.

The Dean of Guild had come to have two Councils, each with a clerk of its own. The 'Council' of which the Letter of Guildry made most was the Dean of Guild Court itself, with its eight lyners, four from the Merchants House and four from the Trades House. But the Lord Dean also had his Council of the Merchant rank, for a long time better known as the Merchants House Directors; and this Council too had its clerk. He was William Henry Hill, who was also the House's Collector, the fourth of a family which had held the collectorship from 1767 to 1837 (see Chapter 4). Before his own appointment in 1866 W. H. Hill had compiled the House's history, *View of the Merchants House of Glasgow.* He was an able lawyer and, no doubt, had a clearer view of the background of the problem which the House and the Dean of Guild Court were facing than any of the others who had to deal with it.

To begin with the Directors seem to have thought that the appointment of the Dean of Guild Court clerk would be 'put upon the same footing as that of all the officers elected by the Merchants House'. But that was a miscalculation. They were not the Lord Dean's 'Council' for this purpose. The city corporation, on the other hand, assumed that the Court clerkship would belong of right to the town clerk they chose and that his fees for work in the Court could be merged in a Corporation Fee Fund.

At this point the very active Lord Dean, Patrick Playfair, publicly protested, no doubt with the advice and support of his Collector. He announced that he and his Court proposed to elect a clerk of their own choosing. For a time it seemed as if there might be a friendly compromise between the House and Court on one side and the corporation on the other. While both sides were obtaining further legal advice the corporation appointed an interim town clerk, Andrew Cunninghame, and the House and Court decided that 'to avoid unseemly conflict' the Lord Dean and his Council should choose Mr Cunninghame as Dean of Guild Court clerk till the end of the House's financial year in October. The Lord Provost, Sir James Watson, was an active member of the House and a future Dean of Guild. Evidently he was ready to see the corporation's claim quietly forgotten.

Patrick Playfair

Patrick Playfair was a Director of the Merchants House from 1862 till 1865. After his term as Lord Dean of Guild in 1873 and 1874, he served as a Director again, and then returned to the deanship in the crisis of 1878–9 (see Chapter 7). Thus it was his lot to serve as Lord Dean during the House's two most serious crises of the 1870s, and at his death the House recorded its appreciation of his 'upright and honourable bearing [and] sagacious counsel'.

Playfair was an East India merchant, operating out of his headquarters in St Vincent Street, who set up a large firm in Calcutta. Around the time of his first deanship he retired from the business and 'devoted himself to works of public and private usefulness' from his Glasgow home in Woodside Terrace and his Ayrshire estate. A quiet man, he was considered not to be an effective public speaker, but acknowledged to have made a useful contribution to the affairs of the city. He was known as a merchant to be 'strictly honourable and scrupulously exact in his dealings', and he was a liberal donor to causes of various kinds, especially religious ones – he was a member of the Free College Church. At the time of his death in 1879 he was a Merchants House Director, sub-dean, a lyner of the Dean of Guild Court, and the House's representative on the board of Allan Glen's Institution.

But the man soon chosen as permanent town clerk of Glasgow was by no means of this mind. J. D. Marwick was a strong-willed lawyer with firm ideas about the dignity of his office. (As Sir James Marwick he later became one of Glasgow's foremost historians.) On his appointment as clerk to Glasgow's town council, *The Bailie* advised: 'If Mr. Marwick has the *savoir faire* to conceal from the honest men that he is slightly above their level, and to "soft sawder" them a little . . . , he will be a valuable official. Let him drive them only with the feather end of his pen, and he may guide them in the way that they should go without eliciting a murmur of discontent . . .'.[21] But this was not Mr Marwick's style. Moreover, in his home city of Edinburgh the Guildry, more or less equivalent to the Glasgow Merchants House, had long ceased to be effectively active and had had to give up its claim to appoint members of the Dean of Guild Court, apart from the Dean himself. He evidently regarded the Merchants House as an anachronism which could become a nuisance. He insisted on his right to be Clerk of the Dean of Guild Court. When the Court, with the support of the House, elected a clerk of its own, James Roberton, professor of conveyancing at Glasgow University, he refused to hand over the official records and papers. The Court's work was paralysed.

Again the useful Andrew Cunninghame had to be brought back to keep it going. Professor Roberton resigned. Cunninghame carried on his work for the Court, in the eyes of the House as temporary Clerk and Assessor duly elected by the Court, and in those of the corporation as the town clerk's deputy – while the two sides prepared to bring the whole problem before the Court of Session. James Marwick, meanwhile, dragged his feet on the matter for two years. Under his guidance the corporation disputed the proper form of procedure. Meanwhile two explosive charges were placed under the feet of the Dean of Guild.

Though its own lyners had supported the Lord Dean throughout the dispute, the Trades House was induced to state that the town clerk was the best possible Assessor for the Guild Court and to hint that the Merchants House was exceeding its powers by intervening on this question. This stance seemed to isolate the House from its natural ally. Dean of Guild Playfair, however, made a firm but diplomatic and friendly reply.

The second explosive may have seemed still more dangerous. Ignoring the corporation's approval in 1869 of the Merchants House's new regulations, Marwick argued that, having ceased to consist only of burgesses, the House was no longer legally constituted. A Dean elected by it was not qualified to sit in the Guild Court or in the corporation itself. Conceivably, even the House's right to its older funds and resources might be challenged.

This was a dangerous argument, however illogical it may seem, for there were town councillors who disliked the presence in the corporation, *ex officio*, of the Lord Dean and the Deacon Convener of the Trades. Perhaps it was lucky that the Dean who followed Patrick Playfair was a man capable of notably persuasive leadership, James King of Campsie. As we have seen, Dean of Guild King made such an impression on the town council that he was later asked by the councillors to allow himself to be elected unopposed as an ordinary member in order that he might be chosen Lord Provost. As the city's chief magistrate he was immensely successful, organising Glasgow's first great International Exhibition in 1888. This was the best possible proof of the practical value to Glasgow of its *ex officio* councillor. Yet, on the basis of James Marwick's argument about burgess-ship every Dean of Guild who took his seat in the corporation till 1885 – including Patrick Playfair, James King himself and ex-Lord Provost Sir James Watson – had to meet a formal objection to his presence, though this was never pressed to the point of excluding him.

Meanwhile the case of the Dean of Guild Court clerkship finally reached the Court of Session in 1876, when the Judge Ordinary decided that the Court had always had the right to choose its own Clerk and Assessor. This was total victory for the House and Court in a sometimes rather anxious comedy that brought to life much of Glasgow's civic past.

The comedy was not quite over, however. Gracefully, Dean of Guild King proposed that Town Clerk Marwick should now allow himself to be elected Clerk of the Court. Mr Marwick replied that he really had no time for the work and could accept the invitation only if the indispensable Mr Cunninghame could continue to act as his deputy.

After a decent interval Marwick withdrew altogether. At last the Court was able to choose a clerk completely independent of the corporation, the Glasgow University professor of Scots law, Robert Berry. Its organisation was strengthened. With the support of the Merchants House it was safeguarded against the effects of an Act of Parliament which might have made it subject to corporation control. The House had obtained for the Court everything that it wanted in 1869.

Building a magnificent home

While the controversy was still seething the Directors were concerned with something more immediately important to the Merchants House itself, the building of a new Hall. In 1873 they found a site that suited them, on the west side of George Square.

The Bank of Scotland was preparing to build at the west end of the Square. It was agreed that the bank's new office and the Merchants' building, though ultimately the work of different architects, should conform to a general pattern. The architect chosen by the House was John Burnet, one of the most notable in mid-Victorian Glasgow. After four years a handsome block looked across the Square to the future site of the City Chambers, the Merchants House occupying the northern corner with West George Street (Figs. 6.5, 6.6). The tower at the corner sacrificed the symmetry of the west side of George Square – but it was a reminder of the earlier tower in the Bridgegate, and, like it, it elevated the ship on its dome to a commanding position on the skyline.

Within this building John Burnet provided a lofty Hall with an open pitch-pine roof (Fig. 6.7). It was designed to display the House's portraits and the 'broads' commemorating benefactors and their legacies. With its range of high windows it too may have been consciously reminiscent of the old Hall in the Bridgegate. The building also contained committee rooms and offices both for the House itself and for the Chamber of Commerce, with other accommodation to be let to business firms: its cost – such was the value of money in the 1870s – was only a little over £32,000. The ancient reliefs, which were the House's most historic possessions, were set up at the entrance to the Hall itself and the Ingram panel above the Directors' Room fireplace.

Fig. 6.5   The new Merchants House building in George Square

Fig. 6.6   The Merchants House building from West George Street
The original entrance was at the north-east corner of the building, and was later altered to become a window of the Committee Room.

Fig. 6.7 John Burnet's Merchants' Hall of 1877
When a later architect, J. J. Burnet, added extra storeys to the building in the redesign of 1907–9, some of the height of the Hall was lost. The ceiling and plasterwork were radically altered, as were the windows, panelling and seating.

By October 1877 some of the offices were already in use, and on 21 November 1877 the Hall was officially opened at a dinner of members, who had most of the city's leading personalities as their guests. Here was a visible sign that, thirty years after its old legal privileges had disappeared, the Merchants House held its place firmly in the life of the city.

Notes

1. J. Kellett, *Railways and Victorian Cities* (London, 1979), p. 212.
2. Merchants House Minutes, 13 Apr. 1836.
3. Ibid., 7 Jan. 1842.
4. Ibid., 31 Jan. 1845.
5. Ibid., 13 June 1845.
6. Kellett, *Railways*, pp. 220–6.
7. MH Minutes, 10 Mar. 1836.
8. John Riddell, *The Clyde: the Making of a River* (Edinburgh, 2000; first published as *Clyde Navigation*, Edinburgh, 1979), pp. 113–15.
9. MH Minutes, 24 May 1858.
10. Ibid., 11 Oct. 1849.
11. James A. Mackay, *The Postal History of Glasgow* (1984), p. 26.
12. MH Minutes, 17 Apr. 1855.
13. Ibid., 7 Oct. 1873.
14. Ibid., 8 Aug. 1849.
15. *Clydeside Cameos: a Series of Sketches of Prominent Clydeside Men*, No. 11, republished from *Fairplay* (London, 1885), pp. 84–91, at p. 90.
16. MH Minutes, 16 July 1862.
17. Ibid., 25 Jan. 1854.
18. William Leggatt, *Account of the Buchanan Institution in Glasgow* (London, 1860).
19. *Glasgow Herald*, 10 Mar. 1858.
20. MH Minutes, 10 Mar. 1868.
21. *The Bailie*, No. 30 (14 May 1873).

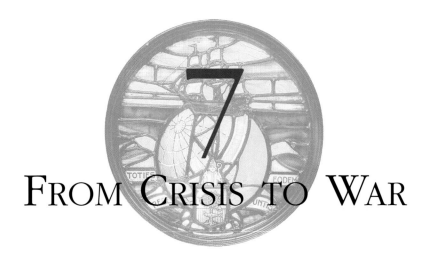

FROM CRISIS TO WAR

The City of Glasgow Bank crash

Less than a year after the opening of the new premises on George Square, when the Directors of the House met there on 1 October 1878 to make their decision on the nomination of a new Dean of Guild, Glasgow was on the edge of the worst financial crisis in its history. The House itself was in a state of minor crisis. The retiring Lord Dean, Sir James Watson, announced that John Muir, who had accepted nomination for the deanship, had withdrawn at the last moment on grounds of ill-health. Another candidate had been found, James Stevenson, a manufacturing chemist, who had been a generous contributor to the mission at Lake Malawi, founded after David Livingstone's death to carry on the missionary-explorer's work in Africa, and had taken a leading role in financing the African Lakes Company. Stevenson was duly elected a week later.

Meanwhile on the same day another meeting was taking place addressing a problem of a quite different order. The result was a telegraph issued late that evening by the manager of the City of Glasgow Bank to all its branches: 'Bank has stopped payment close your door at once and pay nothing whatever other banks will pay the notes.' The *Glasgow Herald* on 2 October broke the dire news: 'The City of Glasgow Bank has stopped payment.'

Established in 1839, the City of Glasgow Bank was the newest of the large Scottish banking companies and, to all appearances, one of the most enterprising. (Despite its name, it had no connection with the Glasgow municipality.) Its head office was in Virginia Street and its 133 branches were spread throughout Scotland and the Isle of Man, but most of its 1,819 shareholders were in Glasgow and the West of Scotland. By the time the bank's affairs had been wound up, all but 254 of them were bankrupt.

There had, of course, been Scottish bank failures before this one, though they were few compared with those in eighteenth- and nineteenth-century England, the United States and other countries. During the financial crisis of 1857 another big Glasgow company, the Western Bank of Scotland, had collapsed, and the City Bank itself had closed down temporarily. But what distinguished the disaster of 1878 was the size of the losses, amounting to £6 million, and the discovery that failure was the result of fraud by directors (two of whom had been recent Merchants House Directors). The charges amounted not so much to villainy, but rather to what has been called 'one of the most astonishing examples of bad banking management on record'.[1] The seven directors were tried, convicted and imprisoned for falsifying the accounts.

The sense of shock was immediate: the *Glasgow Herald* reported on 3 October that 'one could hardly walk a dozen yards in Buchanan Street yesterday afternoon without meeting a friend who found himself in some . . . form of tribulation.' Over the next few days the full extent of the catastrophe sank in. Like all such Scottish institutions of the time except the three oldest, which operated under royal charter or Act of Parliament, the City of Glasgow Bank was an unlimited company. Each of its shareholders was individually responsible for its debts to the full extent of his or her own possessions. To Victorian businessmen the very idea of limited liability had been deeply suspect. The Merchants House had repeatedly protested against proposals in Parliament which would have made it available for banks and other companies. But now, as the unexpected size of the City of Glasgow Bank's losses became known, uncertainty, depression and bankruptcies spread throughout the West of Scotland. A distressingly high proportion of the bank's shareholders turned out to be retired clergymen (many of them Free Church), widows and spinsters, who relied on the dividends – it was still paying out 12 per cent earlier that year — for their modest incomes. Many of the more financially astute shareholders had decamped some time before, probably around the time that the more substantial and reputable businessmen had left the board of directors. For the remaining shareholders, however, the situation was grim, and when the resources of those at the lower end of the property scale were exhausted, successive calls on those who still had some means of payment spread ruin to new circles. Throughout the following year, 1879, there was a bankruptcy in Glasgow almost every day, and among those reduced to poverty were several members of the Merchants House. The failure concided with, and was compounded by, the worst nationwide economic downturn of the nineteenth or twentieth centuries.

Perhaps it is not surprising that, less than a month after his election, Dean of Guild Stevenson should have found himself forced to resign because of a breakdown in health. Precedent suggested that in a case of this kind the most junior ex-Dean available should be brought back to the chair. This had happened in 1868, when Dean of Guild John Ramsay had resigned on being elected an MP. But then the interim Lord Dean who succeeded him had only four peaceful summer months to serve. James Stevenson's successor would have the best part of a stormy year. Sir James Watson may not have been sorry to discover that a paragraph of the Letter of Guildry declaring that no Dean should bear office for more than two years together seemed to exclude him, since he had retired only a few weeks earlier. In such a crisis the business of a leading Glasgow stockbroker must have needed all his attention. The previous Lord Dean, James King, was president of the Chamber of Commerce, and there was a tradition that the two offices should not be held at one time. It was left to Patrick Playfair, who had borne the brunt of the struggle over the Dean of Guild Court clerkship five years before, to undertake the duty during this anxious time (see Chapter 6). He died a year later, not long after the end of this his second deanship, in November 1879, aged sixty-five, his long-term heart condition no doubt exacerbated by the strain.

The Merchants House was at the centre of the effort to relieve the hardship of those worst affected by the bank crash. Accommodation was given free of charge in the Merchants House building for the setting up of a City of Glasgow Bank Relief Fund. William McEwen, the notable ex-Dean and philanthropist (see Chapter 6), and James White, a Director for twenty-five years from the late 1850s, were among the chief promoters of this charitable effort, which distributed £400,000 among those who suffered most from the failure. Most of the House's Directors served on its committees. But years passed before Glasgow recovered completely from commercial loss and unemployment. It is significant that in successive annual reports till 1886 the Directors pointed out that some offices in the Merchants House building were still unlet. The Directors had been considering a proposal to double the entry fee for new members from 10 to 20 guineas, but under the new circumstances this was dropped. It was finally adopted only in 1924.

James White of Overtoun

When James White died in 1884, William McEwen, ex-Lord Dean of Guild and White's colleague on the boards of the Merchants House and other Glasgow charitable bodies, proposed a statue to him in Cathedral Square. The statue was unveiled in 1891 and given over to the care of the Merchants House. A tribute to him at the time by the House's Directors mentioned the 'many instances of his munificent liberality', and he left a legacy of £1,000 to the Merchants House itself.

James White was born in 1812, the son of John White of Shawfield, who with his brother founded the chemical business J. and J. White. James trained in the law and became a partner in a legal practice, but he later joined the family firm and managed the commercial side. He cut down the number of chemicals it produced, eventually concentrating on bichromate of potash, used in the dyestuffs industry and recently introduced to the leather industry, and the firm became its biggest manufacturer anywhere in the world. Other business interests included the Glasgow and South Western Railway, of which he was deputy chairman, and the Royal Exchange, of which he was chairman.

James White's name became associated with relief funds and with helping those in trouble generally. He was one of the originators of the City of Glasgow Bank relief fund, and chaired the *Daphne* relief fund and others. He gave much time and energy to the Deaf and Dumb Institute and was a manager of the Western Infirmary.

He was a generous donor to various city and Free Church projects. Forceful and energetic, his business tactics were described by a contemporary as 'invariably bold and sweeping in their character. Where a less courageous man would shrink from a transaction of thrilling magnitude, he plunges directly into it, and his unfailing success justifies the audacity of his policy.'[2]

The crash had also changed many people's minds about limited liability. When a Bill came before Parliament in 1879 to amend the law relating to liability of members of banking and other joint-stock companies, the Directors gave their general approval, objecting only to the clause by which banks in Scotland would either have to give up their right of issuing notes or close their branches in England: this they felt would 'seriously disturb trade . . . and in Scotland be felt as an almost national calamity'.[3] The petition was presented on the House's behalf, as were so many in the late nineteenth century, by ex-Dean Archibald Orr Ewing, MP, and, the objectionable clause having been withdrawn, the Bill passed into law as the Companies' Act 1879.

Sir Archibald Orr Ewing

Archibald Orr Ewing (created a baronet in 1886) was at one time 'the largest Turkey-red dyer in the world', according to a contemporary. He had begun work in the firm of his brother John Orr Ewing, manufacturer of Turkey-red handkerchiefs, and in 1845 set up his own firm of Archibald Orr Ewing and Co. He soon bought the Levenbank works, five years later acquired the Milton works, and then added another Vale of Leven works, so that by 1866 the Orr Ewing brothers owned all the Vale of Leven calico printing works except those of William Stirling and Sons.

Orr Ewing was a member of the Merchants House from 1852, and a Director from 1857. He was well known as a businessman of uncommon energies and abilities when he was elected Lord Dean of Guild in October 1864, serving the customary two years. His successor as Lord Dean, John Ramsay of Kildalton, entered Parliament in 1868, and Archibald Orr Ewing was recalled to the deanship for the remainder of that year. Among his many services to the House was his undertaking the cost of the printing of the handsome and weighty quarto volume, *View of the Merchants House*, largely the work of W. H. Hill, 'presented to the House by Archibald Orr Ewing, Esquire, of Ballikinrain'.

The House sent two of its Lord Deans to Parliament in 1868, for immediately after completing John Ramsay's deanship, Orr Ewing himself stood as the member for Dunbartonshire and was elected, later defending his seat successfully, and remaining a Conservative MP until his death in 1893. He represented the House before Parliament on many matters. He purchased the estate of Ballikinrain in Stirlingshire in 1862, effecting the transition from Glasgow trader to country gentleman: 'he thinks like a country gentleman, he acts like a country gentleman, and . . . he talks like a country gentleman'. *The Bailie* summed him up: 'laird at Ballikinrain, farmer on the skirts of Ben Lomond, turkey-red dyer in the Vale of Leven, merchant in Glasgow, and . . . one of her most influential and most highly prized citizens'.[4]

It is not surprising that there were few large new gifts to the House during the 1880s. The great wave of large benefactions did not begin until the following decade and after, but many of them came from men and women who must have remembered the days when need was greatest. It is perhaps reasonable to suppose that, in the end, the experience of 1878 helped to strengthen the House for its work in the twentieth century and beyond.

Reforming the pensions

The House did receive one substantial bequest at the time of the bank crash, however. Shortly before the crash it had been told of the splendid bequest of a member, Samuel King, which was to add more than £18,000 to its general funds. Anticipating more applications for charitable aid, the Directors reviewed all the existing pensions. Some pensioners decided that they could do without the House's help and resigned their pensions; most payments were increased. Early in 1879, in an effort to make better use of the mortifications and endowments under the House's control, the Directors applied for and obtained, under the Endowed Institutions (Scotland) Act 1878, permission to increase from the House's own funds most of the minor mortifications and thereafter apply them to pensions, retaining the names but not the conditions of the mortifications. All the pensions now paid at least £5, and most £10, per annum.

Two major bequests of the late nineteenth century

Samuel King was enrolled as a member of the Merchants House in 1870, described as a merchant. He carried on his business from his office in Queen Street. His father was Andrew King, Merchants House member and Glasgow manufacturer; both parents died while Samuel was a young boy, and his brother and sisters died in infancy. At the time of his own death, aged about fifty, in 1878, he was unmarried, living with female relatives in Newton Place. In his will he left the life-rent of this property to his aunt and cousins, and they were willing to have the house sold in return for an annuity from the Merchants House equal to the value of the life-rent. Samuel King also made a bequest to the town of Alston in Cumbria, where his mother had been born, and the residue of his estate was left to the Merchants House, amounting in the end to £18,000.

In the late nineteenth century, as the House reorganised its mortification funds to allow it to direct its charity towards educational objects and needy individuals not covered by the original terms of the bequests, a major bequest was received which allowed it to give regular help to others besides members, their wives and daughters. This was the Morgan mortification, amounting to over £70,000, left by John Morgan of Springfield House, Bishopbriggs. John Morgan was born in 1809, the younger son of the minister of Gretna. He was a merchant in Cartagena, South America, and Trinidad, returning home in 1842 to live with his brother, William Morgan, of Morgan, McEwen and Co., East India Merchants, at Springfield House. John Morgan inherited his brother's fortune, and on his death in 1894 left the greater part of his property to the Merchants House. Two-thirds of the revenue of his estate was to be applied to the Morgan Fund, to further the charitable objects and purposes of the House, and the remaining third to be devoted to the Morgan Bursaries, to be granted by the Presbytery of Glasgow. A memorial board was set up in the Merchants' Hall.

Much of the impetus and organisation of the House's pensions reform of 1879 was owed to William McEwen, who was re-elected Dean of Guild for a second two-year term in 1883, partly so that he could carry through further work on the pension roll.

The reorganisation he carried out raised the level of many of the pensions from £10 to £50. There were now 217 pensioners receiving a total of £5,700 each year, compared with 174 receiving £3,188 thirteen years previously, at the time of the last augmentation. 'In awarding pensions', it was stated five years later, 'the Directors have to exercise much discrimination, and in this delicate and responsible duty they endeavour to afford liberal recognition to Members whose circumstances with age and infirmity call for aid, and their widows and young children to whom the Directors deem the revenues of the House for benevolent purposes are exclusively destined.'[5] The Directors had to remind members that these pensions were not hereditary, and that they were not intended for those who 'having health and ability' should be able to support themselves. There was another augmentation of many pensions in 1902.

The Lord Dean of Guild and Glasgow City Council

The dispute in the early 1870s between Town Clerk Marwick and the Merchants House about the clerkship of the Dean of Guild Court had escalated into a claim by Marwick that the Merchants House was not properly constituted and that the Lord Dean had no right to a seat on the town council (Chapter 6). One lasting effect of this episode was that, from 1874, each Lord Dean upon taking his seat in the council at the start of each new session, had to endure a formal protest about his presence and a statement that the council reserved the right to question the validity of his election by the Merchants House. Perhaps one of the reasons that the formidable William McEwen was recalled to a second deanship in 1883 was to get this matter dealt with once and for all. McEwen made his position clear, stating that 'while willing . . . to take his share of municipal work, he did not consider it consistent either with the dignity of his office or with the rights of the Merchants House, to do so under such a protest'.[6] There ensued an acrimonious exchange of letters with Mr Marwick, and a compromise was reached: the Lord Dean would take his seat at the council table on a protest one last time, in February 1884, and he would make a formal counter-protest as to its inefficacy. Thereafter, honour having been satisfied, no further protests would be made.

It was not the last time that the Merchants House had to defend the right of the Lord Dean to sit on the council. In 1900 an attempt was made by means of the Town Councils (Scotland) Bill to remove Deans of Guild and Deacons from all town councils. The Merchants House, together with the Trades House and representatives from other cities, succeeded in getting this clause removed. Further attacks on the *ex officio* positions on town councils were made in the twentieth century, until voting powers were abolished in 1975 (Chapter 8).

Educational endowments – reformed for the twentieth century

The Endowed Institutions legislation also made possible more direct involvement of the House in educational provision, a subject very much of the moment in the 1870s.

A Provisional Order attached to this Act opened the way for an annual sum of money from James Ewing's legacy 'for Educating, Training and Settling in Business the sons of decayed Glasgow Merchants' to be devoted to four entrance bursaries of £20 each to the Faculty of Arts (which at that time included engineering and mechanics) at Glasgow University; at the same time four more bursaries, of £25 each, named 'The Merchants House Bursaries' were set up, two in medicine, one in arts and one in law. In 1910 the House received applications by six female students for two of its university bursaries, and agreed to present them for the bursary examination, 'in this respect departing from the previous uniform practice of awarding these Bursaries solely to *boys*'.

The Provisional Order of 1880 also enabled the House to apply the funds of the Auldhouse and Wardrop bequests to various scholarships and bursaries for Allan Glen's Institution and the former Mechanics' Institution, which had become the Glasgow College of Science and Arts (see below). This assistance for technical and scientific education for Glasgow boys proved very fruitful, and in a report twenty-six years later the headmaster of Allan Glen's stated that all who had received Auldhouse Scholarships had done well. The House continued to award these bursaries to Allan Glen's boys until the advent of comprehensive education in the 1970s.

In 1909 the House obtained a special Act of Parliament for its own purposes, the Buchanan and Ewing Bequests Act, which enabled it to increase and extend the scope of its educational work. The advent of free secondary education meant that there was now little demand for help with this, and only one applicant had been found in 1908 for funding through the Buchanan and Ewing bequests. The House commissioned Sir Henry Craik, MP, former secretary of the Scottish Education Department, to investigate possible alternative uses. His report recommended that the House should use these funds to support the institutions of higher education in Glasgow, by providing equipment and financing lectureships in new subjects. After the Bill that was drawn up from these proposals had received royal assent, grants of at least £50 (and in practice usually more) were given, for five years in the first instance, to various higher education institutions in Glasgow. The first beneficiaries were Glasgow and West of Scotland Technical College, Allan Glen's Institution, St Mungo's College Medical School (attached to Glasgow Royal Infirmary), Glasgow School of Art and the University of Glasgow (for a Chair of Scottish History and for establishing a scholarship), and the grants totalled £800 for that year.

A commitment to education

Educational provision grew to be one of the House's foremost interests in the nineteenth century, not only in devoting funds which they controlled to bursaries, scholarships and other educational purposes, but also in providing directors for the boards of various educational charities. A list of committees for which the Merchants House had to provide representatives by the turn of the century shows how many of them were educational in nature (see pp. 145–7 below). The Merchants House was also among the bodies that were asked to help in making appointments to the newly created Adam Smith Chair of Political Economy at the university, endowed with £15,000 in 1895 by a Merchants House member, Andrew Stewart. The House did its best to promote the interests of the Royal Infirmary's medical school (St Mungo's College), supporting the case for having it made a college of the university – though this did not happen until 1948.

This educational involvement can only have been enhanced by the presence of a man with a professional interest in education, Dr Walter Graham Blackie, Dean of Guild in 1886 and 1887, the latter the year of Queen Victoria's Jubilee. He was the younger son of John Blackie, of the famous Glasgow publishing business. Walter Blackie was a geographer, who specialised in maps, atlases and gazetteers and made the company into one of Britain's leading educational publishers. (Blackie's printing works at Bishopbriggs were sold to Collins in the 1960s.) He was a Director of the Merchants House from 1867 till 1879, and after his deanship served again till 1892. After the House had succeeded in winning the right to representation on the educational governing board of Hutchesons' Hospital (as distinct from the charitable incorporation of the same name), Dr Blackie was the first appointee and served on the board for many years. He also represented the House on the boards of both the Glasgow General and the Glasgow City Education Endowments.

Addresses loyal and royal

In March 1882 the House expressed its 'abhorrence of the wicked outrage, in the attempt by Hector MacLean, on Her Majesty's life at Windsor . . . and their thankfulness for its providential failure'. Five years later, at the Queen's Jubilee, the House acknowledged with satisfaction 'the judicious and progressive principles which have characterised and the benign influence and effects which have ensued from the legislation of your auspicious reign'. The address continued:

'Science and the Arts have made vast and unparalleled strides and discoveries as wonderful as useful have ensued, the result of which has been to augment the wealth of the nation and to carry comfort to the homes of the people. Religion and learning have been fostered. An acquaintance with and appreciation of the wants of the poor, largely promoted by the kindly interest of Your Majesty and Your lamented Consort, H.R.H. the late Prince Albert, have also during Your Majesty's reign been notably displayed alike by legislation for ameliorating the condition of the labouring classes and in improving the education of the people.

'No less notably has Your Majesty's reign been distinguished by wise and well conceived measures for removing restrictions and impositions which in former times fettered the free development of trade and navigation, of industry and manufactures. And while at the present time the commercial outlook for the Country is neither so prosperous nor the social relations in all parts of the United Kingdom so satisfactory as your loyal subjects would fervently desire we nevertheless hope and pray that by the operation of economic laws the commercial depression which presently prevails may pass away, and by judicious legislation wisely administered all reasonable grounds of complaint may be removed and prosperity and contentment again pervade your realms.'

The list of educational concerns was augmented in the twentieth century, with the extension, in 1910, of representation on the Muirhead Trust, to include a Merchants House nominee. The Muirhead Trust was founded to fund two chairs of medicine at Glasgow University, as well as grants for women's education at the Royal Technical College, and postgraduate scholarships for women at the Royal Samaritan Hospital and the Sick Children's Hospital.

Committees with Merchants House representation at the end of the nineteenth century

- Clyde Navigation Trust
- Clyde Lighthouses Trust

For the Clyde Navigation Trust, see Chapter 5. The Merchants House had been involved in campaigning for a Lighthouse Trust from the mid-eighteenth century (Chapter 5). The Act of 1871, initiated by Sir James Lumsden while he was Lord Provost, restored and confirmed the Trust in its authority and gave the Merchants House the right to appoint one of the trustees. Its responsibilities were now defined as the lighting, buoying and dredging of the Clyde from Port Glasgow down to Little Cumbrae, and as far east and west as the Ayrshire coast and Kintyre.

- Royal Infirmary
- Royal Lunatic Asylum
- Asylum for the Blind
- Lock Hospital
- Lying-in Hospital and Dispensary
- Western Infirmary
- Victoria Infirmary
- Convalescent Home

For the first five of these, see Chapter 5. The Western Infirmary was founded in 1874, and the first chairman was Robert Dalglish, MP, of Kilmardinny (see Chapter 5). The Merchants House gave £500 to the building fund and had two representatives on the board from the beginning. The Victoria Infirmary opened in 1890, after several years of work by its founders. The Merchants' Hall was the venue for the public meeting about the new hospital in 1887, presided over by Lord Provost Sir James King, at which a telegram arrived at the last minute, announcing that the Queen had consented to the hospital being called the Victoria Infirmary of Glasgow. The Merchants House provided a governor from the time of hospital's foundation. The Glasgow Convalescent Home in Lenzie opened its doors in 1873, and the Merchants House was involved in the directorate from the beginning.

- Hutchesons' Hospital

The patrons of Hutchesons' Hospital had included the Dean of Guild, *ex officio*, from its foundation in 1641, and the town councillors, thirteen of whom were Merchants, had always been patrons, but it was only in 1872, under the Hutchesons' Hospital Act, that the Merchants House itself was asked to provide patrons – three – for the governing board of this charitable foundation.

- Buchanan Educational Institution
- Logan and Johnston School of Domestic Economy
- Allan Glen's Institution
- College of Science and Arts
- Anderson's College Medical School
- Glasgow and West of Scotland Technical College
- St Mungo's College
- Queen Margaret College
- Athenaeum Commercial College
- Haldane's Academy of the Fine Arts
- Michael MacMillan's Bequest
- Scott Scholarship and Bursary Fund
- Marshall Trust
- Glasgow General Education Endowments Board
- Glasgow City Education Endowments Board

Before 1860, the only educational board on which the Merchants House was represented was the Buchanan Institution (see Chapter 6). By the end of the century there were many more. The Logan and Johnston School of Domestic Economy was founded in 1868 by the will of Mrs Jean Johnston or Logan, for the educating, upbringing and assisting in life of poor or destitute step-children or orphan girls. By 1886 it had premises in Greenhead Street, where 170 girls received 'a plain English education, including reading, writing and arithmetic, and also sewing and knitting'. The Merchants House provided four of the school's directors. In the twentieth century the school became a pre-nursing college, before being merged into Glasgow Corporation's further education colleges.

Allan Glen's Institution was established by the will of a Glasgow wright who died in 1850 as a school for the sons of tradesmen. About twenty years later its new constitution included the Dean of Guild, *ex officio*, as one of the school's governors, and in 1876 the Merchants House was asked to provide an additional representative. After its reorganisation in 1886, it became known as a school for boys wishing to follow an industrial or scientific career. The Merchants House channelled its Auldhouse apprenticeship funds into the school, as well as to the College of Science and the Arts, the former Mechanics' Institution which later became part of Glasgow and West of Scotland Technical College.

Anderson's College Medical School began its life as part of the 'university' founded by the will of Dr John Anderson in 1796. The medical section separated from Anderson's University and moved to its own premises near the Western

Infirmary in 1888, from which time the House provided a governor. The Glasgow and West of Scotland Technical College also arose out of Anderson's University, and the House sent a representative to its board from 1890. St Mungo's College was the name given to the medical school of the Royal Infirmary – the Merchants House gave regular grants to this from 1909 onwards. Queen Margaret College was set up in 1883 to provide university-level education for women; from 1890 it had its own medical school, and two years later became part of Glasgow University. The Merchants House appointed a governor for the board from 1886.

The Athenaeum was set up in 1847 as a literary and scientific institution which offered public lectures, evening classes and commercial subjects. In 1888 it moved to a splendid new building in St George's Place (now Nelson Mandela Place). The Merchants House contributed a governor from 1901 onwards. Its music school later became the Scottish College of Music, which in turn became the Royal Scottish Academy of Music and Drama, and its commercial college became the Glasgow and West of Scotland Commercial College, later becoming part of the new Strathclyde University. Haldane's Trust was set up by James Haldane, a Glasgow engraver who died in 1866, and from this the trustees financed a new school of art and design, which moved to the McLellan Galleries in 1869 and was known as the Glasgow School of Art and Haldane's Academy. The Merchants House provided two trustees of Haldane's Academy from 1868. The Haldane name was later dropped and the institution became Glasgow School of Art.

In addition to all these responsibilities, the House provided governors for a number of educational trusts, such as the Scott Scholarship, set up in memory of Sir Walter Scott, Michael MacMillan's Bequest, by which MacMillan, a Merchants House member and Glasgow manufacturer, left money for a school for soldiers' children, and the Marshall Trust, which was brought under the Educational Endowments administration in 1888.

- Stirling's Library
- Baillie's Institution

For Stirling's Library, see Chapter 5. Baillie's Institution was established by a deed of George Baillie, a Glasgow lawyer, in 1863, for the 'self-culture of the operative classes in Glasgow' by free public libraries and reading rooms. Under the Educational Endowments Act, the Merchants House elected a governor for Baillie's Institution from 1889.

- Coulter's Mortification for Premiums to Inventors (see Chapter 4)

A splendid bequest

The largest bequest ever received by the Merchants House came in the early years of the twentieth century, in a rather dramatic way. George Arbuthnot Burns, the second Lord Inverclyde, chairman of the Cunard Company and a director of the family shipping firm of G. and J. Burns, was Lord Dean of Guild in 1903 and 1904 (Fig. 7.1).

In October 1905 he died unexpectedly at the age of forty-four. Lord Inverclyde, who had no children, had left a formal will, made in 1901, leaving everything to his widow absolutely, but in the month following his death the Collector, W. H. Hill, reported to the House's finance committee an unexpected message from the late Dean's lawyers:

> *While recently investigating the contents of a handbag belonging to the late Lord Inverclyde which he had left in his business room at his firm's office in Jamaica Street, Lady Inverclyde, his late Lordship's widow, discovered among a number of other papers a document apparently of a testamentary character written by his late Lordship and subsequent in date to that which has already appeared in the public prints. Her Ladyship with whom at the time were the present Lord Inverclyde and Mr Timothy Warren the family solicitor, at once handed over the document to the latter; but it appears that there is considerable doubt both as to its legal validity and effect and in all probability these will require to be determined judicially.*[7]

The new will, dated 9 November 1902, and drawn up therefore soon after his election as Lord Dean, was in the following terms:

> *I leave everything to my wife which I possess, in Trust for her and the Trustees to be chosen by her.*
>
> *After her death I leave everything to the Merchants' House of Glasgow for the creation of a Fund to be known as the 'Inverclyde Bequest'. The income of this Fund is to be allocated annually by the Directors of the Merchants' House to Charities or Institutions connected with Seamen or for the benefit of aged or infirm Seamen or their families. The term 'Seamen' is to include all those who form the crews of Merchant vessels.*
>
> *I wish the Income of the Bequest allocated in the following proportions:–*
> *Seamen and Seamen's charities in Scotland – Two fifths.*
>
> > *do.   Liverpool and Manchester – One fifth.*
> >
> > *do.   Belfast – One fifth.*
> >
> > *do.   New York and Boston – One fifth.*
>
> *I wish in particular that assistance should be given to deserving Seamen who are in distressed circumstances who have been in the Service of the Cunard Company or Messrs. G. & J. Burns . . .*[8]

Lady Inverclyde chose not to contest this unusual will, and an agreement was reached that she should receive £20,000 outright and all the income from the estate for her lifetime. The will was formalised and confirmed by a special Act of Parliament in 1906, and on Lady Inverclyde's death the House received in 1926 the largest contribution ever made to its funds amounting, with an additional £1,000 bequeathed by the fourth Lord Inverclyde (Lord Dean in 1949 and 1950), to £184,147. The income is distributed chiefly through associations or institutions for seamen, and sub-committees in Liverpool and Belfast (and formerly also New York) advise the House's Directors on its use in the specified ports outside Scotland. This bequest revived an old tradition of the House, which showed a special interest in the troubles of seamen and their families as long ago as 1697, with the Seamen's Box that later became the Clyde Marine Society (see Chapter 4).

Fig. 7.1   George Arbuthnot, 2nd Baron Inverclyde (1861–1905)

The framed cartoon, from *Spy* magazine's Men of the Day series, was given to the Merchants House in 1993 by descendants of Lord Inverclyde, in honour of his munificent bequest to the House. George Arbuthnot Burns succeeded to the title and to the chairmanship of the Cunard Company on the death of his father in 1901. He was a very active and strong chairman, and had embarked on a role in public life with his deanship of 1903 and 1904. The article accompanying the cartoon remarks that he was a possible future Lord Provost, but he died in October 1905 after being taken ill with pleurisy on his steam yacht at Wemyss.

Industrialists and philanthropists

The designation of Deans at this time suggests a changing social pattern. Among them had always been found both 'self-made' men who had built up their own businesses and members of long-established merchant families, but in the eighteenth and nineteenth centuries many were both businessmen and lairds, known by the names of their estates as well as of their forebears. In the 1860s John Ramsay of Kildalton (on Islay) followed Archibald Orr Ewing of Ballikinrain (in Stirlingshire), who was later made a baronet. Robert King of Levernholm (1905 and 1906), brother of Sir James King of Campsie, was probably the last Dean to take his style from his lands. He was also the only candidate proposed by the Directors in the twentieth century whose election was contested at an Annual General Meeting – apparently on the ground that the House needed new blood in its management of its affairs. It was characteristic of the House's spirit of moderation and compromise that when he came to retire King proposed the name of his defeated rival, Thomas Mason, who became Sir Thomas after his years in the chair were over (see below).

By the 1870s the iron industry in Glasgow was no longer as important as it had been, but another and even greater industry had been born, combining Glasgow's three great strengths – heavy engineering, iron and commerce – in one mighty leviathan. Glasgow's shipbuilding industry accounted for the launch of over 248,000 tons of shipping in 1880. The first shipbuilder to be elected Lord Dean, in October 1881 (to serve for 1882 and 1883), was Alexander Stephen, who hailed from Dundee. The head of the Clydeside shipbuilders Alexander Stephen and Sons, he gained a worldwide reputation for ship design: 'no builder living has so many vessels afloat of his own individual design', said a contemporary, and he personally made models of most of the vessels constructed by his firm. Their new premises at Linthouse, by Govan, were 'one of the sights of the river', with the huge overhead gantry, the first of its kind on the Clyde, visible from a considerable distance.[9] Stephen patented and developed the construction of composite ships (built with a framework of iron, covered in planking), and introduced the practice of building the ships' machinery at the same time as the hull, and putting the engines and boilers on board before launch – then a revolutionary idea. This latter development, although an advanced construction method, was partly blamed for a dreadful disaster in July 1883, when the *Daphne* overturned in the water after leaving the slipway. An unusually large number of men were on board, working to complete the vessel before the Glasgow Fair, and 146 of them were drowned, trapped in the holds, engine rooms and cabins. A public subscription raised £30,000 for the relief of the bereaved families, and the firm escaped litigation, but the disaster was a huge setback. It happened a few months before the end of Alexander Stephen's deanship, and William McEwen filled in for him during several weeks of absence. Alexander Stephen was the first chairman of the governors of the Glasgow and West of Scotland Technical College, and later represented the Merchants House on that board. He was chairman of Govan School Board, to which he donated a generous sum to provide bursaries for boys of the parish.

John Ure, Lord Dean in 1890 and 1891, had been born in the Bridgegate in 1824. His parents had married and set up home (and shop – John's father was a master baker) there in 1817, the very year in which James Ewing urged the removal of the Merchants' Hall to a less objectionable neighbourhood. The project with which the future Lord Provost Ure was most associated, the improvement of sanitation in the city, must have taken root in the sights – and smells – of his boyhood locality. By all accounts he was lucky to have survived boyhood: his early playground was the Clyde near the Bridgegate and when he was eight years old he was rescued from drowning by the son of one of the bridge toll-keepers and only just resuscitated. He had two other narrow escapes in childhood, and as a boy himself rescued a friend from drowning in a canal and also saved a man who had fallen into the Clyde. Most appropriately, much later in life he was president of the Humane Society, which awarded medals and certificates for life-saving on the Clyde, and still operates a vital life-saving service on the river (see Chapter 9). Ure became a grain dealer and then set up as a flour miller (with his mother dead, dependent sisters and a father in ill health he had given up his hopes of a profession), and in the early 1860s built his new Crown Flour Mills in Washington Street, complete with all the improvements in mechanisation that had been developed by that date. By then his talents for tactful and persuasive public speaking as one of the leaders of the grain business had already come to wide notice, and he was elected on to the town council, becoming Lord Provost in 1880. To his untiring energy and keen common sense, according to the acerbic commentator of *Clydeside Cameos*, 'is due the fact of Glasgow being now so healthy. In order to get thoroughly up in the subject of sanitation he visited the sewers of all the leading towns in the kingdom, carefully inspected their nuisances and pumped their officials. . . . But John not only worked himself; he made everybody else work, and personally saw that the various departments kept up to the time of day. He saw, further, the imperfections of the whole system, and he set himself to work out a scheme of sanitary reform which has been the salvation of the city, but which he had almost to carry at the point of the bayonet.'[10] His other lasting innovation was the building of the new City Chambers in George Square. A previous attempt to set up a competition for the design had broken down amid difficulties and objections, but Provost Ure guided the plan through 'by tact and finesse' and himself laid the foundation stone towards the end of his period of office. The new municipal buildings were completed in 1888, and it must have given John Ure much satisfaction during his deanship a couple of years later to be able to look out from the Merchants House across the square to the magnificent domes and towers of the town council's new home. The town council unanimously pressed him to allow himself to be re-elected as provost for a further three-year period, but he could not be persuaded to abandon his retirement plan of world travel. Even the offer of a knighthood could not make him stay. *Clydeside Cameos* records: 'Within a week after he had doffed the official robes he was on his way to the Antipodes. . . . The State official had to cable him: "Queen wants to knight you; wire reply," to which John answered, "Thanks; would rather not."'[11] He remained plain Mr John Ure to the end of his life (preferring this title even after receiving his honorary LL.D. from Glasgow University), but his fellow citizens knew him as one of the best Lord Provosts the city had ever had – as well as one of its most unaffected, kindly and courteous men.

Another self-made man was James Reid, Lord Dean in 1893 and 1894, who had attended the village school in his native Kilmaurs and worked as a blacksmith's assistant. Later he worked as an engineer in Greenock, before becoming manager of Glasgow's steam locomotive works, Neilson and Co., known as the Hyde Park Works, then located in Anderston, later, famously, in Springburn. He became a partner in the company and later was given the option to buy it, which he did in 1876. His early working habits died hard: he came into work every day at 6 a.m. along with the men, and often worked until late in the evening. His four sons came into the business in 1893 (one of them, Hugh, was a future Dean of Guild, see Chapter 8), and a year later James Reid died of a heart attack, while on the golf course at St Andrews, bringing his deanship to a sudden end.

Sir James King, ex-Lord Provost and ex-Lord Dean, stepped into the breach, and four months later, in October 1894, Hugh Brown was elected Lord Dean. His family had Merchants House connections going back over three or four generations, and he had been a Director from 1861, continuing with few intermissions till his death in 1906. The son of a muslin manufacturer, he ceased to work in the business himself upon inheriting his father's fortune, and devoted his energies to the directorship of various concerns (the Caledonian Railway Company, the Clydesdale Bank, the Tharsis Sulphur and Copper Company, Nobel's Explosive Company) and to a prominent role in the compassionate and voluntary side of public life. He served on the boards of many public and charitable institutions, on some of them as the representative of the Merchants House, but it was with the Royal Infirmary that he became most strongly associated. He was a director of the infirmary for many years, working closely with William McEwen, whom he succeeded as chairman in 1885 (and he in turn was succeeded by future Lord Dean J. D. Hedderwick in 1901). He was one of the founders of the Royal Infirmary's medical school, later incorporated as St Mungo's College, and raised money for it both publicly and privately. He was a great friend to the city's benevolent institutions and was remembered as one of Glasgow's most public-spirited citizens.

Among the Deans and leading members of the Merchants House in the late nineteenth and early twentieth century, the ship-owning side of the shipping industry was well represented. Lord Inverclyde's munificence has already been noted. Sir James Bell, of steamship owners Bell, Brothers and McLelland, was Lord Dean in 1899 and 1900. He was a young Lord Dean of Guild, at under fifty, but already had behind him an outstanding public career, which had left Glasgow a larger, cleaner, brighter city with a more powerful corporation. He was elected unopposed to the town council in 1890, and was made provost in 1892, at forty-two one of the youngest Glasgow provosts of the time. Perhaps it took a man of relative youth and much energy to tackle two of Glasgow's end-of-century problems: purifying the river and bringing into the corporation the independent police burghs, such as Hillhead, Maryhill, Govanhill and Pollokshields. The opening of the sewage works at Dalmarnock marked the beginning of the end of the practice of piping untreated sewage straight into the Clyde, and that alone would have been enough to earn Provost Bell the eternal gratitude of his fellow citizens. The unification of the corporation with the police departments was realised in 1895, at which point Bell was re-elected for a further year to oversee the transition. That was the year of his knighthood. His provostship also saw the elevation of Glasgow to a County of a City, and he became its first Lord Lieutenant. He masterminded the corporation's takeover of the tramways, until then a private company, and brought under the corporation's jurisdiction the multifarious civic trusts: police, parks, water, city improvement, gas and electric light, and so on. It was he who brought electric street lighting to Glasgow, switching on the lights in 1893, having first tried out the new method of lighting in his own house. Sir James served as chairman of the Clydesdale Bank and of the Glasgow and South Western Railway Company. His influence in the shipping industry was put to good effect in 1896, when he mediated between striking engineers and employers, successfully ending a twelve-week strike. He had a long association with the Royal Glasgow Institute of Fine Arts, and owned a fine art collection at his house in Kilwinning. He played a major part in having Glasgow's Art Galleries built from the proceeds of the 1888 International Exhibition at Kelvingrove, and along with Sir James King was in charge of the 1901 Exhibition.

Sir James was succeeded by the House's first banker Dean, Robert Gourlay, to whom the Directors paid warm tribute upon his death in 1916: 'In the management of the affairs of the House his financial knowledge and sound judgment were of great advantage, while the benevolent work of the House appealed strongly to his philanthropic instincts, and afforded a valuable field of exercise for his unique knowledge of old Glasgow Families.'[12] His portrait, by Sir James Guthrie, RSA, was gifted to the House by his son (Fig. 7.2).

Sir Thomas Mason, Dean of Guild in 1907 and 1908, was the first person to serve both as Dean of Guild and Deacon Convener – and one of only two ever to do so. (The other was Robert Robertson in the late 1920s.) He was apprenticed as a youth to his father, a mason, and launched into his first subcontract at the age of eighteen. He went on from strength to strength, and was well established in the construction industry by the time he went into partnership with John Morrison in 1876. Morrison and Mason became one of the best-known building concerns in the West of Scotland, responsible for many major public projects, including several railways, the piers of the Forth Railway Bridge, Queen's Dock, Glasgow City Chambers, the tunnels and reservoir at Craigmaddie for Glasgow's waterworks, Jamaica Street bridge, and the theatre that was later to become the Citizens. Sir Thomas's expert judgement, detailed knowledge of the building trade, and organising genius were in demand for many public offices, but his outstanding public service was for the Clyde Trust, on which he represented first the corporation and then, from 1893 until his retiral in 1919, the Merchants House. He chaired the Trust for the last eleven of these years, and was acknowledged to have been one of the best chairmen that body had ever had. The construction of Princes Dock was one of the many important projects that were undertaken during his period of office. A good listener who was endowed with down-to-earth common sense, he was a very popular figure in Glasgow, and always ready to help any good cause. He was knighted in 1909 for his public services. His association with the Merchants House directorate lasted over three decades and only ended a year before his death, aged eighty, in 1924.

Fig. 7.2 Robert Gourlay, LL.D. (artist: Sir James Guthrie)

Robert Gourlay was a Director of the Merchants House from 1879 until his death in 1916, save for a break of three years and his term as Dean of Guild in 1901 and 1902. When he died it was said that he had been prominent for nearly half a century in every movement for the furtherance of the best interests of the city. Born in 1840, he was educated at the High School and Glasgow University. His father, known as 'Banker Gourlay' was the agent of the Bank of Scotland's first Glasgow branch, and Robert followed his father into banking, rising to be manager. He was a director of the African Lakes Company, the Burmah Oil Company and the Scottish Provident Institution, and was chairman of George Outram and Company, the proprietors of the Glasgow Herald. He had many philanthropic and charitable interests and acted as honorary treasurer for many voluntary societies. Among the charities that benefited from his attention were the Soldiers' and Sailors' Families Association, the Old Man's Friend Society and the Old Women's Home, the Indigent Gentlewomen's Fund, the Royal Glasgow Cancer Hospital and the Glasgow Royal Maternity and Women's Hospital, for which he was instrumental in obtaining the new building. His honorary LL.D. from Glasgow University came in recognition of his many public services. Above all, he was remembered for being 'almost the last survivor of [Glasgow's] notable hierarchy of commerce' and for 'the admirable school in which he was reared, where business concerns were never allowed to overwhelm the social graces of life'.[13] Already in the early twentieth century, his quiet and courteous business manners made him seem like a character from another era.

A continuing public role

In 1905 Glasgow and the House gave a Prime Minister to the United Kingdom for the first time. Sir Henry Campbell-Bannerman was a member and the son of a Director and benefactor, Lord Provost Sir James Campbell, of J. and W. Campbell, warehousemen, of Ingram Street. His Liberal Government, which was to lay the foundations of the welfare state and of centralised town planning, caused the House some alarm by certain of its proposals. Among them was the Land Values Taxation (Scotland) Bill of 1906, also known as the 'Glasgow Bill', promoted by radical supporters of land reform, which aimed to give burghs the right to levy a tax on site values as well as the ordinary rate on rentals. The House asked one of its Directors, Dr David Murray, lawyer, scholar and historian of Glasgow, to represent the case against the Bill on its behalf. A forceful case was made in its petition to Parliament: 'The object of the said Bill is to revolutionise the system of land assessment in Scotland by imposing a discriminating tax against the owners of landed property and of feu duties and ground annuals.' The House, like other such owners, would be called on

> to furnish . . . information about a state of matters which does not exist, viz: the value for which this ground would sell if it had no erections upon it . . .
>
> The promotion of the present Bill is due partly to hostility to the private ownership of land and partly to the extent to which the Local Authorities who have taken up the measure have been increasing their Expenditure and running into debt. In order to avoid the necessity of retrenchment they desire to obtain additional revenue from a class which is limited in voting power . . .[14]

The Bill was twice passed in the Commons and twice rejected by the Lords. Its main points were adopted into the Budget of 1909, but – burdened as Dr Murray had predicted with administrative difficulties and a low return in taxation – it had still not been fully implemented by the time war broke out. To the relief, no doubt, of the Merchants House and other Glasgow landowners, it was extinguished amid the compromises made on policy by the wartime coalition government, and never ignited again. One of its unintended effects, however, was to hold up house building in Scotland.

In the later nineteenth century the House successfully protested against proposals which would have undermined the independence of Glasgow Dean of Guild Court. The Burgh Police and Health (Scotland) Bill of 1888 threatened the constitution and continued existence of the Dean of Guild Court. The Lord Advocate agreed with the House on the importance of the Court's constitution, 'which, by including Lyners elected by the Trades House from among their best qualified members, skilled in building works and architecture, with an equal number of members, experienced in affairs, selected by the Merchants House, formed a Court highly practical in character, and speedy, commercial and satisfactory in its judgments'.[15] In 1903 the Merchants House, along with the Trades House and guildries of other cities, succeeded in having a proviso inserted in the Burgh Police (Scotland) Act that nothing in the Act should alter or affect the rights, constitution, powers or privileges of the Dean of Guild Court. The argument put forward by the Court, and by the Merchants House in support of it, was that it was effective, hard-working and, in a city where the town council itself was the principal litigant before it, independent of the council in its judgments. In 1909 the Housing, Town Planning etc., Bill seemed likely to sweep away the Court's powers altogether in areas approved for redevelopment. Again the House petitioned Parliament, this time in conjunction with the city corporation and the Trades House. With the help of local MPs an amendment was secured safeguarding the Court's jurisdiction. This was the last such battle they had to fight. The main problem throughout the nineteenth century was the lack of building control legislation in Scotland. The Dean of Guild Court could only apply the legislation that existed, and its expertise mainly related to safety of construction. In general the Dean of Guild Court supported reforms to building legislation to strengthen the public health aspect of buildings, and once a stringent code of legislation was in place – beginning with Glasgow's own building legislation under Acts of 1892 and 1903 – the Court's function was to interpret and apply that, thereby taking its constitution and existence out of the firing line.[16]

Another of the city's powerful – and therefore controversial – institutions was the Clyde Navigation Trust. At a time when the Clyde was one of the world's most important waterways, influence over its management was naturally highly prized and sometimes bitterly contested (Fig. 7.3). The House continued to defend its representation on the board of the Trust, won after sustained efforts in the mid-century (see Chapter 6). This brought it, around the turn of the century, along with the Trades House and the Chamber of Commerce, into direct opposition to the city corporation, in a fiercely fought and long-running battle about the Trust's composition. The Merchants House and the other two institutions had thrown in their lot with the directly elected trustees, representing the users of the Clyde, in support of a proposal to increase the numbers of the latter such that they would outnumber the council representatives. The Lord Provost's response was to co-opt numbers of councillors on to the committee that was considering the proposed Bill, in order to vote it out. John Ure resigned the deputy chairmanship of the Trust in protest. (He had returned to public life in this capacity after his retirement tour of the world, but died three months after his resignation, an outcome attributed to the strain of dealing with the warring interest groups about the river that had nearly claimed his life as a boy.) Another battle over representation ensued in 1905, when the House fought a parliamentary Bill to abolish the representation on the Trust by itself, the Trades House and the Chamber of Commerce. Lord Dean Robert King and Director Robert Gourlay attended a House of Lords committee that reduced the representation to just one for each of these bodies, but another petition to the Commons succeeded in restoring the representation to two each. Not all its activity on behalf of the Trust was about representation: in 1883 and 1890 it petitioned Parliament in support of the Trust's efforts to increase the accommodation of Glasgow's harbour, resulting in the development of docks at Cessnock (later named Prince's Dock).

The House's possessions

Some minor improvements had been made to the Merchants House building over the first two decades, with a kitchen range being added in 1879 and electric light in 1895.

Fig. 7.3   The Broomielaw from Brown Street, c. 1885
In the foreground are the passenger wharf and a goods shed. The first Caledonian Railway Bridge
(1878) now marks the upper limit for shipping. Just behind it can be seen the arches of the Jamaica
Bridge (built by Telford, an earlier version of the present bridge), and beyond that the South Portland
Street suspension footbridge. The Victoria Bridge (1854) replaced the old Glasgow Bridge near the
Bridgegate. In the distance is the Albert Bridge (1871). The Merchants' steeple still dominates the
skyline to the left.

In 1907 major alterations were begun to extend the building in order to provide
office accommodation which would bring in additional rents. The architect was John
James Burnet, the more famous son of the building's first designer. He added two
and a half storeys to the building, and changed the West George Street entrance and
made alterations to the Hall at the same time (Fig. 7.4). The former West George
Street entrance had been at the north-east corner of the building. This was now
altered to a window and the entrance vestibule was converted to become the
Committee Room, accessed from the Collector's office next door. The new entrance
was made out of two adjacent doorways in the middle of the West George Street
front. Both entrances, on George Square and West George Street, were provided with
'an Electric Passenger Hoist'. On the first floor level, the present Anteroom was

converted out of the old 'Secretary's Room' (Collector's office). Extensive alterations were made to the Hall: the ceiling was completely renewed, and new frieze and pilasters added; five new windows replaced the six old ones; the benches were removed and the platform altered; new panelling and dadoes were fitted. The work was completed in 1909.

Fig. 7.4 The Merchants House building as altered by J. J. Burnet

At the Necropolis, the House continued to take a close interest in the surrounding area, spending money on improvements, such as railings and access (repositioning the gate at the Bridge of Sighs), the improvement of the layout of Cathedral Square, and the purchase and laying out of new ground. But maintaining the monuments was beginning to be a burden, especially when family or descendants moved away, and in the late 1880s owners were invited to pay a fee to have their monuments looked after by the House for all time to come.

A letter 'to the owners of the Necropolis', 1878

Forty-five years after its opening, the Necropolis was immensely successful from the public point of view – it had expanded eastwards in 1857 and was to do so again in 1894 – but its upkeep was already becoming burdensome to its owners. The poet William Motherwell, little read now but highly esteemed in Victorian times in Britain and America for his romantic poetry on medieval and Norse themes, had been buried there in 1835, and an elaborate monument by the sculptor James Fillans was raised by subscriptions from his admirers in 1851. The Merchants House provided at no charge the plot of ground surrounding his grave for the erection of the monument. In July 1878 the *Glasgow Herald* printed an anguished letter from 'One who has seen Motherwell' complaining about the state of the poet's tomb. He was in the habit of taking visitors round the Necropolis, and had been accompanying a young American gentleman, 'a poet of promise among the rising intellectuals of the United States'. Of the marble bust of Motherwell he writes:

'It is as black as an Ethiopian – covered all over with layers of soot. The bust is placed under a canopy, open at the four sides, through which thick flakes of soot penetrate; and, as no rain falls upon it, they adhere to the bust. There is an accumulation of these sooty particles, rendering the aspect of the dead poet quite undistinguishable. Would that some of the kind hearts that placed it there were still alive . . . and no such complaint as I now make to the directors of the Merchants' House would be allowed to remain unredressed for a day. It is in no spirit of fault-finding that I make this appeal to the present enlightened head of the Merchants' House – Sir James Watson – but for the honour of Glasgow, and my love for the memory of one of her sons of genius . . .'

The House was still concerned for the relics of its past. Having failed to get the ownership of the Bridgegate Steeple transferred to the town council in 1821, the House attempted it again in 1889, again on the understanding that the council keep it and its clock in repair, and on condition that 'the steeple should not at any future time be taken down without the consent of the Merchants House'. The corporation replied that they would accept the gift provided the steeple was conveyed to them unconditionally. Evidently the House felt unable to accept these terms, and nothing more was done. Eight years later when the bell needed renovation, it was reported as 'belonging to the House', and repaired at a cost of £65, paid for by the House. The bell was reported by the founders to be 'in a splendid state of preservation, and altogether a masterpiece in the way of workmanship'. (It was only in 1921 that the ringing of the bell was discontinued.) In 1913, when plans were being made to extend the fish market, the members of the House had reason to be glad that they had not succeeded in conveying the steeple to the town: the council proposed to remove it and asked the Merchants House's approval. The Directors, and indeed the membership at the Annual General Meeting, refused to consent to this. (And when two years later the council was intent on demolishing the Tolbooth Steeple as part of its plans for improving the town cross area, the Merchants House objected to this too, supported by the Glasgow Archaeological Society.)

Fig. 7.5 Coat-of-arms of the Merchants House

The coat-of-arms incorporates the merchants' mark based on the figure 4. Each merchant had his own mark which he branded or painted on his goods, and many of these marks, especially in Scotland, were variations on this symbol. This variant was the one used by the Merchants House of Glasgow. The motto of the House, 'Toties redeuntis eodem', 'So many returning to the same place', is a reminder that not all voyages ended successfully.

The badge of the House, which had been used for many generations, was legitimated by a patent of arms from the Lord Lyon in 1912 (Fig. 7.5). The patent of arms, along with one of the old oak doors from the Merchants' Hall in the Bridgegate and an oak chest made from the beam to which the bell in the steeple had been suspended, are now displayed in the House's Committee Room.

The chest was a bequest from William Henry Hill, the Collector and Clerk who had been the chief official of the House for forty-six years. W. H. Hill was the astute lawyer who guided the House towards the twentieth century while having at his fingertips all the traditions of more than three hundred years of history (Fig. 7.6). From the outset of his appointment to the end, he set an uncompromising standard in his work. Immediately upon his appointment in 1866 he had taken the books in hand, causing the auditor to note the 'marked improvement . . . since our last audit in the Construction of the Books and System of Book-keeping, and of the correct, clear and distinct manner in which the entries are made. We have rarely seen Books kept in so satisfactory a manner.'[17]

Fig. 7.6   W. H. Hill, LL.D. (artist: William M. Pratt)

William Henry Hill was born in 1837, a son of Laurence Hill who had been Collector in the early years of the century (see Chapter 5). He was sent to school in Ayr and in the south of England, where the family owned an estate. A graduate of Glasgow University, he practised law in the family firm of Hill, Davidson and Hoggan. As well as Collector and Clerk of the Merchants House, he was factor to the University of Glasgow, Clerk to the Faculty of Physicians and Surgeons of Glasgow and Clerk to Hutchesons' Hospital, all positions held in his family for generations. He performed a notable service both to the University at the time of its removal to Gilmorehill, and to the Western Infirmary as honorary secretary and treasurer. To all this he added, in 1883, the position of secretary to the Glasgow Chamber of Commerce. Introduced by his father to a love of archaeology, palaeography and Scottish antiquities, he found time amid his busy professional life to research and publish accounts of the history of several Glasgow institutions, notably of course the Merchants House (see Chapter 6), and he owned an important private library at his house at Barlanark. His LL.D. was an honour from Glasgow University in recognition of his contribution to the literature on Glasgow's history. A contemporary described the unmarried Dr Hill as 'unobtrusive in his habits, with a charming naiveté of manner', and recalled his entertainment of friends at his Barlanark residence in the good old country style.

His collectorship was ended only by his death, at the age of seventy-five, in 1912. On the day of his funeral, a special meeting of the Directors was called and they proceeded to the Barony Church for the funeral and then to the Necropolis for the interment. At their next meeting, the Directors noted that Dr Hill during his association with the House had seen the value of its property and investments increase from £84,000 in 1866 to over £400,000 in 1912. They recorded 'their high appreciation . . . of his sound judgment, his administrative ability, and his uniform tact and urbanity. To his constant concern to conserve the interests of the House and uphold its traditions is due in no small degree the regard with which the House is held by the Community.'[18] His partner in the ancestral law firm, James Alexander McCallum, was appointed to succeed him.

Fifteen months earlier, in a coronation address to King George V, the House had prayed 'that Christianity may advance and peace prevail among the Nations: that Trade and Commerce may flourish, and Learning, Arts and Science increase and develop for the well-being of Mankind, adding lustre to the Annals of Your time'.[19] But by 1914 Europe was at war. It was a new chapter not only for Glasgow but for humanity.

Notes

1. S. G. Checkland, *Scottish Banking: A History, 1695–1973* (Glasgow and London, 1975), p. xix.
2. *The Bailie*, No. 221 (10 Jan. 1877).
3. Merchants House Minutes, 9 June 1879.
4. *The Bailie*, No. 683 (18 Nov. 1885).
5. MH Minutes, 9 Oct. 1888.
6. MH Annual Report 1884.
7. MH Minutes, 3 Nov. 1905.
8. Ibid.
9. *Clydeside Cameos: a Series of Sketches of Prominent Clydeside Men*, No. 37, republished from *Fairplay* (London, 1885), p. 288.
10. Ibid. No. 33, p. 257.
11. Ibid., p. 260.
12. MH Minutes, 13 Mar. 1917.
13. *Glasgow Herald*, 28 Dec. 1916.
14. MH Minutes, 11 May 1906.
15. MH Annual Report 1888.
16. Andrew Jackson, *Glasgow Dean of Guild Court: A History* (Glasgow, 1983), pp. 93–6.
17. MH Minutes, 30 Sept. 1867.
18. Ibid., 18 Oct. 1912.
19. Ibid., 13 June 1911.

THE AGE OF BEQUESTS

The twentieth century was as full of disturbance and change as any of the preceding centuries of the Merchants House's existence. The welfare state emerged, doubtless bringing with it the assumption that old-fashioned benevolent work would cease to be important or even possible. Yet during the course of the century, the resources and many of the activities of the House expanded faster than they had ever done before. Its old task of providing for members and their families in distress was as necessary as ever, but it also began to help people who would have had no claim on it in former days – people with neither membership qualification nor mercantile connections. It is remarkable how, even in years of depression, its financial strength continued to grow. It reorganised its funds and its machinery for payment, and put in place important membership reforms. The old Merchant Guild remained a working institution in the life of the city.

The First World War

From the outset of the war of 1914–18 the House contributed as generously as it was able to the various war relief funds, such as the Soldiers' and Sailors' Families Association, the British Red Cross Society, the Lord Provost's Fund for the Relief of Dependants of Glasgow Soldiers and Seamen, and the Belgian Relief Fund.

Along with other Scottish institutions the House protested against Government regulations under which the holders of the new War Loans or their heirs, and the heirs of Scottish military officers, had to apply to the Bank of England or English courts in London for legal title to their property. It was only when a member and former Director of the House, the future Prime Minister, Andrew Bonar Law, became Chancellor of the Exchequer, that the necessary concessions began to be made (in 1917). Bonar Law had been brought up by his Glasgow relations from the age of twelve, and worked in their office from the age of sixteen. He became a junior partner in William Jacks and Company, a firm of Glasgow iron merchants, and was chairman of the Glasgow Iron Trade Association. He was a member of the Merchants House from the beginning of the century, and a Director from 1901 till 1903; he was at this time MP for a Glasgow constituency.

By 1918 the House's grants to public war funds might have adversely affected its own pensioners, if it had not been for two generous bequests received during the war years. The Schaw and Hamilton Mortifications made possible a war bonus to pensioners in 1918, and the following year 'in view of the probability that the cost of living will not be brought back to the pre-war standard' the war bonus was replaced by an increase in the pensions, to 25 per cent above the pre-war rate – though the Directors were aware that 'this does not in any way represent the increase in the cost of living consequent on the War'. In 1920 they decided to bring the pensions to a level 50 per cent above the pre-war rate, although 'even this does not represent an increase adequate to meet the increased cost of living'.

The bequests that made this possible were particularly important because they allowed the House for the first time to give help to women who were not widows or daughters of members. The first of these was the legacy of Miss Marjory Shanks Schaw, who died in 1915. Miss Schaw's bequest of £10,000 was for providing pensions to maiden ladies resident in Glasgow over fifty years old, 'who had seen better days'. Before this bequest was a year old, the Directors reported: 'The very large number of applications received – many times more than the Income provided will avail for – shews that generous as the Bequest was, the need for assistance among the deserving class intended to be benefited is greatly larger.' Some of those whom the Directors wished to help were ladies who, while having a Glasgow connection, were not resident in the city, and they applied to Miss Schaw's trustees for a further grant from the residue of her estate free of the condition of Glasgow residence. The trustees granted a further £10,000, bringing this bequest to £20,000 in total.

> **Miss Marjory Shanks Schaw**
>
> Marjory Shanks Schaw was the sister of Archibald Shanks Schaw, a Glasgow iron merchant who died in 1889. In 1891 she gifted £40,000 to the Royal Infirmary for a convalescent home in memory of her brother, which was built at Bearsden and opened in 1895. She gave an additional £15,000 to endow it, and took a keen interest in the home and visited it regularly. When she died in 1915 at over ninety years of age, she left an estate valued at over £500,000 to be distributed among charitable institutions in and around Glasgow.

The second large wartime bequest was that of two sisters, Miss Mary Hamilton and Miss Hamilton L. Hamilton, whose mortification of £40,000 came to the House in 1916. Hamilton's Mortification could be spent on help not only for women and children but also for 'necessitous and deserving' men who, if they had been members of the House, 'would have been deemed worthy of its benefits'. The Misses Hamilton were the daughters of James Hamilton of Ascogbank in Bute, tobacco importer in Glasgow, and his wife Jane Ponton or Hamilton, whose portraits they also bequeathed to the House, along with the portrait of their brother Patrick. These two bequests (the last to be known by the old Scots term 'mortification') set the Merchants House on a course of benevolence that it has followed ever since.

Of course, in contributing to Glasgow institutions such as hospitals and colleges, it had for a long time had wider charitable interests than that of merely looking after its members, but it was now able to extend this wider benevolence to individuals and not just institutions.

The Merchants House War Relief Fund

In 1917 the Lord Dean, Hugh Reid, looking ahead towards the end of the war, foresaw that members of the mercantile community and their families would have peculiar difficulties to face. Those who had served in the Forces would have to re-establish themselves in business or, if they were young men, would have to make a new beginning of their working lives. Hugh Reid proposed that a Merchants House War Relief Fund should be created to meet these needs. To found it he gave £10,000 in memory of his eldest son, killed in action in France in 1915.

An appeal went out to members, and by October 1918 £40,000 had been raised. At its peak the fund reached over £54,000. It was divided into two parts, one to provide interest-free loans or grants to help people establish or develop their businesses (including ex-servicemen not connected with the Merchants House), and the other to give pensions or other help. The first was to be terminable when the special post-war needs were met. The capital of the second was to be maintained and eventually merged with the general funds of the House. This was a far-sighted and imaginative plan to strengthen a new generation in the business life of Glasgow. In practice, however, it came up against particularly intractable problems during the 1920s and 1930s, when business depression in the West of Scotland was almost continuous and not even the most enterprising and active could be sure of finding a foothold in trade. In the end more than a third of the repayments of the interest-free loans proved irrecoverable. But the encouragement of the fund did help many men, young and old, to make a new start, and it eased the lives of others who had had to give up hope of regaining the position in life they had held in 1914. By 1938 the terminable section of the Fund was almost exhausted, though it was not finally closed down till 1961. The permanent section continued to be used to raise the level of pensions granted by the House.

Hugh Reid left his mark on Glasgow in many ways (Fig. 8.1). He was the son of James Reid, Dean of Guild in 1894, who had begun life as a blacksmith's assistant and became head of the Hyde Park Locomotive Works (see Chapter 7). Hugh began his working life as an apprentice in the Hyde Park Works, and served the firm for nearly sixty years. Under his directorship it became the largest railway locomotive building operation in Europe, and supplied engines to all parts of the British Empire. Hugh Reid joined the Merchants House in 1892 and was a Director almost continuously from 1899 until his death in 1935, and Dean of Guild in 1917 and 1918. In 1917 he was made an honorary burgess for his services to Glasgow, and three years later he was knighted for his services to the community, especially during the war. His generous giving to the community where his workforce lived created Balgray Park in Springburn and various other public facilities.

Fig. 8.1   Sir Hugh Reid, Dean of Guild 1917 and 1918

'Like his father . . . Sir Hugh was an exceptionally fine example of the best type of Glasgow businessman – eminent in business and eminent in public service. . . . [He was] a man of tireless energy and strong purpose, of great ability, rapid in thought and action, yet full of tact, of great kindness of heart and openhanded generosity and liberality.' (Merchants House Annual Report 1935)

When he was elected Dean of Guild in October 1916 he determined to use his position as head of the Dean of Guild Court to do something for Glasgow's terrible housing problem. As soon as he accepted office, he proposed that preparations be made for tackling the problem of slum housing and of providing workers' houses when the war ended. This resulted in the Special Committee on Housing, on which Reid served as an *ex officio* member of the town council. By October 1918 seven blocks of flats were nearing completion in Garngad and others were in preparation. The first of his two annual reports for the Court, in October 1917, identified the problem of infant mortality as primarily a housing problem. He called for a joint approach by the municipal authorities and private enterprise to solve what he saw would be the city's most pressing need after the war.

The House can seldom have been more useful than it was between the wars, when economic crisis struck at the lives of many in the business community and there was a need for the renewal and expansion of a whole series of Glasgow institutions. Part of its response to this was in contributing towards the building or endowment of many colleges, schools and hospitals.

Merchants House benevolence between the wars

Grants were given to the following organisations:

1925 Royal Hospital for Sick Children (building fund)
     Glasgow and West of Scotland Commercial College (building and endowment fund)
1926 Victoria Infirmary (new wing)
     Ear, Nose and Throat Hospital (building fund)
     St Andrews Ambulance Association (building new HQ)
1927 Royal Cancer Hospital (radium fund)
1928 Royal Infirmary (Canniesburn building fund)
     Glasgow Dental Hospital (building fund)
     Glasgow and West of Scotland College of Domestic Science
1929 Victoria Infirmary
     David Livingstone Memorial
1931 Eye Infirmary
     Cathedral Organ
1932 Development Board for Glasgow and District (to promote industrial development and the establishment of new industries in Glasgow district; two Merchants House representatives on the board)
1933 Glasgow Council for Community Service in Unemployment (help and services for unemployed; two Merchants House representatives on the board)
     Glasgow Civic Society ('to work for a more beautiful city'; a Merchants House representative on the Society)
1934 Royal Hospital for Sick Children (orthopaedic department)
1935 Victoria Infirmary
     Glasgow Council for Community Service in Unemployment
1936 Scottish National Development Council
     Anderson College of Medicine (building needs)
1937 Scottish Empire Exhibition of 1938
     Ear, Nose and Throat Hospital (extension)
     Glasgow Humane Society (new house for officer)
1938 Glasgow Deaf and Dumb Mission
     Anderson College of Medicine

Bequests between the wars

The Directors also had to consider, with practical humanity and at the same time with detailed discrimination, applications for help from a widening range of men and women in hardship. There was a distinct need for funds which could be used more freely than some of the older bequests. In 1921 the House received £10,000 'for such purposes as the Dean of Guild and Finance Committee may determine'. The bequest was from William J. Chrystal in memory of his son Lieutenant Ian C. Chrystal, who was killed in France in 1917, and of his daughter Eleanor. William Chrystal had been a member of the House from 1866, and a Director for several periods from 1890 until his death. A notable chemist, he was head of the chemical manufacturing firm, John and James White (see Chapter 7 for James White), which latterly he ran from its offices in the Merchants House building. He was of too retiring a nature to be a public figure in city affairs, but he was active in many of the city's institutions: a governor of the Royal Technical College, where he took a great interest in the chemical department; donor of radium equipment for the Glasgow Cancer Hospital; a director of the Chamber of Commerce; and chairman of the Royal Exchange for many years. His bequest to the Merchants House was particularly useful because it was free of restrictions and allowed the development of benevolence in new directions.

In 1925 the House received £2,000 from Miss Rebecca Edgar's bequest. Miss Edgar had left a will dividing her estate 'among such of the Benevolent, Charitable and Religious Institutions in Glasgow and Greenock as her Trustees . . . might think proper'. The Merchants House made an application to the trustees for a share of the bequest, for a class of person for whom the House had hitherto been able to do very little: 'deserving widows in reduced circumstances, of men who, while not in business on their own account in Glasgow, should appear to the Directors to have been useful in carrying on the business life of the City'.[1] This, together with the Chrystal Bequest, enabled the House to embark on assistance for a new and expanding category of Glasgow people: 'owing to modern developments, many who do important business work in Glasgow and exercise supervision and control in large businesses cannot be described as carrying on business on their own account, though doing more important work than many who have that qualification'.[2]

It was a category of beneficiaries that future testators and donors were encouraged to bear in mind. In 1933, Sir Frederick C. Gardiner (Dean of Guild in 1923 and 1924, and a Director for over twenty years), and his brother William Guthrie Gardiner, created the Gardiner Fund, 'in order that the Directors may be enabled . . . to deal with more cases of those who have no membership claim in the House, direct or indirect, but who while not in business on their own account, have occupied important and responsible positions'.[3] The brothers and their trustees eventually added £8,500 to their gift of £10,000. This made a substantial increase to the funds set aside for assisting the growing class of men who had held managerial positions, and their dependants.

Another great Glasgow shipowner, Lawrence Glen, left one-third of his estate in 1938 – finally amounting to over £65,000 – 'for the general charitable and benevolent purposes of the House without any restriction for membership qualification'. Lawrence Glen founded the shipowning and shipping company Glen and Co., which owned and managed several shipping companies, including the Scandinavian Shipping Co., and did a very large amount of trade with Scandinavian countries. He was responsible for much philanthropic work and giving in Glasgow, all done behind the scenes, in accordance with his modest and retiring personality.

It was in 1926 that the Inverclyde Bequest (see Chapter 7) started to operate, with committees in England, Ireland and the United States administering the part of the funds, and reporting annually to the Directors. The Scottish share was distributed among various carefully selected seamen's charities.

The Gardiner brothers

The shipping firm of James Gardiner and Co. was founded by the brothers James, Frederick and William Gardiner, who were cousins of Sir James Guthrie the artist. The brothers were sons of the manse, and attributed much of their self-discipline and later public spirit to the influence of their mother, who had brought up a family of eight on a slender stipend. After long and strenuous working lives, culminating in the firm's sale of a fleet of fourteen cargo steamers to the government in 1917, William retired from the business, and he and Frederick gave and raised very large amounts of money for charitable and educational organisations. The two brothers jointly endowed four chairs at Glasgow University, in organic chemistry, physiological chemistry, bacteriology and music, and later founded a lectureship in pathology in connection with the Sick Children's Hospital (the endowments totalling £94,000).

Frederick suffered from asthma all his life, and had spent six years in New Zealand for the sake of his health, returning to join his brothers' business. Although he was a major benefactor of Glasgow University, his delicate health as a child and young man had deprived him of school and university, and he used to claim, without foundation, 'I am completely uneducated.' He had largely made up for his lack of formal education by reading and was a great lover of literature. He personally gave £20,000 to various youth organisations and charities, and jointly with his brother William's trustees gave £20,000 to the Western Infirmary for a new medical institute.

William lived in Stirling and was instrumental in getting the new Stirling Royal Infirmary built. He was by nature a shy and retiring man, and did not follow his brother into public life. His great forte was in extracting charitable donations from unlikely sources, and stories were told of his bold approaches to donors.

Other important benefactions of this time included £5,000, 'to be used as the Directors think proper', left by Dr Robert T. Moore, Dean of Guild in 1925 and 1926. Robert Moore was the first Doctor of Science and the first civil engineer to be Dean of Guild. He had distinguished himself as a student at Glasgow University (from the age of fifteen), and served his apprenticeship as a civil engineer in the mining industry. He had a career of outstanding brilliance and became an authority on all branches of mining in his home country and abroad, including South Africa, Calcutta and San Francisco. He was a director of Dixon's Blazes, the Dalmellington Company, Clyde Ironworks and several other mining companies in Scotland, and a director of the Clyde Valley Electricity Company.

The Second World War

The Second World War was much more clearly anticipated than the first. In April 1939, a sub-committee of Directors was already considering the safeguarding of the building against air raids. Air-raid shelters were provided in the basement, blackout and fire-fighting equipment was supplied, and arrangements were made for the officer of the House and his family to be available at all times 'for the defence of the roof which is flat'. A committee was appointed from among the House's tenants to manage the shelters and the fire-watching, which gave rise to months of disputes and negotiations between the tenants and the Directors.

The only damage done to the Merchants House building was mercifully slight, and occurred on 18 September 1940, when the building was struck,

> . . . *a basement window in Messrs. Robb and Crosbie's office having been broken by a small splinter from a bomb which fell in George Square, and a square of plain window glass (not stained glass) of the Hall was broken by a lump of concrete (apparently thrown up from the pavement in George Square broken by the bomb) which struck the wire netting protecting the cupola over the entrance to the Hall at 30 George Square and bounced off it against the glass.*[4]

The portraits were put into storage, arranged by Dr T. Honeyman of the Art Galleries, for the duration of the war. The marble busts of James Ewing and James Buchanan were stored in the basement, along with the memorial boards and the model ship. The statue of Kirkman Finlay was too heavy to be moved and had to remain where it was, as did the Archibald Ingram bas-relief over the fireplace. The stained glass windows had to take their chance as well, and fortunately survived unscathed. Special blackout curtains were ordered for the Hall.

The Directors were asked for their consent for the Bridgegate Steeple to be used as a stance for fire-watching. This they gave, on condition that the local Fire Prevention Committee would make good any damage done in the course of their operations, and that 'every precaution would be taken to prevent attracting the attention of the enemy'. They were not much reassured by a reply from the secretary of the committee that 'he was sure none of the fire fighters would be inclined to advertise to the enemy the position of the Steeple as their own framework would be of more consequence than a lifeless Steeple'.[5]

During the war the House of course contributed to the various organisations for war work and war relief: the City of Glasgow Central War Relief Fund, the British Red Cross Society, the St Andrews Ambulance Association, Glasgow YMCA, the Clydeside Air Raid Distress Fund, the Glasgow Sailors' Home for Additional Wartime Accommodation, and the Shipwrecked Mariners' Society, among several others.

New regulations

One of the Directors during the war years was a man with the instincts of a reformer, John Dallas, who felt that the qualifications for membership of the House should be made clearer (Fig. 8.2). He also wanted to review the arrangements for choosing Directors and the committees which carried on the active work of the House, and advised that the system of paying pensions and the attention given to each case should be overhauled in a way which would ensure greater care for individual needs. It was appropriate that his campaign should have begun at a time when thoughts were beginning to turn towards the creation of the post-war welfare state; in this way the House was able to adapt to meet the new situation.

Fig. 8.2   John Dallas

John Dallas's business career began in the Royal Bank of Scotland, and he later joined the firm of Dallas Ltd., warehousemen, of which he became head. From 1904 until 1908 he served as councillor for the Cowcaddens ward, which was one of the outlets for his lifelong interest in social work, in particular the improvement of housing. He was a member of the Merchants House from 1905, and a Director from 1938 almost continuously until his death in 1950, aged seventy-seven.

As regards membership the House had, in fact, been broadening its base – moving away, almost imperceptibly, from the insistence that all members should be independent business or professional men towards the acceptance of executives who might not always be proprietors, partners or directors of their firms. The Directors of the House were free to choose any who 'may be considered eligible'. In 1942, when John Dallas's proposals were discussed, the Dean of Guild was, for the first time since banker Robert Gourlay at the turn of the century (Chapter 7), a man whose work had been done solely as an executive: Sir Robert Bruce, former editor of the *Glasgow Herald*.

It was decided that men 'of known substantiability and good repute established in Glasgow, or in the West of Scotland with Glasgow connections', might become members if they were:

(a) in business on their own account 'to a substantial extent, or in good practice in a recognised profession other than the Ministry', or

(b) directors, managing directors, managers or other principal officers 'in a considerable business, corporate body, or authority', or

(c) men 'of like standing and qualifications' established elsewhere in Great Britain who were sons of members, or

(d) men 'of recognised eminence or otherwise possessed of qualifications which in the opinion of the Directors would make them desirable Members of the House'.

This was a wider foundation for the twentieth century and one which still preserved the special character and traditions of the Glasgow Merchants.

In the nomination of members for election by the House as Directors new arrangements were made in 1943 to encourage the regular choice of a proportion of new men, without losing the advantages of experience in the work. Every member was to be free to propose names for election at the Annual Meeting, but to ensure that all vacancies were filled, the Directors were to be careful to nominate the required number of candidates. After some years of discussion and experiment the House formally recognised a tradition by which former Lord Deans remained Directors *ex officio*.

In 1942 the Directors were still grouped, as they had been for about a century, in three standing committees. Of these the Committee on Finance, Pensions and Adjustment of Business, which included all the ex-Deans, had for a long time been in effect the executive of the House for most matters. The other two, on Bursaries – covering all the educational interests of the House – and on the Necropolis, were smaller and met less often. In 1943 a new Committee on Pensions was set up to deal with what was unmistakably one of the main functions of the House. Four years later this committee took over educational work also. The permanent Bursaries and Necropolis Committees ceased to exist, the bursaries being dealt with by the Pensions Committee and the Necropolis by the Finance Committee. All Directors were then able to specialise in either the management of finance and general questions or in the House's social work.

The Necropolis

Indeed the Necropolis Committee was soon to lose its reason for existence. The idea of 'a Père la Chaise' had little appeal for twentieth-century Glaswegians, who had ceased to think much about cemeteries, and the House could no longer draw any profit from what had once been its boldest investment. From the mid-1920s onwards members were reminded in every Annual Report that 'from the point of view of revenue the Necropolis is not a desirable asset'. The Necropolis account was in permanent deficit, as the sale of burial places could meet only a fraction of the running costs, and this was a drain on the finances of the House.

As early as 1939 the Directors had considered building a crematorium on the Necropolis to increase the income from it, but at first this was rejected as too expensive. Ten years later, however, serious consideration was again given to the idea. A Provisional Order of Parliament was obtained for the erection of a crematorium in 1950, and an architect was commissioned to draw up plans and obtain costs. A sub-committee of the House presented the case to the Directors in 1952:

The House had performed a needful public service when it had turned the Firpark
into a Necropolis at a time when Cemeteries were much needed. Cremation was
merely a later development of the same work. . . . [T]he House had a duty to maintain
the Necropolis in good order and . . . it would be justified in erecting a Crematorium
which would not only pay for itself but also cover the annual loss on the Necropolis
and so provide additional revenue for the charitable purposes of the House.[6]

There was at this time no public crematorium in Glasgow. The projected costs,
however, were high, and the House's financial position had become weaker with
a fall in the value of its stocks and shares. Matters not in the control of the Merchants
House might stand in the way of its success: the corporation was known to be
considering building a crematorium, which would probably have fairly low charges.
There was a distinct possibility that the project might put the House to considerable
financial loss. And it was felt that 'to some slight extent at least it might affect the
dignity of the House'.[7] After careful consideration of all aspects, the sub-committee
recommended that the plan to build a crematorium should be postponed indefinitely.

In 1966 a special sub-committee on the Necropolis succeeded in negotiating
a transfer of the cemetery to Glasgow Corporation, on payment by the Merchants
House of £50,000 (nearly half of which represented the funds received by the House
for the upkeep of particular monuments).

Reorganisation of pensions

The new structure of committees was the first part of the reorganisation. The second
part, also urged by John Dallas, was concerned with the administration of pensions.
He was anxious that the fullest use should be made of the funds of the House –
during the War and just before it, when needs had been rather less pressing, these
had sometimes been allowed to accumulate. He urged that scales of payments should
be adapted both to the rise of prices and to the development of state Old Age
Pensions. Pensioners, he argued, ought to be visited in their homes by Directors,
who could get to know them and their circumstances. In 1949, shortly before the
death of John Dallas, the first Lady Visitor, Miss Joanne G. Warren, was appointed to
maintain such contacts.

John Dallas left a bequest to the House of £10,000, to establish the Simon Dallas
Fund for Maiden Ladies, in memory of his brother. It was for daughters of
businessmen 'whose financial circumstances have substantially deteriorated; . . .
preference shall . . . be given to any ladies who have given loyal and devoted service
to aged parents'. After all his years of work for the House, he had a clear idea of the
kind of social situation he wanted to alleviate:

The reduced value of money, the heavy burden of taxation and the limited income
derived from small investments have changed the position of many maiden ladies of
good education, and, without limiting the power of the Directors, I may say that the
object of this bequest is partly to assist those, the amount of whose income may
disqualify them for Government Old Age Pensions. The ownership of any capital,
other than a dwelling house, in excess of £1,500 should be taken into consideration

in deciding upon grants, and it is my wish that the pensioner be visited at least every
second year by a Director of the House, and that grants . . . be sent to the recipients
each half-year by post and that such recipients be not required to call for payment. [8]

John Dallas also dedicated a window in Glasgow Cathedral to the memory of his
brother Simon. This window is between the Merchants House window (Fig. 8.3) and
the Trades House window – a position that might be regarded as symbolic, as John
Dallas had a foot in both camps, so to speak. He was a member of six of the Trades
Incorporations, and Deacon of the Tailors Incorporation in 1920. In 1922 he was
elected Collector of the Trades House, and helped to inaugurate the Commonweal
fund of that House. He was known by the many public and charitable bodies in
which he was involved for his progressive outlook and his ability to put
improvements into practice. The residue of his estate, amounting to between £60,000
and £70,000, formed the Dallas Benevolent Fund, to be administered by eight
trustees, including one from the Merchants House, for the benefit of people in
reduced circumstances.

A steady stream of bequests and gifts

Other important legacies came to the House at this time, including one of £19,400 in
1947 from David Johnstone Smith, a public-spirited accountant and a former Director
of the House, whose grandfather, Stewart Smith, had been Dean of Guild in 1829 and
1830. The bequest in 1953 from Merchants House member P. D. Ridge-Beedle of
three-quarters of his estate eventually totalled £38,800. Each of these major bequests
left the House free to use the money for those in need without membership
restriction.

Sir George Arthur Mitchell, Dean of Guild in 1933 and 1934, chairman and director
of several colliery companies, was a nationally respected authority on mining and the
coal and steel industries. His will established a Trust Fund, from which the Merchants
House was granted £10,000, for the purpose of giving grants to charitable institutions
or associations in the city. Smaller sums of money could be put to good use too: an
anonymous gift of £1,000 by an ex-Director in 1958 made it possible for all
pensioners to be granted the means for taking a holiday.

A legacy of 1965 gave the House the William Clements Simpson Bequest Fund of
some £20,000, to help 'necessitous Christian widows or unmarried daughters' of
Glasgow merchants or professional men, and to make grants to charitable institutions
and organisations in the city and its environs. In 1966 the House received from
Daniel Duncan, Dean of Guild in 1961 and 1962, investments to the value of £9,497,
the income to be used for charitable purposes other than educational.

In the first part of the twentieth century the House took on many responsibilities of
an educational nature, providing representatives on the boards of many institutions
and endowments, especially after the Educational Endowments (Scotland) Acts 1928
to 1935 reconstituted or amalgamated several of Glasgow's educational trusts and
endowments. It also acquired a major educational bursary of its own, thanks to one
of the more unusual legacies in favour of the House between the wars. George Craig

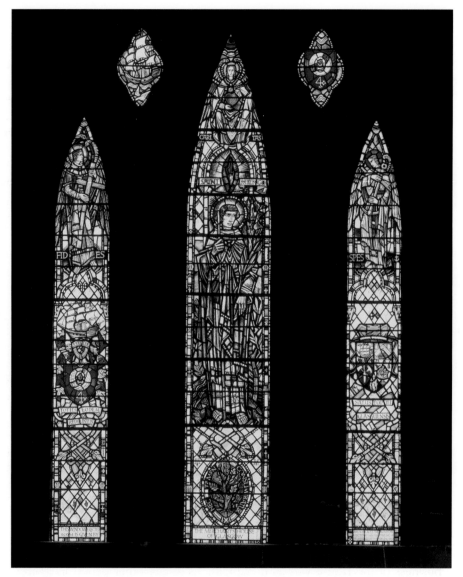

Fig. 8.3   The Merchants House window in Glasgow Cathedral (artist: William Wilson)
The first meeting of the Society of Friends of Glasgow Cathedral was held in the Merchants House in 1935. One of its first projects was the renewing of the stained glass. Several years later the Society asked the Merchants House to provide a window and suggested William Wilson as artist. The central panel depicts St Mungo holding the hazel branch upon which he breathed, causing it to burst into flames. The coat-of-arms of the House and that of the Dean of Guild Court are in the side-lights. Faith, Hope and Charity represent the benevolent purposes of the House. (Wilson's original sketch had a design based on the signs of the zodiac in the side-lights, but this did not meet with the Directors' approval.) The top-lights show the ship and the badge. A service of dedication for the window was held in November 1954. In the same year the House met the cost of the remodelling of four of the pews in the quire, with the badge of the House on the side panels.

was a consulting chemist and chemical engineer who left his estate, after payment of legacies, to the Merchants House 'for the upbringing, training and educating of orphans, of Scottish parentage exclusively, with the object of dissociating them from their surroundings (which could throw them back a generation) and making them worthy citizens, or eminent citizens if further help can effect it'. A minute of 1931, the year of George Craig's death, explained a little of the background to the legacy:

> . . . Mr Craig considered that he and the other members of his family had been handicapped in early life by lack of advantages. . . . [W]hat he had in view is to provide secondary education for orphan children considered to have abilities which would benefit by training in better schools, to be supplemented in the case of those who shew sufficient ability by training in a University.[9]

It was not until 1959 that the assets, valued at £58,377, were received by the House. By this time it was found that the terms of the will could not be literally carried out and it was necessary to obtain the authority of the Court of Session to a cy pres scheme to give effect to the general intention of the testator. This enabled the fund to begin in 1960 paying out grants to schoolchildren and students, especially those with some difficult circumstance in the family background. It was also necessary in 1959 to consider how far the funds must be invested in trustee securities.

This led, in 1960–1, to a further reorganisation of the whole funds of the House. A Financial Adviser was appointed, and after the Directors had obtained a favourable opinion from W. I. R. Fraser, QC (later Lord Fraser, a Senator of the College of Justice), the funds were rearranged in three groups: a 'General Pool' of those which were not restricted to trustee securities and where there was power to spend capital; the 'Hamilton Pool', where investment powers were unrestricted, but capital must not be spent; and a Trustee Pool, including the great majority of special mortifications and bequests, where trustee securities must be held. The arrangements for the last pool were modified to take advantage of the wider power of investment of trust funds allowed by the Trustee Investments Act 1961. There was a temporary drop in the value of the House's funds as a result of these changes, but they put its financial affairs on a more firm foundation for the future.

The twentieth-century collectorship

The business of the House was as demanding as at any other period in its history, and it was well served by its two collectors. Dr James A. McCallum died in April 1948, still in office after thirty-six years' service as Collector and Clerk (Fig. 8.4). He had helped to guide the House through a time of rapid social change. 'His high sense of duty, courtesy and dry humour', the Annual Report recorded, 'won for him the esteem and affection of all who knew him and, not least, those who were the beneficiaries of the House, to whom he was a wise, kindly and sympathetic friend'. James Alexander McCallum, LL.D. had become a partner in Hill and Hoggan in 1896, after a brilliant university career and several years of lecturing in jurisprudence. His work involved him in close connection with some of the city's oldest institutions: Hutchesons' Hospital; Hutchesons' Educational Trust; the Royal College of Physicians and Surgeons (he was made an honorary fellow, the first laymen ever to attain this honour); and of course the Merchants House. 'Had one not known the variety of his other interests,' stated his obituary,

> *one might have thought that Dr. McCallum lived for that ancient institution. To him, its very stones were dear. It may be that sometimes his veneration for its traditional practices caused him to attempt to delay innovations, but his motive was always understood and respected. No Dean of Guild and no director who ever had the privilege of serving the House with him could fail to marvel at the unerring instinct with which he guided its affairs.*[10]

He presented Glasgow University with his large and important collection of engravings and etchings, which had previously all been displayed on the three floors of his office, where he used to invite favoured friends on a Sunday afternoon to view them. A bachelor, he lived at the Western Club, and returned to his office every evening after dinner. A friend once, after dining with him, said that he was going home. 'So am I,' said Dr McCallum. 'The office is my home.'

Fig. 8.4 James A. McCallum
Collector of the Merchants House, 1912–48

In 1947 T. L. Grahame Reid, WS, a descendant of James Hill of Cartside (see Chapter 4), and a great-nephew of Dr W. H. Hill (Chapter 7), was appointed Joint Collector and Clerk (Fig. 8.5). On Dr McCallum's death, T. L. Grahame Reid became the sole Collector and Clerk, only the third to hold the position in a hundred years, and the fifth of his family to do so. He too continued in office until his death, in 1969, by which time the family had provided Collectors for 135 out of 200 years. He was also a descendant of Helen Hutcheson, sister of the brothers who founded the famous Hospital, with which he was, again, closely associated in a professional capacity. His colleagues in the Merchants House summed him up:

> *Character today is in some senses an old fashioned word but it still conveys to us a man possessed of individuality, integrity and high moral qualities and that is exactly what he was.*[11]

He was succeeded in the Collectorship by his colleague in Hill and Hoggan, J. D. Mackenzie.

Fig. 8.5   T. L. Grahame Reid
Collector of the Merchants House, 1948–69.

An unbroken succession

This period saw a shift in the background of Deans of Guild. The succession of captains of industry that stood at the helm throughout the later nineteenth century began to give way to the distinguished accountants and lawyers who have filled the office in the later twentieth century and beyond. The tradition of shipowners had continued, represented by Sir Frederick Gardiner, and also George W. Service (Dean of Guild in 1931 and 1932), Claud A. Allan (1935 and 1936), William Cuthbert (1939 and 1940), and Lord Maclay (1953 and 1954). The only shipbuilder to be Dean of Guild in the twentieth century, in 1921 and 1922, was Sir Alexander Gracie, engineering director and then chairman and managing director of the Fairfield Company, though there were Deans from other engineering backgrounds: Robert T. Moore (1925 and 1926) and Sir George A. Mitchell (1933 and 1934), both respected authorities on mining. Charles Ker (1927 and 1928) was the first Chartered Accountant to be elected Dean, and he was followed by quite a succession, including Andrew S. Macharg (later Sir Andrew) in 1943 and 1944, D. Norman Sloan in 1945 and 1946, Norman MacLeod in 1947 and 1948, and Sir David Allan Hay in 1951 and 1952. The first solicitor to be Dean of Guild was Richard H. Barclay, in 1975 and 1976.

The last days of council representation

The House's internal organisation was in a healthy condition by the middle of the century, but its external affairs were more problematic. The position of the Dean of Guild and Deacon Convener on the city corporation had come under attack in 1935, when the corporation brought a Bill before Parliament for a wide-ranging programme of reforms. It was opposed by an equally wide range of institutions that included the Merchants House, Trades House, Chamber of Commerce and Faculty of Procurators. The Bill was rejected on its second reading. Another attempt to exclude *ex officio* representatives from the council in 1944 was just as vigorously resisted:

> *The Houses have chosen men of ability and standing for these offices, who have been desirable acquisitions to the Corporation, and now they form the direct means by which the business community of Glasgow, which the two Houses represent, can express its opinion in the Corporation.*[12]

An incident in 1949 brought the issue to the fore again and focused unfriendly attention on the *ex officio* members. These positions had become more delicate as elected councillors had come to be organised in political parties during the course of the century. For sixteen years the Labour Party had enjoyed a majority on the council, but this was beginning to be encroached on by candidates of the other main group in Glasgow, the Progressive Party. The Progressives, though not aligned to any national party, were dominated by Unionists from the start. They had their origins in a former loose grouping of Moderates of various non-Socialist parties and individuals; they took an anti-Labour, anti-nationalisation stance and campaigned on reining in public expenditure, preserving civil liberties, and improving housing and social welfare. At the council elections of 3 May 1949, fifty-six Labour councillors and fifty-five of the Progressive Party were returned. This left the two *ex officio* members of the council, the Dean of Guild and the Deacon Convener, holding the balance of power. The new Lord Provost was due to be elected on 6 May, and all Glasgow waited to see what would happen. The Dean of Guild, Lord Inverclyde, was in France, and flew back in time to take his place in the packed council chamber. He and the Deacon Convener, Douglas Macnaughton, voted for the Progressive candidate, Victor Warren (later Sir Victor, a former Unionist parliamentary candidate), who was duly elected by a margin of one vote.

There was outraged protest from the council's Labour group, which immediately renounced control of all the convenerships of the various committees, and continued to refuse to compromise and accept the Progressives' offer of coalition government – in effect surrendering the city to Progressive control. They did not deny that the *ex officio* members had the statutory right to vote, but they argued that 'for the Progressive Party to take advantage of the adventitious aid of members not returned by the electorate is to endanger the foundations of democratic government'.[13]

Supporters of the Dean and Deacon's action argued that it was not so very undemocratic an outcome: though the Progressives were left with one fewer seat, they had actually taken 30,000 more votes. Some even argued that this redress of an electoral imbalance was a reason for retaining and valuing these historic seats on the council.[14] A parliamentary inquiry, which reported the following year, concluded that the offices were outmoded and had been abused, but did not deem further action to be appropriate at the moment. By 1952 Labour were back in control of the council.

Relations between the council and the two former 'burgess institutions' were very badly strained by the affair. The corporation attempted to abolish the *ex officio* seats on the council in 1957, but this was resisted by the Merchants and Trades Houses and ultimately rejected by the Commons.

A Private Member's Bill by Willie Hamilton, MP in 1964 resulted in a compromise. The Bill proposed to exclude *ex officio* members from the corporations of Glasgow, Edinburgh, Aberdeen, Dundee and Perth. There were prolonged negotiations and it was finally agreed that Deans of Guild and their colleagues should retain their places on the city councils but with the right to vote only in committees, not in full council meetings. The change became law in August 1965, as part of the Local Government (Scotland) Act 1947 (Amendment) Act 1965. It was the last flourish of the Merchants and Trades Houses' assertion of the right to a formal voice in city affairs.

The House's handbook of 1971–2 could still describe the Merchants House as 'an Elective Incorporation, connected with the Municipality' and 'a Political Association, in so far as, when occasion requires, it takes cognizance of questions affecting the social, commercial, and other interests of the community'. In fact its political role had been falling into abeyance in the course of the century – it joined other groups in putting pressure on the government over the taxation of land values in 1931, and it supported the Faculty of Procurators in 1935 in (unsuccessfully) opposing measures in the Housing (Scotland) Act. But otherwise its representations to Parliament were largely confined to opposing the city corporation's attempts to exclude the Dean of Guild and Deacon Convener from the council. In 1972 when the Royal Commission was due to report on the position of non-elected posts in local government, both Merchants House and Trades House were prepared to accept that these would be abolished. The new order took effect from 1975. Perhaps the surprising thing is that they had retained their formal 'connection with the Municipality' for so long.

New institutions for a new age

Although the House had held on to a voice in the government of the city in 1965, it did not protest when the creation of a new Clyde Port Authority on 1 January 1966 broke its old links with the administration of Glasgow's river. The Clyde Navigation Trust, on which it had two representatives, and the Clyde Lighthouses Trust, on which it had one, disappeared under the new organisation.

When the National Health Service was created the endowed hospitals, which the House had helped to found or support, lost their independence, and there was no longer any need for representatives on their governing bodies. By that time, the House had representatives on around fourteen of these hospital boards, including all the main Glasgow hospitals. In 1948, however, the new authority for these matters, the Western Regional Hospital Board, invited the House to recommend individuals to serve on the boards of management of the various groups of hospitals. An active interest dating from 1787 when the House subscribed for the building of Glasgow's first general hospital, the Royal Infirmary, was thereby continued. At the same time, in order to maintain the voluntary objects and encourage public interest in hospital services and patient welfare, the Glasgow Hospitals Auxiliary Association was formed, to which the House sent a representative. In 1974 the regional hospital boards were replaced by Health boards, with no business representation, and thus ended another chapter in the House's public service.

The years between 1914 and 1975 had seen crises and storms both for the nation and for the House, but it was the important work done quietly in the background that, as so often, secured and strengthened the House's role for the next generation. The augmentation of its funds by generous donors had made it one of Glasgow's foremost charitable organisations. Vital work was done in reorganising and securing the funds, in extending the assistance of the House to a wider class of beneficiary, in broadening the membership, in reforming the committee structures, and in updating the administration of pensions. At a time of enormous social and economic change in Britain, these changes ensured that the Merchants House would continue to make a difference to the lives of Glasgow people for the rest of the twentieth century and beyond.

Notes

1. Merchants House Annual Report 1923.
2. Ibid. 1927.
3. Ibid. 1933.
4. MH Minutes, 4 Nov. 1940.
5. Ibid., 6 Oct. 1941.
6. Ibid., 10 June 1952.
7. Ibid., 10 Mar. 1953.
8. Ibid., 6 March 1950.
9. Ibid., 1 June 1931.
10. *Glasgow Herald*, 5 April 1948.
11. MH Minutes, 14 Jan. 1969.
12. MH Annual Report 1944.
13. *Glasgow Herald*, 13 May 1949.
14. *The Bulletin*, 18 May 1949.

FOUR CENTURIES YOUNG

The House and the city

When the Local Government (Scotland) Act 1973 abolished non-elected posts on town councils, the Merchants House accepted with grace the end of the Lord Dean of Guild's position on Glasgow's local governing body. Lord Dean of Guild William MacKinlay saw the House safely through the transition, and its independence and control over its assets were preserved. Lord Provost Peter McCann, first Lord Provost of the new Glasgow District Council, extended an official invitation to the Dean of Guild and the Deacon Convener to attend meetings of the council, as honorary members, without the right to speak or vote. It was a courteous and welcome acknowledgement that the council valued formal links with the Merchants House and Trades House, and that the Lord Dean and Deacon Convener still had a role to play in the civic life of the city. The Lord Dean of Guild was – and still is – the second citizen of Glasgow.

Although formal links had been preserved, relations were not cordial – the events of the past three decades had cast a rather chilly pall over the relationship. It was thanks to the efforts of one man in particular that this was lifted – George Teacher Dunlop, Lord Dean in 1981 and 1982. In October 1981 he invited Lord Provost Michael Kelly to attend a quarterly meeting of Directors, the first official visit of a Lord Provost to the Merchants House. The Lord Provost addressed the meeting, and mentioned his appreciation of the close ties between the Merchants House and the District Council. George Dunlop's successor as Dean, Bonar G. Hardie, continued to foster this friendly relationship, as have Lord Deans since.

Upon the reorganisation of the municipal structure that took place in 1995–6, there was official confirmation that the Lord Dean would continue to be invited to attend meetings of the full council in an honorary capacity. Successive Lord Deans have been very regular attenders at these meetings. They speak only on their first appearance, when they are welcomed, and on their last, at the end of their period of office, but their presence on the council is a sign of the close interest they take in matters affecting Glasgow. During the local authority elections there is a fortnight's interregnum, during which the Lord Provost stands aside. At these times the Lord Dean and Deacon Convener deputise for the Lord Provost – for example, by hosting civic receptions.

In the course of the municipal year, the Lord Provost and bailies are required to attend an ever increasing number of civic events. The availability of the Lord Dean and his wife to attend these events in support of the provost and bailies is seen by the council as a very valuable contribution to civic affairs and the promotion of the life and business of the city. The historical background and activities of the Merchants House and its leader are often of interest to visiting dignitaries and guests with whom they come into contact on these occasions. During each deanship, hundreds of such events are attended: Lord Dean James S. Laird noted in July 1999 that, in the brief period since his appointment at the beginning of March of that year, he had represented the Merchants House on eighty-six occasions. In the course of special year-long city initiatives, such as the 1988 Garden Festival, there is increased civic entertaining, and an opportunity to raise the profile of the House, as when Lord Dean Peter Paisley, in his capacity as director of Glasgow Opportunities, led a reception for His Royal Highness The Prince of Wales in the Merchants' Hall on the occasion of the Prince's visit to Glasgow in April 1988.

In a reciprocal gesture of courtesy, several Lord Deans have invited the Lord Provost of their time to become a full member of the House. Others have invited the Lord Provost to dinner in the House. On a personal level, several provosts have found that the moral support of a second citizen outside the hurly-burly of local politics makes their job less isolated. The most notable example in recent years was the 'exceptional support' given to Lord Provost Pat Lally by Lord Dean David McVicar at the time of his expulsion from the Labour Party (on charges from which he was later fully exonerated).[1]

The Lord Dean's other major function before local government reform had been to preside over the Dean of Guild Court. This was formally abolished in May 1975 and replaced by the Building Control Committee of the District Council. The Lord Dean of Guild at the time was Richard Barclay, the first solicitor to hold the office, and it was his task to wind the Court up. The Court's offices, which were practically its only remaining asset, were sold, and the Dean of Guild and his eight lyners with the Deacon Convener formed the Dean of Guild Court Trust to administer the residuary funds. This was achieved only after seeing off a challenge from the District Council to the trust's right to the funds. Lord Deans William MacKinlay and Richard Barclay and their fellow Directors, along with their Trades House counterparts, succeeded in preserving the Court as an independent trust with control over its assets, and the council's interest was represented by the appointment of three additional trustees nominated by the council. The Letter of Guildry provided that the fines of the Court were to be used for 'ony guid and godlie workis as they think guid', and so the funds of the trust are now used for charitable purposes, particularly to support appeals which are connected with the city's built heritage. In an echo from the Glasgow of four hundred years ago, four 'Lyners and Brethren' are still appointed annually to be trustees of the Dean of Guild Court Trust on behalf of the Merchants House. In 2002 the trust donated £30,000, payable over three years, to the Kelvingrove Refurbishment Appeal Trust, in support of its complete refurbishment of the city's landmark museum and art gallery. It has pledged to provide a substantial contribution towards the cost of erecting a monument in the Merchant City to honour 400 years of the Merchants House and the Trades House, 1605–2005.

Fig. 9.1   The Lord Dean of Guild and ex-Deans, 1983–2004
Back row: James S. Laird, David McVicar, Morrison Dunbar, J. H. Forbes Macpherson, David H. Galbraith, Geoffrey C. C. Duncan.
Front row: Peter C. Paisley, Bonar G. Hardie, Andrew H. Primrose, Alastair K. Denholm, David W. Duguid.

A benevolent institution

As the Merchants House enters its fifth century, having relinquished its political role, benevolence to the people of Glasgow and West of Scotland continues to be its primary object. Historically the House had directed its benevolence towards those with membership qualifications or, latterly, with some connection with the mercantile community, but during the twentieth century applications from such persons became less frequent and the House reorganised its funds to enable it to give assistance where it was needed. The Pensions Committee welcomed applications from deserving people without membership qualification, whose circumstances had changed and who found themselves in need of help. The friendly contact and assistance that the House has been able to offer have eased the lives of many hundreds of Glasgow people over the years, especially, but not only, the elderly.

In September 1978 the first pensioners' tea parties were held in the Merchants' Hall, attended by more than a hundred of the House's pensioners and their friends. Housebound pensioners were visited by Directors over the course of the year. These events were replaced a few years later by pensioners' lunches, always well attended and much enjoyed. A Christmas gift and a winter heating allowance, sums which have been increased over the years, are given to all the pensioners, and 'precepts', or grants for special purposes such as installing a shower or paying for a television licence, are often given.

Mrs Penelope Robinson was Lady Visitor from 1981 till 1999, personifying the House's friendship and usefulness to very many pensioners over that time. She was succeeded by Mr Ewan Macbeth from 1999 till 2003. Mrs Mary McNicol was appointed towards the end of 2003, taking over the role of Visitor as well as that of secretary, the latter post on the retiral of Miss Anne Walsh who had been an efficient and welcoming presence in the Merchants House office for thirty-three years.

Pensioners of the House

Mrs Penelope Robinson, Lady Visitor, 1981–99:
'All the pensioners – there were about a hundred of them – had some connection with business people of Glasgow. One was an old lady who lived to a hundred. Her father had had a little manufacturer's agency, her brother was killed in the Glasgow Highlanders in the First World War, so this lady took the business on – she never made any money at all, she just had her basic pension, and a tiny bit extra. Others were unmarried daughters of war widows – First World War widows – who were expected to stay and look after mother, and were trained for nothing, and when mother died they were in their sixties and seventies, and they had nothing – they had never had enough money to pay National Insurance, some of them didn't even have an old age pension, or just the very basic one. One lady, whose father was killed in the Boer War, had worked in a shipping office all her life and been given a pension of £2 a week – she was very grateful for it – she had spent her whole working life as someone's secretary and she got £2 a week, but that at that time was just enough to put her above the income support level, so she got the minimum in benefits. When I first started, the Merchants House pension was £300 a year – and that £300 could make a lot of difference.

'It wasn't their fault that they were struggling – some had just had rather dreary lives. It meant so much to them to have that little extra to cover emergencies, or to go on a bus trip – or they might spend it on a wedding present for a great-nephew or great-niece, and that meant a lot, it gave them a sense of pride. I very much admired them. It was a delightful job and I enjoyed it enormously. I certainly enjoyed talking to them and I think they rather enjoyed my visits. I was someone to talk to and tell if they'd had a bad day. The Merchants House made a big difference to a lot of my old ladies.

'One of the elderly ladies – a delightful person, who was living in a nursing home and had no relatives – asked me if I would take her little dog after she died. I had wee Sandy – a thirteen-year-old Yorkshire terrier – for six years. She was so relieved that I had agreed to take "her most precious possession" – and the pleasure was mine, he was a lovely little dog, and after he came to us he went on holidays and did things he had never done in his life!'

The work of the Visitor and of the committees of the House would not be possible without the backup of a dedicated team. The role of Collector, filled since 1985 by David Ballantine, has changed over the years from a managerial to an advisory one. The Collector is involved in all the developments of the House, especially with regard to legal matters, and for some years has had an assistant on the administrative side. From 1969 until 1986 this was John McFarlan, a stalwart of the House who returned after his retiral for several years to help with the pension work. In 1986 A. Dick Barr was appointed Assistant to the Collector, and dealt with administration and management in the office until 2001, when A. James K. Dykes took over as Assistant Collector. The Officer of the House since 1989 has been Ted Norman.

The experience of the House in administering investment funds, interviewing pensioners, considering applications from appeals and charities, and making grants, is very considerable. In 1992 the funds of the Glasgow Corn Trade Benevolent Association, totalling some £190,000, were taken into the care of the Merchants House, to be administered by the House on condition of maintaining the existing pensioners of the Association. The revenue is applied preferentially for the benefit of the Corn Trade pensioners (twelve in 1992), who were brought under the aegis of the Merchants House, and who are visited and invited to the pensioners' lunches along with the Merchants House pensioners. The expertise of the House is thus used for the benefit of a small charity, reducing its administrative costs and securing the objects of its benefactions for the future, and this is a function that the House hopes to extend to other such trusts and charities in years to come.

As public sector budgets have become more restricted for cultural and welfare purposes, the House has received an increasing number of appeals for assistance from charities and institutions previously sustained by public grants. Many such appeals, for specific projects, are received each year, and all are given close attention by the Finance Committee at its monthly meetings. Assistance is given to organisations of various kinds in Glasgow and the West of Scotland, including those that care for the disabled, elderly or ill; those concerned with the welfare and advancement of young people; educational institutions; organisations for the promotion of music, theatre and the visual arts; and those with which the Dean of Guild is connected in an honorary capacity or on which the Merchants House is officially represented (see below).

Beneficiaries of Merchants House grants in 2003

Age Concern Scotland
Bobath
Braendam Family House
Breast Cancer Care Scotland
British Blind Sport
British Red Cross
Citizens Theatre
Clyde Sail Training Trust
Common Wheel
CommunicAbility
Cosgrove Care/Walton
Craigholme School

Cruse Bereavement Care
Doors Open Day
East Park Home
Elpis Centre
Embroiderers' Guild
Girl Guiding Glasgow
Girls' Brigade: Greater Glasgow
Glasgow – the Caring City
Glasgow Braendam Link
Glasgow Old People's Welfare Association
Hansel Village
HIV-Aids Carers Family Support
Hopscotch Holidays for Kids
Lead Scotland
Mark Scott Foundation
Momentum (ReHab Scotland)
National Association of Toy and Leisure Libraries
National Burns Memorial Homes
National Listening Library
National Youth Choir of Scotland
National Youth Orchestra of Scotland
REACT
Sargent Cancer Care Children Scotland
Scottish Opera
Scottish Refugee Council
Society of Friends of Glasgow Cathedral
Starter Pack
Tenovus
Trades House Exhibition
Tron Theatre
Viewpark Family Centre
West of Scotland Schools Symphony Orchestra
Westbourne Music
Young Enterprise (Scotland)

In 1991, at the time of the first Gulf War, the House presented a cheque for £10,000 to the Soldiers', Sailors' and Airmen's Families Association (SSAFA). The presentation, to Lord Provost Susan Baird, honorary president of the Glasgow branch of the SSAFA, was made at a reception in the Merchants House, at which Lord Dean Morrison Dunbar said that the occasion was a fitting way of showing the city's appreciation of its high regard for our armed services. Another connection with the armed forces has been forged by the hospitality given over the years from 1990 to the captain and officers of HMS *Glasgow*.

Fig. 9.2   The Merchants House model ship

This fine model of an early nineteenth-century trading vessel is on display in the Directors' Room of the Merchants House. Models of merchant, as opposed to naval, vessels of this period are quite rare. There is a similar model in Amsterdam by a Dutch shipwright who served his apprenticeship on the Clyde, and it is likely that this model is by him. A Glasgow history of 1797 mentions a model ship suspended from the ceiling in the old Merchants' Hall in the Bridgegate: this model could just conceivably be of that date, but it is perhaps unlikely that it was the same one, as a model for suspending from a ceiling would be built to a different standard and scale.

Bequests and bursaries

This kind of sustained giving is only possible because of the generosity of those who have continued to make bequests to the House for charitable purposes. In 1981 the House received the largest bequest by far of recent times, a legacy of £88,484 from a bachelor member, Mr W. M. Waugh, who had been in business as a coal importer, and had lived in retirement at Seamill Hydro. The sum was to be used at the discretion of the Directors 'for the charitable purposes' of the House. There were smaller, but still important, bequests, of £4,000 in 1970 from Mrs Mary Gatherar, and £5,844 in 1982 from Miss W. B. Craig. In 2002 the House received a bequest of £50,000 from the estate of Mrs Jessie Wood Stirrat.

The Inverclyde Bequest remains the largest ever given to the House, and it continues to be distributed in the proportions stipulated by the second Lord Inverclyde to seamen's charities in Glasgow, Liverpool and Manchester, Belfast, and New York and Boston. The Pensions Committee each year, with the help of committees in Liverpool and Belfast, examines applications and accounts, and distributes funds to several charitable societies and missions to seafarers: £59,000 was distributed in 2003. There is now no committee in the USA, but instead the funds are distributed directly to two charities which continue to satisfy the terms of the bequest: the Seafarer's Friend (formerly the Boston Seamen's Friend Society) and the Seamen's House YMCA in New York. In 1993, at a lunch in the Merchants House, a plaque was unveiled commemorating the Inverclyde Bequest by Mrs Torrie and her son Robin McLean, members of the family, and a framed copy of a *Spy* cartoon of the second Lord Inverclyde, the only known portrait of him in existence, was gifted to the House and hung in the Committee Room (see Chapter 7).

The Inverclyde Bequest in the twenty-first century

The Scottish Nautical Welfare Society
'We continue to pay regular grants to our beneficiaries, who have worked for a significant part of their lives in the Merchant Navy and now, following illness or retirement, are experiencing difficult times. We have regular personal contact with them, and visit those who are housebound or in hospital. The Social Club is a focal point for retired seafarers, where they can come for lunch and to enjoy social events.'

Sir Gabriel Wood's Mariners' Home, Greenock
'The Inverclyde payments allow us to provide "extras" for our residents, such as activities, outings, physiotherapy and aromatherapy.'

The Mission to Seafarers Scotland
'We undertake pastoral and welfare work with seafarers and their families, with the emphasis on bereavement and cases of seafarers in ill health or retired and needing respite breaks. We also organise ship visits to help seafarers deal with loneliness and financial worries experienced while far from home.'

The Mersey Mission to Seafarers, Liverpool
'We look after the welfare of seafarers who visit the ports of the Mersey. From our diary of September 2003: Latif the Turkish seafarer who nearly lost his arm in a lifeboat accident has been released from hospital and is now staying in a local B & B so that he can visit the hospital for further treatment. Tasliman, an Indonesian seafarer who suffered a damaged elbow after an accident at sea, was in hospital for surgery and we helped in getting him to the airport to go home. We sent a fax of his details to the German Mission in Jakarta and asked them to look after him. We received a call from the Coastguard about an injured fisherman who had been taken to the Isle of Man for treatment. We contacted the Royal National Mission to Deep Sea Fishermen on the island and they visited him.'

The Mission to Seafarers (Northern Ireland)
'In 2003 the Mission staff in Northern Ireland made over 2,000 visits to ships in the Port of Belfast and welcomed nearly 14,200 seafarers to our centres in Belfast and Lisahally. During this year there have been sixty-three welfare cases, some of whom needed financial assistance. The grant provided by the Inverclyde Bequest Fund is usually set aside to support those seafarers who are hospitalised and can be left behind when their ships sail.'

The Northern Ireland Veteran Seamen's Friend (Belfast)
'The Veterans are going from strength to strength. The numbers were up for both the dinner and the summer outing.'

Seafarer's Friend (Boston, USA)
'The year 2003 has been very successful for the Seafarer's Friend. We have seen a dramatic increase in visits to merchant vessels. In September we made 100 visits in the port of Boston, MA alone. Our visits are more vital than they have ever been. Seafarer detention has increased greatly in American ports due to a broad response to the attacks of Sept. 11, 2001. Among detained crew, our most popular service is our onboard mobile phone, which allows seafarers to call home despite their inability to go ashore. We continue to increase our services thanks to your help.'

Seamen's House YMCA, New York
'Seamen's House is a program of the YMCA of Greater New York that offers a range of health education, fitness and technology programs for both active and retired seafarers in the Port of New York and New Jersey. From stress reduction and HIV/AIDS education to fitness programs in union halls and on board ships, Seamen's House has received an overwhelming demand for services.

'In 2003, despite the growing security measures around active seafarers, we have continued to work on board ship bringing Seamen's House services to mariners from all corners of the world. Our technology services, with wireless laptops and free email accounts, continue to prove wildly popular, and our health and wellness program has also improved the lives of active seafarers and the twelve retired seafarers who live in our building.'

The House continues to give grants, relatively small now, from the Buchanan and Ewing Bequests each year (for five years at a time) to several educational institutions in Glasgow: currently the University of Strathclyde, the Chair of Scottish History at the University of Glasgow, a Russian Lectureship at the University of Glasgow, the University of Strathclyde School of Business Administration, Glasgow School of Art, the Institution of Engineers and Shipbuilders in Scotland (Students' Section), the Royal Scottish Academy of Music and Drama and Glasgow Caledonian University.

In 1992 a new Merchants House bursary was established which recalled some of the House's most ancient connections. The Bogle family traces its Glasgow merchant connections back to the Letter of Guildry (two merchant Bogles are recorded in 1605), provided Deans of Guild in the eighteenth and nineteenth centuries, and in the early nineteenth century owned Gilmorehill, where Robert Bogle built a mansion. Both land and house were sold in 1845, and twenty years later were acquired by the University of Glasgow, as the site of the new campus. Later in the century the family, no longer in business as merchants, left Glasgow to live on the Continent. The new bursary, under the name Bogles of Gilmorehill, was donated by Miss Ellen Bogle and her brother Robert Bogle, whose great-great-grandfather Robert had bought the Gilmorehill estate and built the mansion. The endowment of £50,000 was to institute an annual bursary, to be administered by the Merchants House, for a home postgraduate student undertaking a taught masters degree in the Faculty of Divinity or the Faculty of Social Sciences at the University of Glasgow.

The £50,000 donation was realised from the sale of the Bogle family silver, which had lain undisturbed in a Glasgow bank vault for a century. When the family had left Glasgow in the nineteenth century, five chests of silver had been deposited in the vaults of the Union Bank of Scotland. These had been transferred to the Bank of Scotland, and in 1987 Ellen Bogle, then retired, decided to have them opened. The lead-lined oak chests were found to contain a magnificent collection of silverware and silver plate. The contents of three of them were sold, the proceeds going to the bursary fund, and from the other two chests the Bogles presented to the House a pair of candelabra, a tea tray and a salver, which are used on special occasions. A board recording this splendid donation was commissioned, in the style of the House's mortification boards, and hung in the Committee Room, with a plaque recording the presentation to Lord Dean Geoffrey Duncan on behalf of the House. A lunch was held for Miss Bogle in June 1992 at which the presentation was formally made.

The Bogle fund, the first new fund for educational purposes to be established by the House for over thirty years, stimulated a review of all the bursaries and scholarships administered by the House. The individual Merchants House bursaries had been replaced in the late 1970s by the Merchants House Travelling Scholarship, an annual bursary to a Glasgow University student or new graduate to enable the recipient to spend time abroad, either to further career plans or acquire fluency in a foreign language. In 1992 a similar travelling scholarship was instituted for the University of Strathclyde. The bursaries are presented in person by the Lord Dean of Guild in the Merchants House, a gesture that gives expression to the bond between the House and the universities. Two bursaries founded in the seventeenth and eighteenth centuries are still being awarded by the Merchants House: the John Craig Bursary, founded in 1697, for distinction in one of the first-year philosophy classes, and the Boyd and Sanders Bursary, an amalgamation of two bursaries, founded, respectively, in 1635 by Zachary Boyd (see Chapter 3) and in 1728 by Robert Sanders (Chapter 4), for distinction in the first year Bachelor of Divinity course (this had fallen into disuse because the amount was too small to be of use, but was augmented and revived in 1992).

The George Craig Trust Fund, established in 1960, for 'the education of children with the object of making them worthy or eminent citizens', has continued to be administered by a special committee of the House. With around twenty to thirty beneficiaries in any one year, over the years it has provided financial assistance to many pupils at fee-paying schools (who no longer receive government assisted places) and students in higher education. In the 1990s awards to students outnumbered those to pupils by a factor of almost 3 to 2, reflecting the difficulties faced by many undergraduates in funding their university education. In 2003 an increase in expenditure for this fund was made possible by transferring funds from the free revenue of the Morgan Mortification (see Chapter 7), which has helped to keep the level of assistance such as to be of real use, and to satisfy some of the increased demand, especially for assistance with students' higher education expenses.

Fig. 9.3 The royal visit for the jubilee of the Queen's accession, May 2002
His Royal Highness the Duke of Edinburgh meets sub-Dean James S. Laird, ex-Lord Dean David McVicar and Collector David Ballantine.

Historic ties and contemporary connections

One of the historic functions of the Lord Dean of Guild is to act as a director of various institutions and bodies founded for the public good. When Hutchesons' Hospital was founded in 1639 and 1641 by the brothers George and Thomas Hutcheson, they nominated the Dean of Guild as one of the patrons. An Act of Parliament in 1872 extended this representation to include three further members of the Merchants House annually elected to serve as patrons. These functions are still being faithfully carried out year after year by the Lord Dean and his three fellow patrons. The Merchants House presence on the board of this charitable organisation is now more important than ever: in recent years the foundation has in effect been run by the patrons from the Merchants House and Trades House.

Helping to run Glasgow institutions is therefore a very ancient part of the House's work, and public trusts still actively seek the involvement of the Merchants House today. The Merchants House has been represented on the board of the Glasgow Building Preservation Trust since its inception as the Bridgegate Trust in 1982. Lord Dean George Dunlop was a founder and the first chairman, and David Duguid (Lord Dean in 1985 and 1986) was the House's first representative on this body, which rescues, restores and rehabilitates historic buildings. The first project of this new organisation was the renovation of the old fishmarket and its transformation into the Briggait Centre, and so it was particularly appropriate that the House as owner of the Merchants' Steeple in the Briggait should have been involved. Over the years the House has supported the Building Preservation Trust as it has restored and found new uses for, among other buildings, the 'tobacco merchant's house' at 42 Miller Street and St Andrew's in the Square, the important eighteenth-century church off Saltmarket where many merchants used to worship.

The Clyde Maritime Trust, set up in the 1990s to conserve and interpret the maritime history of Glasgow and the Clyde, in particular by restoring and opening to the public Glasgow's Tall Ship, the *Glenlee*, invited the Merchants House to provide a representative for their board in 2003.

Fig. 9.4 The Lord Dean of Guild's chain of office

In recent years the Lord Dean has been invited to join, *ex officio*, the boards of the Glasgow Humane Society (a director) and the Citizens Theatre, and the St Mungo's Prize Committee. He is also the vice-president *ex officio* of the Society of Friends of Glasgow Cathedral. The first meeting of the Friends was held in the Merchants House in 1935, and the House has supported this society with regular grants in recent years. The House has taken a particular interest in the Cathedral since the creation of the Necropolis in the 1830s (see Chapter 5), and in the 1950s gave a lasting memorial in the form of the Merchants House window (see Chapter 8). In the past couple of decades it donated £15,000 for an oak floor for the visitor centre and a similar sum for the organ fund. In 2001 Lord Dean Alastair Denholm led a large delegation of Directors and members attending a ceremony of Kirking of the Merchants House at the Cathedral, initiating what is hoped will be a new tradition.

The Glasgow Humane Society

The Humane Society of Glasgow was founded in 1790 to encourage the rescue of drowning persons and the recovery of bodies from the Clyde. Other cities, including London and Paris, already had such organisations. In 1788 the will of Glasgow merchant James Coulter left £200 in the care of the Faculty of Physicians and Surgeons to set up such a society in Glasgow (see Chapter 4).

A meeting was convened at the Tontine Tavern in August 1790 at which the society was founded. The first president was Gilbert Hamilton, a prominent merchant and Director of the House, who was elected Dean of Guild two months later (see Chapter 5). One of the other directors elected at that meeting was David Dale, the great textile industrialist and mill reformer, who was also a Director of the Merchants House for many years.

The first minutes of the Society laid down that premiums were to be given 'to such as shall exert themselves for recovery of people in danger of death from drowning or other accidents. To the person who first employs the Drag, five shillings, to him who actually finds the body, 5/- or 10/6, or more according to the time elapsing from the disappearance of the body, the highest premium being always given to him who finds the body in the shortest time, to those who assist in carrying the body to a receiving house, or in any other way, premiums in proportion to their exertions and success.'

Soon more bequests swelled the funds, including one of £300 from Laurence Coulter, James Coulter's brother, and a few years later the Society built a boathouse on the riverbank at Glasgow Green, and a house for receiving bodies. In 1859 instead of merely giving prizes to those who rescued people and recovered bodies, the society employed an Officer, and has done so ever since. In a remarkable record of continuity, there have been only four Officers from then till the present: George Geddes I and George Geddes II, and another father and son, Ben Parsonage and George Parsonage.

Over the years the Merchants House has given occasional grants to the Humane Society for such things as building a new house for the Officer. But in recent years, the connection has become firmer than ever. Patrick Barns-Graham, Lord Dean in

1977 and 1978, was for several years chairman of the Society. In April 1978, at a lunch in the City Chambers to honour Ben Parsonage for fifty years of life-saving work (and at least a thousand people rescued), on behalf of the Merchants House he presented Ben with his portrait, commissioned by the House from his son George. In 1980 the Trades House and the Merchants House shared the cost of a new engine for the boat, and further grants were given in 1985 and 1989. In 1990, for the bicentenary, the Merchants House gave a grant of £2,000, and in 1994, 'in view of the very long-standing connection with the Society', the House contributed £6,000, one-third of the cost of a new pontoon barge. In 1998 a grant of £2,000 was made to the Friends of Glasgow Humane Society.

Public institutions and trusts with Merchants House representatives in 2004

- Hutchesons' Hospital (4 patrons, 2 of them members of the executive committee)
- Glasgow Chamber of Commerce
- Glasgow Nursing and Medical Relief Association (formerly the Glasgow District Nursing Association)
- The Muirhead Trust
- Glasgow Educational and Marshall Trust
- General Convocation of the University of Strathclyde
- Adam, Bell, Gibson and Stewart Trust
- Glasgow City Council Central Area Management Committee
- Baillie's Institution
- Dallas Benevolent Fund
- Glasgow Building Preservation Trust
- Clyde Maritime Trust (the *Glenlee*)

The Lord Dean is appointed to the following:
- Adam Smith Chair of Political Economy (representative to the University Court, University of Glasgow)
- National Burns Memorial Cottage Homes, Mauchline (honorary president, *ex officio*)
- Clark (Mile-end) Bursary Fund (trustee)
- Association for the Relief of Incurables (trustee)
- Glasgow Humane Society (a director, *ex officio*)
- Society of Friends of Glasgow Cathedral (vice-president, *ex officio*)
- St Mungo's Prize Committee (*ex officio*)
- Citizens Theatre (*ex officio*)

A building to be proud of

In 1986 Prime Minister Margaret Thatcher commented favourably on the recently improved reputation of the city: 'The people of Glasgow, whose forefathers pioneered trade around the world . . . are now putting these same qualities to work

Fig. 9.5   The Merchants' Hall

in successfully transforming Glasgow.'[2] The Merchants House has played its part in this regeneration of the buildings and streets of central Glasgow which started in the early 1980s and has given the city a place on the international tourist trail. The Glasgow's Miles Better campaign gave a terrific boost to the city's image and economy, the 1988 Garden Festival was closely followed by the year as European City of Culture 1990, and in 1999 Glasgow was United Kingdom City of Architecture and Design. In 2004 Glasgow has launched itself again as Glasgow: Scotland with style. As the city became newly conscious of the glories of its Victorian heritage, columns, pediments and architraves emerged from under thick layers of grime. The exterior of the Merchants House building was the subject of restoration and stone cleaning in the early 1990s, and further refurbishment was carried out in 2001. The globe and ship on the dome now form part of the city's illuminated skyline, in the Lighting Up Glasgow initiative of the new millennium.

The hidden glories of the interior were brought before the public gaze too. The Merchants House, under Lord Dean David Galbraith, took part in Glasgow's first Doors Open Day in September 1990, an idea pioneered by Glasgow, as part of the City of Culture programme, and which has now been taken up by other towns and cities in the country. Over 500 people visited on that first Doors Open Day, to be shown round the superb first-floor interiors by a team of Directors and staff. The House thereafter has made regular grants to Doors Open Day and has continued to open its own doors on the appointed day to a steady and increasing stream of admiring visitors from both home and abroad.

In the last decade of the twentieth century, the Merchants' Hall became a greater asset than ever to the House, with more letting for functions than at any time in the past. Thorough redecoration of the Hall, a rolling programme of portrait cleaning, new seats to replace the old benches, new lighting, fine new lavatories, servery and kitchen facilities have made the Hall a superb venue for dinners, concerts, receptions and large meetings. With its good acoustics, it was found to make a particularly fine concert hall, and at the end of 1989 a Steinway grand piano was purchased, as the Merchants House's contribution to Glasgow's forthcoming year as European City of Culture. The inaugural concert for the new piano, organised by Westbourne Music, was held on 23 January 1990, with soloist Antony Goldstone playing Bach, Beethoven, Chopin and Mussorgsky. This marked the start of Westbourne Music's series of lunchtime concerts in the Hall throughout the City of Culture year, encompassing folk, classical ensemble, cross-genre works and new commissions. It was hailed by the critics as 'one of the most thoughtful music ventures in the whole city of culture calendar'. Westbourne Music's lunchtime concerts thereafter became a regular fixture in the winter months. The concerts, informal affairs with a friendly atmosphere, attract many people who prefer a daytime to an evening event, along with business people from nearby offices, and students from the Royal Academy. World premières and several avant-garde events have kept them in the public eye.

The Merchants House lunchtime concerts

'In this secular cathedral, the composer Rossini, the three musicians, the guest speaker, the notables on the wall, myself, and all those in the audience suddenly in my imagination became everyman and universal. I am grateful to them and thankful for this joyful occasion in Glasgow.'
Edward W. Milner, *The Herald*, 8 October 1992

'[The performers] don't usually take much persuading because it's a lovely hall to play in. . . . We've got a fantastic piano. We're very lucky to have a very good Steinway – and there aren't many halls which do.'
Stephen Strugnell, administrator of Westbourne Music: *The Glaswegian*, 2 December 1999

A musical highlight was the Chopin recital in September 1998, to mark the 150th anniversary of Chopin's appearance at the previous Merchants' Hall in Hutcheson Street (see Chapter 6). The pianist, Murray McLachlan, narrator, Scott Cooper, and soprano, Patricia McMahon, were dressed in period costume, to represent Chopin, his valet, and Madame Giulietta Adelasia. The Polish Consul was invited to attend, and the event was a sell-out and much enjoyed by all present. All the proceeds, along with a generous grant from the House, went to Marie Curie Cancer Care, who used the money to refurbish and modernise their Marie Curie Hunters Hill Centre.

Lettings in the rest of the building, always an important object, have become crucial to the income of the House, particularly since the phasing out of tax relief on dividends from the late 1990s. When tenants have vacated the premises, the opportunity to upgrade the accommodation has been taken, which in turn brings in increased rents. Major work was done on the office accommodation in 1979–81, necessitated by the Offices, Shops and Railway Premises Act 1963, when the offices were reduced in number and increased in size, the water and electrical services were renewed, and a new lift was installed. The House's original tenant, and one of major importance, is Glasgow Chamber of Commerce, and in the mid-1990s there was major upgrading of the Chamber's offices. In 1996, Lord Dean Forbes Macpherson inaugurated the company Ship Venture Limited to take on responsibility for the refurbishment and commercial letting of those parts of the property not used by the Merchants House itself, in order improve efficiency and maximise the income from the building.

Lady members

The most radical development in the last few decades has been one that has taken its place in the House's structure so quietly that its impact has been almost imperceptible. After nearly four centuries as an all-male institution, the House opened its doors to lady members in September 1997, with the admission of the first lady member, Her Royal Highness The Princess Royal. Discussions on the admission of lady members had gone on as far back as 1982, but the matter was not pursued. By the mid-1990s, however, there were many women in leading positions in city firms from which membership was drawn, and it seemed increasingly anomalous that they should be excluded. Assisted by Collector David Ballantine, Lord Dean Forbes Macpherson took the initiative in presenting to the Directors the desirability of amending the resolution concerning eligibility for membership. The Directors' Resolution of 12 July 1943 referring to 'men' was safely amended to 'men and women' (and 'sons' to 'sons and daughters'). No change was needed in the Regulations, as they referred only to 'all persons who in the time coming may be considered eligible by the Directors', and members at the Annual General Meeting of March 1997 willingly agreed with Dean of Guild Macpherson that a woman by any definition was a person.

Soon after this an approach was made to the Palace and there was ready agreement by the Princess. An invitation was sent to Her Royal Highness to visit the Merchants House to sign the Gold Book. The visit took place on 5 September 1997 (the first official royal engagement since the death of Princess Diana six days previously). The royal visitor was taken upstairs to the Directors' Room, where the ex-Lord Deans of Guild were assembled to be presented to her. From there she was escorted into the Hall, where she met the staff and the Directors and their wives. She was then introduced to four of the House's pensioners, and conversation flowed for several minutes. Finally she took her place on the platform, where Lord Dean David McVicar made a short speech and ex-Dean Forbes Macpherson gave a résumé of the House's history. Her Royal Highness then signed the Gold Book and was presented with a cheque for £5,000 for The Princess Royal Trust for Carers, which the House had supported in the past (with a grant of £6,000 in 1994–6). The visit was a great success

Fig. 9.6   Princess Anne signs the Gold Book, September 1997
Lord Provost Pat Lally and Lord Dean David McVicar look on.

and was enjoyed by all present, particularly by the pensioners, to whom the royal visitor had chatted easily and informally.

There are now around thirty lady members of the House, and doubtless many more to come. The first woman Director, Professor Janet B. I. McDonald, Chair of the Citizens Theatre, elected in 2002, has been joined on the board by retired Lady Visitor Mrs Penelope Robinson, Dr Helen Laird and Miss Catriona Reynolds.

A progressive House

Rooted as it is in the traditions of guild and city, the Merchants House is nevertheless a forward-looking institution. Under Lord Dean Andrew Primrose the Regulations have been thoroughly revised for the first time in thirty years. As befitting a twenty-first-century organisation, eligibility for membership has been broadened and clarified, and the rules for electing Directors have been updated too, with a maximum term of office for Directors of nine years.

Increasing involvement of members in the activities and traditions of the House is another of the initiatives of Andrew Primrose's deanship. This marks a shift in emphasis for the House. A golf outing to Western Gailes Golf Club in September 2003 proved very popular, as did a concert by the George Penman Jazzmen in December. The first ever Members' Dinner took place in February 2004, with Lord Provost Liz Cameron as the guest of honour. A presentation by the Cunard QM2 team, Carnival Cruising Cunard, was well attended in March. An updated video was made in 2003, highlighting the House's present activities in the context of its past history and the development of Glasgow. All these developments aim to give the House a higher profile among members and draw in new and younger members, ensuring that the Merchants House will continue to thrive in the century ahead.

The quatercentenary

The Letter of Guildry was signed on 6 February 1605. On Sunday 6 February 2005 a civic service is to be held in Glasgow Cathedral to commemorate the historical links between the Merchants House, the Trades House and the city council. A Fanfare for the occasion has been commissioned from John Wallace, Principal of the Royal Scottish Academy of Music and Drama, a world-renowned trumpeter and member of the Merchants House. On the evening of the following day the two Houses will be honoured by a civic banquet in the City Chambers. Many of the civic themes for 2005, including the Lord Provost's Procession, will portray the contributions of the Guildry to the development of the city.

The council and the two Houses plan to commission a monument within the Merchant City to highlight significant events in their history and to link the Merchants' Steeple, Merchants House, Trades Hall, Cathedral and City Chambers with the monument in an historical walking trail.

Within the Merchants House itself, the pensioners will receive gifts to commemorate the quatercentenary, and members and their guests will celebrate with a banquet. A fine wooden lectern has been commissioned by the ex-Deans from Michael Visochie, a local craftsman. The House will honour its maritime roots with events on the Clyde during the summer, including a visit to HMS *Ocean*, built in Govan, which is returning to the Clyde as part of the celebration of the bicentenary of the Battle of Trafalgar.

The Merchants House of Glasgow is a unique institution. No other town in Scotland has an independent organisation that has contributed so much prosperity, wielded so much power and performed so much service in the course of four centuries. Its home still has a commanding situation in the city's central square, just as its former home commanded the river and the earliest Glasgow bridge. Its early members, in protecting their trading rights and privileges and becoming prosperous men, laid down the basis of Glasgow's prosperity. Daring in trade and pioneering in manufacture, they insured themselves and their fellow members against disaster by contributing to a benevolent institution that has sheltered thousands of Glasgow families from destitution. In their desire to preserve the status of their guild they took a leading role in the government of the city, bringing to it their ideals of fiscal and social responsibility. Over the centuries they have adapted to change without losing sight of their traditions. This is what has given the Merchants House its strength. It is part of the fabric of Glasgow and the city is the richer for it.

Notes

1. Pat Lally, *Lazarus Only Done It Once* (London, 2000), p. vii.
2. John Struthers, *Glasgow's Miles Better: They Said It* (Glasgow, 1986).

Deans of Guild of Glasgow

The list dates from the Letter of Guildry in 1605. The election of Deans of Guild took place in October until 1957, and in March thereafter. It has been usual from early days for Deans to be re-elected to serve a second year. The dates below correspond with those given on the boards in the Merchants' Hall, and give the full year after the October election: 1610 means October 1609 till October 1610; 2000 means March 2000 till March 2001.

1	Matthew Turnbull	1605	1606
2	Archibald Faulds	1607	
3	William Sommer	1608	
4	George Mure	1609	
5	James Bell	1610	1611
6	William Weems	1612	
7	James Bell	1613	1614
8	John Lawson	1615	1616
9	John Rowat	1617	
10	Colin Campbell	1618	1619
11	John Rowat	1620	1621
12	Colin Campbell	1622	
13	Matthew Turnbull	1623	1624
14	Patrick Bell	1625	
15	Matthew Turnbull	1626	
16	Colin Campbell	1627	1628
17	Patrick Bell	1629	1630
18	John Barns	1631	1632
19	Henry Glen	1633	1634
20	John Barns	1635	1636
21	James Hamilton	1637	1638
22	Walter Stirling	1639	1640
23	James Bell	1641	
24	John Barns	1642	1643
25	Henry Glen	1644	1645
26	Andrew Cunningham	1646	

27	James Hamilton	1647	
28	William Dunlop	1648	1649
29	John Graham	1650	
30	William Dunlop	1651	1652
31	James Hamilton	1653	1655
32	John Bell	1656	1657
33	James Campbell	1658	1659
34	James Barns	1660	
35	Frederick Hamilton	1661	1662
36	John Barns	1663	1664
37	Frederick Hamilton	1665	
38	James Pollock	1666	
39	John Walkinshaw	1667	1668
40	John Anderson	1669	
41	Frederick Hamilton	1670	
42	Robert Rae	1671	
43	John Walkinshaw	1672	1673
44	John Caldwell	1674	
45	Frederick Hamilton	1675	1677
46	Ninian Anderson	1678	
47	Robert Campbell	1679	1681
48	Hugh Nisbett	1682	1683
49	John Fleming	1684	
50	Robert Cross	1685	
51	George Johnston	1686	
52	Robert Campbell	1687	1688
53	William Napier	1689	1690
54	James Peadie	1691	
55	John Leckie	1692	1693
56	John Cross	1694	1695
57	John Aird	1696	1697
58	Robert Rodger	1698	1699
59	John Aird	1700	1701
60	Robert Yuill	1702	1703
61	John Aird	1704	1705
62	John Bowman	1706	1707
63	Thomas Peter	1708	1709
64	Thomas Smith	1710	1711
65	Robert Yuill	1712	1713
66	Thomas Smith	1714	1715
67	Adam Montgomery	1716	1717
68	Thomas Thompson	1718	1719
69	James Peadie	1720	1721
70	Gilbert Buchanan	1722	1723
71	John Stark	1724	1725
72	James Peadie	1726	1727

73	Hugh Rodger	1728	
74	Andrew Buchanan	1729	1730
75	William Cunningham	1731	1732
76	Andrew Ramsay	1733	1734
77	Arthur Tran	1735	1736
78	John Gartshore	1737	1738
79	James Robertson	1739	1740
80	George Bogle	1741	1742
81	Matthew Bogle	1743	1744
82	George Bogle	1745	1746
83	John Brown	1747	1748
84	George Bogle	1749	1750
85	George Murdoch	1751	1752
86	Robert Christie	1753	1754
87	John Bowman	1755	1756
88	Archibald Ingram	1757	1758
89	Colin Dunlop	1759	1760
90	Archibald Ingram	1761	1762
91	George Brown	1763	1764
92	Arthur Connell	1765	1766
93	John Coats Campbell	1767	1768
94	Archibald Smellie	1769	1770
95	George Brown	1771	1772
96	James Buchanan	1773	1774
97	John Coats Campbell	1775	1776
98	Hugh Wylie	1777	1778
99	Alexander McCaul	1779	1780
100	John Coats Campbell	1781	1782
101	James McGrigor	1783	1784
102	Alexander Brown	1785	1786
103	William Coats	1787	1788
104	Alexander Low	1789	1790
105	Gilbert Hamilton	1791	1792
106	John Dunlop	1793	1794
107	John Laurie	1795	1796
108	Robert Findlay	1797	1798
109	Archibald Smith	1799	1800
110	John Laurie	1801	1802
111	Robert Carrick	1803	1804
112	John Laurie	1805	1806
113	James Black	1807	1808
114	John Hamilton	1809	1810
115	Robert McNair	1811	
116	Daniel Mackenzie	1812	1813
117	John Guthrie	1814	1815
118	James Ewing	1816	1817

119	Henry Monteith	1818	
120	Robert Findlay	1819	1820
121	William Smith	1821	1822
122	Mungo N. Campbell	1823	1824
123	Robert Dalglish	1825	1826
124	Alexander Garden	1827	1828
125	Stewart Smith	1829	1830
126	James Ewing	1831	1832
127	James Hutchison	1833	1834
128	James Martin	1835	1836
129	William Brown	1837	1838
130	James Browne	1839	1840
131	William Gray	1841	1842
132	Hugh Cogan	1843	1844
133	John Leadbetter	1845	1846
134	James Bogle	1847	1848
135	Andrew Galbraith	1849	1850
136	William Connal	1851	1852
137	James Hannan	1853	1854
138	Robert Baird	1855, to 7 August 1856	
139	William Connal, Interim Dean	from 22 to 25 August 1856	
140	William Brown	from 9 Sept. to 7 Oct. 1856	
141	John Jamieson	1857	1858
142	Thomas Buchanan	1859	1860
143	Sir James Lumsden	1861	1862
144	Alexander Ronaldson	1863	1864
145	Sir Archibald Orr Ewing, Bt.	1865	1866
146	John Ramsay	1867	1868
147	Sir Archibald Orr Ewing, Bt.	1868	
148	William McEwen	1869	1870
149	Alexander Ewing	1871	1872
150	Patrick Playfair	1873	1874
151	Sir James King, Bt.	1875	1876
152	Sir James Watson	1877	1878
153	James Stevenson	from 8 Oct. to 20 Nov. 1878	
154	Patrick Playfair	1879	
155	James Buchanan Mirrlees	1880	1881
156	Alexander Stephen	1882	1883
157	William McEwen	1884	1885
158	Walter Graham Blackie, Ph.D., LL.D.	1886	1887
159	William Walls	1888	1889
160	John Ure, LL.D.	1890	1891
161	John Guthrie Smith	1892	1893
162	James Reid	from 10 October, 1893 to 23 June 1894	
163	Sir James King, Bt., LL.D.	to 9 October 1894	

164	Hugh Brown	1895	1896
165	Donald Graham, C.I.E.	1897	1898
166	Sir James Bell, Bt.	1899	1900
167	Robert Gourlay, LL.D.	1901	1902
168	The Right Hon. George Arbuthnot, Lord Inverclyde	1903	1904
169	Robert King	1905	1906
170	Sir Thomas Mason	1907	1908
171	Matthew Pearce Campbell	1909	1910
172	Francis Henderson	1911	1912
173	Sir John Archibald Roxburgh, LL.D.	1913	1914
174	James David Hedderwick, LL.D.	1915	1916
175	Sir Hugh Reid, Bt., C.B.E., LL.D.	1917	1918
176	Richard H. Hunter	1919	1920
177	Sir Alexander Gracie, K.B.E., M.V.O., D.L.	1921	1922
178	Sir Frederick C. Gardiner, K.B.E., LL.D.	1923	1924
179	Robert T. Moore, D.Sc.	1925	1926
180	Charles Ker, LL.D.	1927	1928
181	Robert Robertson, B.Sc., M.I.C.E.	1929	1930
182	George W. Service	1931	1932
183	Sir George A. Mitchell, LL.D.	1933	1934
184	Claud A. Allan	1935	1936
185	J. A. Ralston Mitchell	1937	1938
186	William Cuthbert	1939	1940
187	Sir Robert Bruce, LL.D.	1941	1942
188	Sir Andrew S. Macharg	1943	1944
189	D. Norman Sloan	1945	1946
190	Norman MacLeod, C.M.G., D.S.O.	1947	1948
191	The Rt. Hon. John Alan, Lord Inverclyde	1949	1950
192	Sir David Allan Hay, K.B.E.	1951	1952
193	The Rt. Hon. Lord Maclay, K.B.E	1953	1954
194	W. H. Marr	1955	1956
195	Sir Ian F. C. Bolton, Bt., K.B.E., D.L., LL.D.	1957	1958
196	Harry Yates	1959	1960
197	Daniel Duncan, D.L., J.P.	1961	1962
198	J. Martin Baxter	1963	1964
199	Brig. J. W. H. Gow, C.B.E., D.L., J.P.	1965	1966
200	Thomas G. Robinson, O.B.E., T.D., D.L.	1967	1968
201	Peter B. H. Brown	1969	1970
202	Ross T. Haddow, M.C., J.P., C.A.	1971	1972
203	Peter B. H. Brown	from 31 Jan. to 6 Mar. 1973	
204	William M. Mackinlay, C.B.E, J.P., LL.D.	1973	1974
205	Richard H. Barclay, T.D., M.A. (Cantab.), LL.B.	1975	1976
206	P. A. Barns-Graham, T.D., C.A.	1977	1978
207	William A. P. Jack, C.B.E., F.R.I.B.A, F.R.I.A.S., F.S.A.S.	1979	1980
208	George Teacher Dunlop	1981	1982
209	Bonar Graeme Hardie	1983	1984

210	David W. Duguid	1985	1986
211	Peter C. Paisley	1987	1988
212	David H. Galbraith	1989	1990
213	Morrison Dunbar, F.R.S.A.M.D.	1991	1992
214	Geoffrey C. C. Duncan	1993	1994
215	J. H. F. Macpherson, C.B.E., D.Univ.	1995	1996
216	David McVicar	1997	1998
217	James S. Laird	1999	2000
218	Alastair K. Denholm, D.Univ., F.Univ.	2001	2002
219	Andrew H. Primrose	2003	2004

COLLECTORS OF THE MERCHANTS HOUSE OF GLASGOW

1	Archibald Faulds	1605
2	Robert Bogill	1624
3	John Herbertson	1632
4	John Gilmour, younger	1633
5	William Hyndschaw	1642
6	Cuthbert Campbell	1650
7	James Barnes	1656
8	Thomas Davidson	1657–8
9	Andrew Gibsone	1659–60
10	John Luke	1661–2
11	John Cauldwell	1663
12	Peter Gemmill	1664
13	John Corse	1665–8
14	John Craig	1669
15	George Herbertsone	1670–2
16	John Stirling	1673
17	James Biskett	1674–5
18	George Muirhead	1676–7
19	James Stirling	1678–9
20	William Napier	1680–3
21	William Anderson	1684–5
22	James Bogle	1686–7
23	Andrew Scott	1688–9
24	John Ritchie	1690–1
25	John Coats	1692–3
26	Robert Boyd	1694–5
27	John Anderson	1696–7
28	Andrew Scott	1698–9
29	John Buchanan	1700–1
30	Robert McGoun	1702–4
31	James Smyth	1705–6
32	William Gow	1707–8

33	John Whythill	1709–10
34	James Christie	1711–36
35	John Riddell	1737–49
36	William Robb	1750–1
37	James Barrie	1752–3
38	John Wilson	1754–8
39	Ebenezer Monro	1759–63
40	John Carlile	1764–6
41	James Hill	1767–88
42	James Hill and James Hill, jnr	1789–90
43	James Hill, jnr	1791–1818
44	Laurence Hill, LL.D.	1819–37
45	Robert Buntine	1837–50
46	Archibald Newall	1850–8
47	John Smith	1858–66
48	William H. Hill, LL.D.	1866–1912
49	James A. McCallum, LL.D.	1912–48
50	T. L. Grahame Reid, W.S.	1948–69
51	J. D. Mackenzie	1969–85
52	David A. R. Ballantine	1985–

Assistant Collectors

John McFarlan	1969–86
A. Dick Barr	1985–2001
A. James K. Dykes	2001–

SELECT BIBLIOGRAPHY

The pre-1958 archives of the Merchants House of Glasgow are held by Glasgow City Archives in the Mitchell Library. A selection of published sources consulted by the author is listed below.

Anderson, James R., *The Burgesses and Guild Brethren of Glasgow*, vol. 1: *1573–1750*; vol. 2: *1751–1846*, Edinburgh, 1925

Bell, Sir James, and Paton, James, *Glasgow: its Municipal Organization and Administration*, Glasgow, 1896

Blair, George, *Biographic and Descriptive Sketches of Glasgow Necropolis*, Glasgow, 1858

Butt, John and Ponting, Kenneth (eds), *Scottish Textile History*, Aberdeen, 1987

Devine, T. M., *The Tobacco Lords: a Study of the Tobacco Merchants of Glasgow and their Trading Activities c.1740–90*, Edinburgh, [1975] 1990

Devine, T. M. (ed.), *Scottish Elites*, Edinburgh, 1994

Devine, T. M. and Jackson, Gordon (eds) *Glasgow*, vol. 1: *Beginnings to 1830*; vol. 2 (W. H. Fraser and I. Maver, eds): *1830–1912*, Manchester, 1995

Devine, T. M., *Scotland's Empire, 1600–1815*, London, 2003

Ewing, James, *View of the History, Constitution and Funds of the Guildry, and Merchants House of Glasgow*, Glasgow, 1817

Fisher, Joe, *The Glasgow Encyclopedia*, Edinburgh, 1994

Gibb, Andrew, *Glasgow: the Making of a City*, London, c.1983

Gibson, John, *The History of Glasgow*, Glasgow, 1777

Gourlay, James, *A Glasgow Miscellany: the Tobacco Period in Glasgow* [privately printed, no date]

Graham, Eric J., *A Maritime History of Scotland, 1650–1790*, East Linton, 2002

[Hill, W. H.] *View of the Merchants House of Glasgow*, Glasgow, 1866

Jackson, Andrew M., *Glasgow Dean of Guild Court: A History*, Glasgow, 1983

Kellett, John R., *Railways and Victorian Cities*, London, 1979

Lumsden, Harry, *Bibliography of the Guilds of Glasgow*, Glasgow, 1928

Mackay, James A., *The Postal History of Glasgow*, [Glasgow] 1984

[James Maclehose (ed.)] *Memoirs and Portraits of One Hundred Glasgow Men*, 2 vols, Glasgow, 1886

McUre, John, *A View of the City of Glasgow and an Account of its Origin, Use and Progress*, Glasgow, [1736] 1830

Maver, Irene, *Glasgow*, Edinburgh, 2000

Murray, David, *Early Burgh Organization in Scotland*, vol. 1: *Glasgow*, Edinburgh, 1924

Oakley, C. A., *Our Illustrious Forbears*, Glasgow, 1980

Reid, J. M., *A History of the Merchants House of Glasgow*, Glasgow, 1967

Renwick, R., Lindsay, J. and Eyre-Todd, G., *History of Glasgow*, 3 vols, Glasgow, 1921–34

Riddell, John F., *The Clyde: the Making of a River*, Edinburgh, [1979] 2000

Senex [Robert Reid], *Glasgow Past and Present*, 3 vols, Glasgow, 1884

Smout, T. C., 'The early Scottish sugar houses', *Economic History Review* 2nd series, 14 (1962)

Smout, T. C., *Scottish Trade on the Eve of Union, 1660–1707*, Edinburgh, 1963

Smout, T. C., 'The development and enterprise of Glasgow 1556–1707', *Scottish Journal of Political Economy* 7 (1964)

Smout, T. C., 'The Glasgow merchant community in the seventeenth century', *Scottish Historical Review* 47 (1968)

Tweed, J., *Biographical Sketches of the Honourable the Lord Provosts of Glasgow*, Glasgow 1883

INDEX

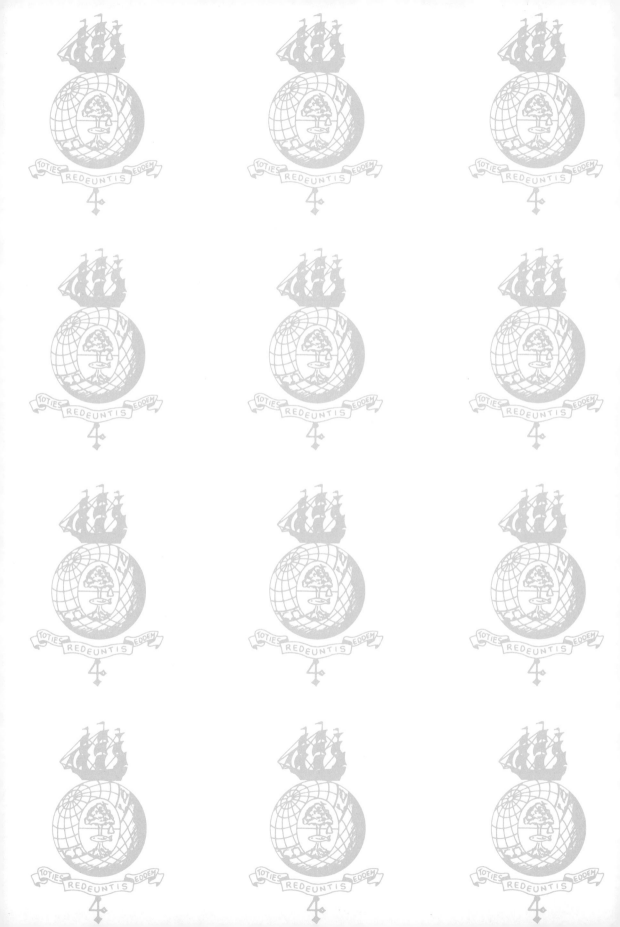